Why International Cooperation
Is Failing

Thomas Kalinowski is a Professor at the Graduate School of International Studies, Ewha Womans University in Seoul, Korea. He holds a PhD in Political Science from Free University Berlin. He teaches International Political Economy, Comparative Political Economy, International Organizations, and Sustainable Development. His recent research has focused on bringing the Comparative Capitalist perspective into the investigation of international cooperation and conflict. His key contribution to the study of Comparative Capitalism has been to help overcome the euro-centric perspective within Comparative Political Economy by systematically including East Asia in the field.

T0323636

Why International Cooperation Is Failing

How the Clash of Capitalisms Undermines the Regulation of Finance

THOMAS KALINOWSKI

OXFORD
UNIVERSITY PRESS

Great Clarendon Street, Oxford, OX2 6DP,
United Kingdom

Oxford University Press is a department of the University of Oxford.
It furthers the University's objective of excellence in research, scholarship,
and education by publishing worldwide. Oxford is a registered trade mark of
Oxford University Press in the UK and in certain other countries

First published 2019
First published in paperback 2022

Published in the United States of America by Oxford University Press
198 Madison Avenue, New York, NY 10016, United States of America

British Library Cataloguing in Publication Data
Data available

Library of Congress Cataloging in Publication Data
Data available

ISBN 978-0-19-871472-9 (Hbk.)
ISBN 978-0-19-287144-2 (Pbk.)

DOI: 10.1093/oso/9780198714729.001.0001

Preface to the Paperback Edition

Attempts to better understand international conflict and cooperation are a constant work in progress. When revising this book for the paperback edition, I had to limit myself to corrections and minor revisions without the possibility of major updates. Thus, it might seem that this investigation of the (often failed) attempts to regulate international finance with a focus on the period since the Global Financial Crisis of 2008/09 is already outdated and primarily of historical interest. Indeed, there is no shortage of new crises and conflicts from trade wars to climate change, from the COVID-19 pandemic to the Russian aggression in Ukraine. Still, I think this study remains relevant for at least two reasons. Firstly, finance remains at the heart of our global political economy where another financial crisis is only a matter of time. Secondly, and more importantly, this book remains useful for conceptual reasons. The purpose of this book has been to illustrate a way of investigating international conflict by tracing its origins to domestic political economies. This approach remains helpful as it tries to escape a superficial agency orientation while avoiding the pitfalls of over-theorizing. International crises often seem overwhelming and create a glut of ready-made explanations – ranging from the grand abstractions of international relations theory to the fantastical conspiracies about seemingly almighty world leaders. This book offers an alternative, practical path of investigation that does not rely on the premises of grand theories about the "anarchy of the international system" and that rejects the focus on individual leaders and elites in explaining political economic developments. The global political economy is neither shaped by universal laws (as the physical world is) nor by the psychological quirks and egoisms of a few individuals (as private lives often are). As influential as some so-called leaders may seem when displaying their high heels of power from private jets to state dinners and military parades, their power is only relevant in the context of the political economy they represent.

The alternative "second image" approach presented in this book traces the sources of international cooperation and conflicts to their domestic origins by combining approaches from international political economy and studies of comparative capitalism. In other words, an investigation that follows a truly *global* political economic perspective that is not primarily centered on nation-states and their international relations. The central argument of the book is that international conflicts are the result of the way our global economy is structured as a competition between different "models of capitalism". Amid intensifying economic globalization since the 1970s, distinct versions of capitalism with distinct economic structures, institutions, policies, and ideologies have emerged. In these distinct national and transnational forms of capitalism, different dominant business factions have used economic transnationalization to increase their leverage over governments and civil society and most importantly labor unions. US financialization, the European integration process and East Asian export orientation are three distinct expressions of contemporary global capitalism and at the same time follow a distinct domestic institutional path dependency. These different models of capitalism in the US, the EU and East Asia are economically integrating while politically competing over the way this process of integration is governed. It is this dialectic – the unity and internal contradiction – of contemporary global capitalism that constitutes its dynamic. This dynamic has created vast financial wealth but has also been a driver of massive inequality, crisis and conflict. Among those conflicts is the way international finance is regulated internationally. Just as finance constitutes a *social* relationship between creditors and borrowers, the governance of global financial relations constitutes a *political* relationship between states at the international level. Governments politically represent "their" respective domestic political economies in international organizations and institutions.

To briefly illustrate the book's central argument: US finance-led capitalism has a strong preference for open capital accounts that ensure the business model of being the financial center of the world. Consequently, the US has little interest in reducing global financial instability as this exactly constitutes the basis for financial hedging and selling financial products around the world. At the same time, the US plays a very constructive role internationally when it comes to macroeconomic policies that allow central banks and governments to manage crisis situations. Unfortunately, the EU has shown little inclination for such an active role of the state as the internal dynamics of the euro and the European Single Market are based on an austerity consensus limiting the active role of its member states. When it comes to monetary policies, the European Central Bank has managed a partial break with this path dependency and became more active. At the same time, the EU and its member states have been (unsuccessful) lobbyists for a "New Bretton Woods" that would supplement its regional Economic and Monetary Union with a stable global currency system. Unfortunately, not even East Asian G20 members that are facing severe problems with currency management themselves, support such a new global monetary system. Instead, the East Asian G20 member states China, Japan, and South Korea have developed strong national self-help strategies to protect themselves against global financial volatility and erratic exchange rate movements. On the other hand, when it comes to active government interventions in crisis management East Asian countries have been very cooperative and invested substantially in national competitiveness. A strategy that will, however, further increase global economic imbalances with the rest of the world. In sum, the different models of capitalism take different positions within a "trilemma triangle" of macroeconomic policies, financial regulation, and management of currencies. This placement is not just the result of choices made by governments, but they rest on a whole political economy of path-dependent economic structures, institutions, and policies. It is this complex political economic structure that we need to investigate if we want to understand the origins of international cooperation and conflict in order to effectively anticipate and address such global challenges. I hope this book can be a small contribution to this path of inquiry.

I would like to thank all my students that provided feedback and suggestions for corrections for this paperback edition. In particular, I want to thank Pauline Vanardois for helping me to compile the revisions for this edition. I wrote this book with the students of my Global Political Economy and Comparative Political Economy courses in mind. I want to equip them with a textbook that helps them to go beyond textbook knowledge. Above all, I want students to think for themselves about the problems of the global political economy using the academic tools provided to them by books like this. Remaining critical of textbook explanations is vital in any academic effort. Theories are always just tools to be used for *our own* research. They should never be accepted as dogmas that offer explanations *by themselves* without the need of a critical inquiry. There are no shortcuts to interpreting and (hopefully) changing the world other than to explore the workings of human society by ourselves.

Thomas Kalinowski, May 2022, Seoul

Acknowledgements

Academic work, just like any kind of work, is never the achievement of an individual alone. It is built on the published works of others, on discussions with colleagues and friends, and on institutions providing funding and an intellectually stimulating atmosphere. Many aspects of international conflict and the diversity of different models of capitalism that are covered in this book are already well researched and could be approached through literature research alone. In particular, I was fortunate to be able to rely on a vast amount of literature that helped me to understand the global role of the US and the spread of US finance-led capitalism. To gain a better understanding of the global role of an emerging euro capitalism and the importance of the rise of East Asia for the global political economy, I have additionally conducted numerous interviews with decision-makers in the European Commission and national governments in Europe and Asia, as well as experts in these countries. Their willingness to share their insights with me is greatly appreciated.

Funding is important to do research, and I was very fortunate to receive several grants that helped me to work on this book over the years. In particularly, I would like to thank the National Research Foundation of Korea,[1] the Korean Institute for International Economic Policies, the Japan Foundation, Ewha Womans University, the German Academic Exchange Service (DAAD), Heidelberg University, and the Deutsche Gesellschaft für Internationale Zusammenarbeit (GIZ) for financing some of my research in Europe, Korea, China, and Japan.

Even more important than money is time to think and write as well as an intellectually stimulating atmosphere. One of the great privileges of a professor is to have time off during the semester breaks and sabbaticals. The Max Planck Institute for the Studies of Societies (MPfG) in Cologne, the Jeju Peace Institute, Heidelberg University, Wissenschaftszentrum Berlin (WZB), the University of Duisburg-Essen, Tokyo University, and the German Institute for Global and Area Studies (GIGA) in Hamburg hosted me during my

[1] This work was supported by the National Research Foundation of Korea (NRF) Grant funded by the Korean Government (MEST) (NRF-2010-812-B00011).

research on this book. They were terrific hosts and provided me with the environment to bring this book to a completion.

No book would be ever completed without the right balance between critique and encouragement. I want to thank all my colleagues and friends who have provided valuable feedback for my research on this book and the related journal articles. In particular, I want to thank Stefan Niederhafner, Hyekyung Cho, Andreas Noelke, Martin Hoepner, Nobuhiro Hiwatari, Werner Pfennig, Sigurt Vitols, Werner Pascha, Aurel Croissant, and Patrick Koellner. At crucial points during the long (and long-delayed) process of research and writing, they provided support and helped me to keep going. My assistants Yara Yamout and Ilknur Karaduman provided very valuable work in collecting and updating statistics.

Finally, I want to thank the team at OUP, the reviewers, and the copy-editor, Hilary Walford for their patience and efficiency.

Contents

List of Figures

List of Tables

List of Abbreviations

AMF	Asian Monetary Fund
ATTAC	Association for the Taxation of Financial Transactions and Citizens' Action
B20	G20 Business Forum
BIS	Bank for International Settlements
BWS	Bretton Woods System
CAP	Common Agricultural Policy
CC	comparative capitalism
CDO	collaterized debt obligation
CDS	credit default swaps
CDU	Christian Democratic Union
CFIM	Coordination Framework for Implementation Monitoring
CIPE	Comparative International Political Economy
CMEs	coordinated market economies
CMI	Chiang Mai Initiative
CP	Communist Party
CPE	comparative political economy
CRD	Capital Requirements Directives
DAAD	German Academic Exchange Service
EAEC	European Atomic Energy Community
EBA	European Banking Authority
EC	European Community
ECB	European Central Bank
ECJ	European Court of Justice
ECSC	European Coal and Steel Community
ECU	European Currency Unit
EDP	Excessive Deficit Procedure
EEC	European Economic Community
EFSF	European Financial Stability Facility
EMCF	European Monetary Cooperation Fund
EMS	European Monetary System
EMU	Economic and Monetary Union
EPB	Economic Planning Board
ERM	Exchange Rate Mechanism
ESGP	European Stability and Growth Pact
ESM	European Stability Mechanism

ETUC	European Trade Union Confederation
EU	European Union
Euratom	European Atomic Energy Community
EWC	European Work Councils
FDI	foreign direct investment
FAZ	Frankfurter Allgemeine Zeitung
Fed	US Federal Reserve System
fintech	financial technology
FSAB	Financial Service Action Plan
FSB	Financial Stability Board
FTT	financial transaction tax
G-SIFI	global systemically important financial institution
GATT	General Agreement on Tariffs and Trade
GIGA	German Institute for Global and Area Studies
GIZ	Gesellschaft für Internationale Zusammenarbeit
HICP	Harmonized Index of Consumer Prices
HPAE	high-performing East Asian economies
IEO	Independent Evaluation Office
IMF	International Monetary Fund
IPE	international political economy
L20	G20 Labour Forum
LMEs	liberal market economics
LTCM	Long-Term Capital Management
M&A	mergers and acquisitions
MfPG	Max Planck Institute for the Study of Societies
MiFID	Markets in Financial Instrument Directive
MITI	Ministry of International Trade and Industry
MNC	multinational corporation
OECD	Organization for Economic Cooperation and Development
OMT	Outright Monetary Transaction
OTC	over the counter
PIN	Public Information Notice
PPP	purchasing power parity
SDR	Special Drawing Right
SEA	Single European Act
SIFI	global systemically important financial institution
SME	small and medium-sized enterprise
SMP	security markets programme
TARP	Troubled Asset Relief Program
TEU	Treaty on the European Union
TFEU	Treaty on the Functioning of the European Union
UAW	United Auto Worker

UK	United Kingdom
US	United States
VoC	varieties of capitalism
WTO	World Trade Organization
WZB	Wissenschaftszentrum Berlin

1

Introduction

Problems of international cooperation are usually conceptualized in dichotomies of optimistic 'liberal' theories or pessimistic 'realist' views of international political economy (IPE). From the perspective of liberal institutionalists, obstacles to international cooperation are seen as collective action problems that are merely transitional. From this perspective, rational actors cannot agree on global solutions for global problems because governments fail to transcend short-sighted national egoisms. International cooperation and international institutions such as organizations, rules, and norms are viewed primarily in terms of their function and their effectiveness in influencing the behaviour of nation states. From such a functionalist perspective, calamities such as the global economic and financial crisis since 2008 are viewed as regulatory failures that can be solved by improving international institutions—for example, by introducing improved capital requirements for banks or by introducing a financial transaction tax to curb international financial flows.

From the realist perspective, on the other hand, conflicts at the international level are seen as the result of power struggles between states that are the quasi natural result of an anarchic international system. Realists believe that we live in a Hobbesian world in which the life of nation states is solitary, nasty, and brutish and that cooperation between them is short-lived. Without a global leviathan, the world is seen in constant conflict and zero-sum games of national interests undermine cooperation. For example, the US is promoting its own interest by spreading the gospel of financial liberalization through the 'IMF–Wall Street-Treasury Complex'. China 'manipulates' its currency to become more competitive, and the European Union undermines macroeconomic coordination with its austerity bias and obsession with stability. As the competition of national power is the driving force of conflicts, those accounts explicitly or implicitly lament the lack of a 'global leader' that would provide 'hegemonic stability', as the UK did under the gold standard until 1929 and the US did under the Bretton Woods System (BWS) from 1944 to 1971.

Although both approaches could not be more different in their interpretation of the world, they both follow a top-down, deductive approach in which

Why International Cooperation Is Failing: How the Clash of Capitalisms Undermines the Regulation of Finance. Thomas Kalinowski, Oxford University Press (2019). © Thomas Kalinowski
DOI: 10.1093/oso/9780198714729.001.0001

the behaviour of actors is explained based on general assumptions made about the 'nature' of the international system. Both mainstream approaches deduct national behaviour from a speculative construction of the international system as liberal and institutionalized or power based and anarchic. This book departs from such a top-down approach. Instead of subsuming cases under different theories of IPE, this book investigates international conflicts and cooperation by looking at their domestic origins. Katzenstein's critique of top-down approaches to IPE still holds. 'In itself a global approach to meeting global needs appears to be an ineffective way of trying to cope with the problems of the international political economy. The management and the analysis of interdependence must start at home' (Katzenstein 1978: 22). This book aims to contribute to such a bottom-up research strategy inspired by a tradition of 'second-image' approaches to international relations that see international conflicts as the result of 'defects' within states (Waltz 1959; Kalinowski 2015b). Unlike Katzenstein and the constructivist school of IPE, however, this book focuses not on discourses and identity but on the material origins of conflicts. In short, a second-image IPE approach investigates conflicts in the international political economy by tracing the origin of these conflicts to the domestic political economies. At the same time this book differs from critical IPE approaches in the tradition of studies of imperialism or world system theories that focus on US (or Western) dominance as the source of international conflicts as well as neo-Marxist transnational approaches that see the rise of a global capitalist class transcending nationalist competition. Although inspired by critical approaches of IPE that question the nation state as the central player in global capitalism, this book goes beyond the nation state in a different way by building on studies of comparative capitalism.

The central hypothesis of the book is that if we want to understand international economic conflicts and competing preferences for international institutions we need to investigate the domestic origins of these conflicts. These domestic origins are not primarily conflicting nationalistic strategies but they are seen in the context of a competition between different models of capitalism. These models of capitalism are not just political strategies but institutional and structural path dependencies that emerged as distinct reactions to the challenges of economic globalization. This book tries to show that a combination of an international political economic understanding of the interdependence of different models of capitalism and a sophisticated understanding of their distinct internal dynamics found by studies of comparative capitalism (CC) offers substantial value added to our understanding of international conflict and cooperation. IPE and CC complement each other, as IPE studies have a sophisticated understanding for international conflicts as a result of global interdependence but lack a deeper investigation of the origins of this interdependence. Studies of IPE thus tend to create the illusion of a convergence towards one global capitalism that can be understood through the lenses of IPE theory alone. Studies of CC or comparative political economy (CPE), on the other hand, have a deep understanding of the domestic driving forces of different models of capitalism but lack an understanding of how these domestic models interact globally. Thus, CPE studies tend to exaggerate path dependency and create the illusion that capitalism can still be understood in terms of national institutions and structures. The capitalism of the twenty-first century is neither entirely global nor national, but it is constituted by the global interdependence of domestic (national and regional) models of capitalism.

In order to illustrate the value added of such a critical second-image IPE approach, this book focuses on the problems of the international rules governing finance and traces the problems back to their origins in the domestic political economy of competing models of capitalism. More specifically, the book focuses on the global role and interdependence of the three most important models of capitalism: US-style finance-led capitalism (Chapter 3), European integration-led capitalism (Chapter 4), and East Asian state-led capitalism (Chapter 5). When it comes to the conflicts about international cooperation in regulating finance, the book focuses on four major conflicts in the G20: international macroeconomic coordination, currency management, rules for international banks, and capital controls.

While such a Comparative International Political Economy (CIPE) approach can be useful in understanding other international conflicts as well, I have chosen to focus on finance, because it is the nerve centre of the global economy and connects the different capitalist models through the flow of credit and investment. Since the collapse of the BWS in 1971, the globalization of finance has been a major source both of economic wealth as well as of crisis. So far, all attempts to create a comprehensive global system that would provide a similar degree of stability amid financial globalization have failed. Global finance reminds us of the manic depressive patient described by Susan Strange as 'erratically manic at one moment, unreasonably depressive at others' (Strange 1998: 1). Indeed, global finance is a patient that is a danger not just to himself but to others as well. The global financial crisis of 2008 and the ongoing crisis management since then are only the latest reminder that international financial markets need sound regulation and oversight. How to organize this regulation and oversight of an inherently unstable global financial system and how to manage the financial crises that nevertheless occur comprise one of the most important and challenging political questions of our time. Better to understand the causes of financial crisis and the regulatory failures and to uncover the hidden mechanisms behind financial crises and regulatory failure form an important academic problem and a political challenge. Only a better academic understanding of the problems of international cooperation can also help to overcome them. In other words, this book deals with the question why, despite the obvious problems of the current crisis-prone international financial system, is there so little success in creating international institutions that effectively regulate international finance, prevent financial crises, and help manage crises when they occur? This book departs from an often-found (mis-)interpretation of financial crises as the result of a specific finance-led or financialized (US)-model of 'neoliberal' capitalism and rather sees financial crises such as the global financial crisis of 2008 as a result of a globalized economic system that is driven by the competition of different models of capitalism. Just as finance constitutes a social relationship between economic actors (sellers and buyers, creditors and debtors) at the domestic level, it constitutes a political relationship between different models of capitalism at the international level. As these different economic interests can only be mitigated and balanced but never be completely reconciled, political conflicts are inevitable.

In short, this book conceptualizes international conflicts as a result of a competition of domestic political economies or, in other words, a competition of capitalisms. I combine approaches of international political economy, looking at the domestic origins of international conflicts, with studies of comparative capitalism, providing a deep understanding of the diversity of capitalisms and the concept of path-dependent change. The argument is that different models of capitalism compete to complement their domestic institutions with compatible institutions at the international level. The problem is a political one, because, from a national perspective, international regulations at the global level are used as tools in a much broader competition of capitalisms within the international division of labour. At the same time, government leaders are bound by the path dependency of the respective models of capitalism. This argument should not be misunderstood as an excuse for inaction at the global level, because, as we shall see, the different models of capitalism are not static, but are altered by changing domestic economic structures and balances of power. This means that international cooperation is possible but it always has to be considered in connection with institutional and structural changes at the domestic level. For example, curbing erratic international financial flows is connected to the way consumer and mortgage credits in the US are regulated. A cooperation on exchange rates and global economic imbalances deficits would require a strengthening of organized labour in East Asia pushing for an economy based on domestic consumption. Finally, more active macroeconomic coordination would depend on substantial changes in the way the European Union is constructed. What is required are not simple policy fixes but deep institutional and structural changes of domestic political economies, including the changes in the internal balance of power between different societal interests.

1.1. The Empirical Problem in Brief

Before we can explore the second-image IPE approach and follow the origins of international conflicts to its origins in different models of capitalism, it is necessary to sketch the empirical problem. Why is investigating international financial regulation a good way to understand the problems of international cooperation and regulation?

1.1.1. The Global Financial Crisis and the G20 Process since 2008

The global economic and financial crisis since 2008 has brought the discussion about financial regulation, financial globalization and finance-led 'neoliberal' growth model of the US (and to some degree the UK) into the political and academic mainstream. A huge number of options for crisis management and institutional reforms that could help to prevent future financial crises were proposed, ranging from tougher regulations of banks, a new international currency system ('new Bretton Woods'), to the introduction of financial transaction taxes. Unlike in the past, when such proposals were primarily discussed at academic conferences, civil society forums, and on the political fringes, they now became mainstream and were taken on by national governments and international organizations. The crisis started in the US subprime mortgage sector, but quickly spread to other sectors and countries. Unlike previous financial crises since 1945, the financial and economic crisis since 2008 has been truly global and thus needed a coordinated global response. After the collapse of Lehman Brothers in September 2008, the crisis reached truly global dimensions, and national governments came to the conclusion that only an internationally coordinated effort could prevent a collapse of the world economy.

In order to prevent such a catastrophic event, comparable to the world economic crisis of the 1930s, the G20, which included all countries that were deemed 'systemically relevant' for a functioning global financial system, was upgraded from a meeting of finance ministers into a leaders' forum.[1] Members 'designated the G-20 to be the premier forum for our international economic cooperation' (G20 2009c). Besides the immediate crisis management, the G20 set itself the formidable goal of 'reform[ing] the global architecture to meet the needs of the 21st century' (G20 2009c). Although the G20 has covered many issues over the years, the most important ones, which have dealt with crisis management and global financial regulation, can be divided into four major areas:

1. international coordination of macroeconomic stimulus programmes to revive the global economy;
2. improvement of international standards for banks and other financial institutions;
3. problems of erratic international financial flows and measures to curb them;
4. issues of currency competition and a new global monetary regime.

If we look back, the results of the G20 process are mixed. On the one hand, a further deterioration of the global economy was averted. Most importantly, the international cooperation has (so far) prevented a rise of extreme nationalism that would threaten world peace, as in the 1930s. On the other hand, in only the first two areas has there been some kind of progress, while the global governance of financial flows and a new monetary system remain largely academic discussions at this point. Most analysts have judged that, after the immediate stabilization of the world economy, the G20 process 'lost momentum' (Walker 2010) and, in particular, global financial regulation has 'run out of steam' (Véron 2011). Despite initial expectations, the G20 led not to a major makeover of the international system but rather to an incrementally changed status quo (Helleiner 2014). Indeed, since 2012 the G20 has substantially lost both its focus on financial reform as well as its willingness to implement substantial reforms. Even in the first four crucial years from 2008 to 2012, conflicts and competition between different preferences for international institutions became increasingly visible. As the acute crisis situation, with the

---

[1] The G20 members are Argentina, Australia, Brazil, Canada, China, the EU, France, Germany, India, Indonesia, Italy, Japan, Mexico, Russia, Saudi Arabia, South Kora, South Africa, Turkey, the UK, and the US.

possibility of a catastrophic collapse vanished, the willingness to cooperate internationally diminished and conflicts of interest deeply embedded in competing models of capitalism resurfaced.

1.1.2. Conflicts in the G20

The creation of the G20 acknowledged that the G7, let alone one hegemonic power alone, would be unable to ensure global financial stability. When it comes to global financial stability, there are now at least nineteen 'systemically relevant' countries, plus the European Union (EU). The G20 was originally created in 1999 at the level of finance minister after the Asian financial crisis. It expanded to the level of leaders during the global financial and economic crisis in 2008. Of course, not all G20 members are equally important when it comes to considering rules on international financial regulation and cooperation. Most important are, obviously, the US, as the only remaining superpower and the largest financial market, the European Union, as a unique regional integration project and the world's largest economy, as well as East Asian G20 members China, Japan, and South Korea.[2] East Asia is not just the rising world region economically; countries in the region already have some of the world's largest currency reserves. The dynamics and the crisis of world economic and financial relations as well as their governance are dominated by cooperation and conflict between these three centres. Given the diversity of these regions and countries and their economic models, it is not surprising that there are many conflicts of interests. Within the four fields of the G20 agenda mentioned, the main conflict lines can be very roughly identified as follows (for a more comprehensive introduction see Chapter 2):

1. a conflict between expansionary macroeconomic policies, favoured by the US and East Asia, versus more conservative macroeconomic policies, favoured by the EU;

2. a conflict between the EU and the US about bank regulation on issues such as higher capital adequacy for banks (Basel 3), favoured by the US, versus a better regulation of financial products, financial institutions, and bonuses, favoured by the EU;

---

[2] I refer to these three countries and their economic models as 'East Asia' or 'East Asian capitalism', although they would more precisely be described as North-East Asian. Geographically at least North Korea, Mongolia, and Taiwan belong to North East Asia as well, but they neither belong to the G20 nor do they play a significant role in the issues discussed in this book.

3. a conflict between the EU as well as East Asia, which both prefer to limit the flow of volatile international financial flows, on the one hand, and the US, which wants to keep capital accounts open and unregulated, on the other hand;

4. a conflict between the US, which prefers market-determined currency exchange rates, and the EU as well as East Asia, which both value currency stability.

These conflict lines and the positions and perspective of countries in these conflicts are, of course, painted with a very broad brush for the purpose of our investigation. As we will see more clearly in Chapter 2, this categorization means neither that East Asia or even the EU are unified actors nor that the EU and East Asia have the same goals about details on how to regulate international financial flows. The described issues are the main conflict lines that emerge from many of the secondary and tertiary conflicts that will be brought to the surface throughout the book.

In the investigation of the problems just described, this book is dealing with some of the major questions within the field of IPE. Why is it difficult to cooperate, despite the high costs of non-cooperation? What are the deeper political economic underpinnings of these conflicts? How are the international conflicts connected to domestic social conflicts with different (groups of) countries? Or, to formulate it in a more casual way, why do sensible governments and smart decision makers take positions that prevent international cooperation, undermine global stability, and might even provoke severe international conflicts? For example, why would the US not agree to even the tamest limits on international financial flows like a financial transaction tax of 0.01 per cent? Or why does the European Union prefer a deflationary policy and low growth rates over even the most modest Keynesian fiscal stimuli? Finally, why are East Asian countries unable to kick their addiction to export surpluses that contribute to global economic imbalances and 'currency wars'?

1.2. A Critical Comparative IPE Approach

The questions raised by this book are certainly not new, and scholars in the past have approached the same or similar questions from different theoretical perspectives and with different analytical toolboxes. In this book, I try to show that a critical comparative IPE approach is a very useful way to investigate the problems that have been described. In this section, I will very briefly review and criticize established mainstream theories of IPE to show in which way this approach builds on previous research but also where it is different from previous studies. Those readers not interested in theories of international political economy might be tempted to continue directly with the empirical investigation, beginning in Chapter 2. But I hope they will stay with me in order to get a grasp not just of the flaws in the international regulation of finance but also of the shortcomings in the way that we try to understand these flaws. For scientists, giving an explicit explanation of the process of building on existing theories, and offering a critique of them, is an important part of their endeavour—different from artists who might cite or reject previous works without making such an explicit explanation. Critique is here meant not in a neopositivist way of falsifying existing theories but rather in the original meaning of distinguishing our own work from those criticized (*kritikē* (Greek) = to set apart/differentiate). My approach provides a synthesis where 'old theories' are not simply replaced by new ones, but in Hegel's sense of *aufgehoben*, with its double meaning of abrogated *and* preserved.

Academic research is not just a purpose in itself but has the goal of understanding and explaining natural and social phenomena or, in Max Weber's words, of contributing to the 'disenchantment of the world' (Weber 1958: 133). In order to change the world, we first have to get a proper understanding of it and to understand it we need to build on existing theories, strip them of their residual magic, and adjust them to the ever-changing empirical reality. Theories are tools that help us to understand the empirical world by uncovering mechanisms that cannot be understood by mere observation and description of the reality. Observing the staggering take-off of an Ariane rocket from the European space port in Kourou, French Guiana, we can see that the rocket turns fuel from its gigantic tanks into kinetic energy and hot gases. This observation, however, does not help us much to understand how a rocket works and what laws of nature it depends on. For this, we need (at least) an understanding of theories of chemistry (a carbon source releases energy when reacting with oxygen) as well as an understanding of theories of physics, most notably Newton's third law (the action of outflowing burning gas in one direction causes the reaction of pushing the rocket in the opposite direction). Similarly, by looking at G20 summit statements or different negotiation positions of member countries, we grasp only the superficial level of international conflicts. Leaders, their negotiations, and their statements are just the surface of the deeper-rooted institutions and structures at work. Even the statements of US President Trump and the most powerful people in the world are either surface movements of underlying tectonic shifts or mere tweets that will be irrelevant in the long run. For our understanding of international conflicts and cooperation, it is important to understand the underlying forces of power, the struggles of interests, and their origin in competing models of capitalism. Theories can guide us to search for the deeper causes by looking at underlying institutional constraints or even more fundamental structural driving forces, such as the relationship between the international and the domestic struggle of interest. Unfortunately, the international political economy is far more complex than rocket science. In IPE, actors and their policies are connected through relationship, shaped by institutions and underlying structures. The IPE is not simply the sum of these subsystems that can be analysed separately, but the result of dynamic interaction between these systems. The chemical and physical processes in a rocket work independently from each other and they work independently from our understanding of these processes. The political negotiation process at a G20 summit, however, cannot be neatly divided from an international political economic understanding of the mechanism of international institutions such as the G20 or a comparative political economic understanding of the internal dynamics and interest within the different camps. In this sense, social science is different from basic rocket science and similar to cutting-edge physics, where it is the intersection and tension between theories (say Einstein's relativity theory and Planck's quantum theory) that advance our understanding of the world and not the accumulation of specialized knowledge as such. Of course, specialized research is very important, but the combination of specialized research is equally important, because it not only adds to our understanding of the world but also immunizes us against the hubris of confusing theories of IPE with the realities of IPE itself. My purpose is thus to create not a hermetic model of knowledge but a contribution to the debate of understanding that is open to and invites future research and critique. Let me now explore and critique some of the relevant theories and their processes of 'systematic over-simplification'[3] so that the reader can follow the process of my own understanding of this topic.

1.2.1. The Problem of Realist and Liberal Top-Down Approaches of IPE

Approaches from a 'realist' tradition are the most widely used analytical lenses to investigate conflicts in the international political economy. In a

---

[3] In the words of Karl Popper (1992: 44), science is 'the art of systematic over-simplification—the art of discerning what we may with advantage omit'.

Machiavellian and Hobbesian tradition they highlight the important aspect of power in international relations and human society in general. From this perspective, international relations are conceptualized as the 'rise and fall of great powers' (Kennedy 1987) and conflicts are interpreted as the 'natural' consequence of the anarchic structure of the international system. For realists, economic power translates directly into political and military power regardless of domestic political and economic structures. For the case of China, Mearsheimer, for example, argues:

> If China becomes an economic powerhouse it will almost certainly translate its economic might into military might and make a run at dominating Northeast Asia. Whether China is democratic and deeply enmeshed in the global economy or autocratic and autarkic will have little effect on its behavior, because democracies care about security as much as non-democracies do, and hegemony is the best way for any state to guarantee its own survival.... China and the United States are destined to be adversaries as China's power grows.   (Mearsheimer 2001: 4)

The competition of sovereign nation states is at the centre of the realists' analysis, and the lack of international cooperation is seen as a victim of this competition. Consequently, cooperation is seen as opportunistic and short lived, with few incentives for nation states to obey international rules if they are in contradiction with the (short-term) national interest.

These approaches of power-based 'realpolitik' are often transferred to the economic sphere, where, for example, conflicts about monetary policies appear as 'currency wars' (Rickards 2011). In journalistic works and political discussions, references to national interests or 'national egoisms' that prevent international cooperation are common. International economic conflicts are constructed as 'natural', while international cooperation are seen as (mostly short-lived) exemptions. According to the influential 'hegemonic stability theory' (Kindleberger 1986), international cooperation in global economic regulation works only when there is one hegemonic power taking over the responsibility for the stability of the system and enforcing compliance. In other words, a stable international system can be achieved only if the national interest of the hegemonic power is identical with the global interest for systemic stability. Instability returns when rising powers undermine the hegemony of the leading power without taking charge or the hegemonic power abandons its role as a stabilizer of the international system. This was exactly the situation during the global economic crisis in the 1930s. 'When every country turned to protect its national private interest, the world public interest went down the drain, and with it the private interest of all' (Kindleberger 1986: 290–1).

The liberal institutionalist view of IPE offers a much more optimistic perspective than the 'realist' view, as it acknowledges the importance and effects of international institution. In this perspective, international organizations such as the UN and particularly the EU, but also institutions such as the G20 or the Basel rules on capital requirements for banks, do alter the behaviour of nation states. In some cases, international institutions are not just persistent but even lead to more cooperation in other areas. These functionalist spillover effects can be observed particularly in the European integration process, but the extension of the finance minister G20 to the leaders G20 amid the global economic crisis in 2008 is another example. Liberal institutionalists such as Nye and Keohane argue that the increasing economic and political interdependence leads to more political cooperation between states and the construction of international institutions (Keohane and Nye 1977). As interdependence grows, international problems and conflicts emerge that cannot be solved by individual countries or through bilateral solutions but only through multilateral international cooperation. From this perspective, building international institutions is a rational choice, and the failure of international cooperation can be explained by short sightedness, national egoisms, and the lack of understanding that international cooperation leads to better outcomes. Conflicts are seen as transitional problems in the process of institutionalizing international relations. For example, from a liberal institutional perspective, the rise of East Asia and the resulting global economic imbalances and international conflicts are not the result of a strategy of East Asian countries, and in particular of China, to gain global dominance, as realists would claim, but rather evidence of a 'transitional anxiety' (Ikenberry, 2008: 26) created by the trend toward an inevitable multipolar world.

In other words, from the liberal viewpoint, international cooperation is seen from the perspective of its effectiveness to solve international conflicts and problems. This functionalism of liberal IPE studies corresponds well with those in the field of mainstream economics who evaluate institutions primarily from the perspective of their effectiveness to stimulate economic growth and reduce transaction costs. Economists tend to have a rather technocratic understanding of the world, seeing problems as technical and the result of suboptimal regulation. Unlike the classics of political economy, from Adam Smith through Karl Marx to John Maynard Keynes, contemporary mainstream economists have largely eliminated the political aspects such as concepts of power from their research of the political economy and focus on models limited to economic variables. These economic models are shaped by an (often implicit) functionalist bias in the sense that institutions are evaluated from the perspective of the role they play in reducing transaction costs and ultimately creating an optimal solution. In these models, the economy is viewed as a more (by neoclassical economists) or less (by neo-Keynesian economists) self-regulating machine that can be more (neo-Keynesians) or less (neoclassics) adjusted and optimized through the buttons and levers of economic policy. Crises are interpreted as regulatory failures in the adjustment of the economic machinery, and crisis management is seen in terms of regulatory and institutional reform. For example, financial markets can be brought under control by pulling the lever on the regulation of capital requirements for banks or derivatives. Global economic imbalances between the US and East Asia are seen as a problem of 'currency manipulation' that can be solved by switching the exchange-rate regime button from 'state intervention' to 'market'.

Within such a mechanical concept, international political economy is imagined as a machine in which a certain number of buttons and levers (independent variables) create a certain outcome (dependent variable)—*ceteris paribus*. Through a careful analysis of the machinery, we can derive a perfect setting of buttons and levers to create the optimal outcome. Technocratic 'ideal-solution' and optimal settings are the logical consequence of such a neopositivist view of society, regardless of whether the (implicit or explicit) normative reference point is the free market, Keynesian social engineering, or even totalitarian control over society. Studies of economists focus on technical solutions, such as the best way to regulate banks in Basel 3, the most effective way to curb volatile international flows, or the most rational way to manage currencies. Their studies are highly normative in the sense that they assume that there is an ideal solution, which is then compared with the deficient implementation in reality.

This book agrees with the liberal institutionalist view of the importance of international institutions, but it rejects the functionalist perspective on institutions. At the same time, it dismisses the realist perspective that sees international conflicts as the result of an anarchic world system. Instead the book follows an inductive historical approach that investigates the genesis and the dynamics of international cooperation and conflicts and draws conclusion from these observations for the hidden mechanisms of the international political economy. Instead of viewing international relations as a product of the nature of the international system, international cooperation is seen as the outcome of interdependent domestic political economies with their internal conflicts and defects.

1.2.2. The Second-Image Perspective

While realist and liberal mainstream approaches of IPE differ fundamentally from each other, they both remain trapped in a top-down perspective in which international conflict and cooperation are to a large degree explained by the theoretical construct of an anarchic or institutionalized global system. This top-down approach has for a long time been criticized, in particular by structuralists within the realist camp. Kenneth Waltz's 'second-image' approach to international relations is among those studies that are more useful for our purpose (Waltz 1959). In Waltz's second-image perspective, it is not defects in the anarchic international system or the competition of antagonist national interests that lead to international conflicts and wars; rather 'defects in states cause wars among them' (Waltz 1959: 83). By defects, Waltz means undemocratic constitutions implying that a world of democracies could live in something like Kant's 'perpetual peace'. Such a second-image view seems to be a good point of departure to investigate the domestic sources of international cooperation in the field of global economic governance. The structuralism of such a 'second-image IPE' approach assuming that conflicts in international cooperation are created by 'defects' within domestic political economies (Kalinowski 2015b) is one of the methodological tools of this book (see also Nölke 2015a, b). From this perspective, for example, East Asian dependence on exports that contribute to global imbalances is caused by the 'defect' of weak labour unions and collusion between state and business. Or the reluctance of the US to regulate financial flows is the result of a process of financialization in which financial arbitrage has become the dominant business concept. Finally, the reluctance of the EU to implement Keynesian policies to stimulate the economy and create jobs is the result of the defect of the Maastricht Treaty and its 'convergence criteria'.

While a second-image approach helps to focus on the domestic origins of international conflicts, it does not offer a deeper investigation into these origins. They remain limited by their focus on a constructed 'national interest' without recognizing the contradictions within nation states. Approaches of critical IPE have long been fillings this gap and are thus very important for this book.

1.2.3. Critical International Political Economy

Often critical IPE is used as another term for (neo-)Marxist approaches, but in this book critical IPE is used more broadly for approaches that share the author's scepticism about functionalist liberal solution disregarding structural factors of power but at the same time rejecting the methodological nationalism of realists. From the critical perspective, international cooperation is not a rational choice to overcome collective action problems and find the 'optimal setting of the machinery' but a political process of interest struggles. However, it is not an international political process in the sense of a realist competition of sovereign nation states but rather the result of domestic and international political economic dynamics. The constructivist research agenda is promising in the sense that it investigates the causal relationship between what actors are and what they do (Wendt,1992: 424), but it limits itself to the investigation of ideas and identity without looking at the underlying political economic foundations. Unlike what social constructivists such as Wendt (1992) believe, identities are not the basis of interests but rather the expression of underlying interests that still need to be discovered. The US identity of a hegemonic power based on its role as the financial centre of the world is the result of its domestic political economy and the associated interests of capital account liberalization and market-based exchange rates, and not the other way around. Wendt's critique of realists remains important, because conflicts are indeed what states make of them, but they make them not as a choice but rather as a result of the distinct domestic political economies and the resulting interests. Countries can end hostilities by deciding not to be enemies any more, but this will not solve their underlying political and economic conflicts. Actors and their identity are merely the surface of underlying domestic institutions and structures. As scholars from a neo-Gramscian-inspired IPE school point out, there is a strong connection between the crisis of global capitalism and the crisis of domestic models of capitalism. It is what Gill (2012) and others in the Gramscian tradition of IPE are calling an 'organic crisis'—a crisis that is long-term, structural and multi-layered as opposed to a mere regulatory failure or a failure of global governance.

Traditionally studies of imperialism go back to Hobson, Lenin and Luxemburg, who argue that international conflicts arise from the competition about economic expansion and the externalization of domestic conflicts. Originally, the focus was on the conflicts that arose from the competition between established powers that already divided the world (markets) among themselves and rising powers that wanted their 'place in the sun'. These critical thinkers helped overcome realist approaches that see conflicts as the natural consequences of an anarchic system and instead highlighted the historically embeddedness of these conflicts in social and economic struggles. In many other ways, however, these traditional imperialist approaches are very similar to the views of modern realists, as they both fail to transcend the nation-state level. Later studies of imperialism did transcend the nation state but limited themselves to the conflicts between centre and periphery as well as the competition between developed countries to exploit the global South. The important contribution of World System Theories (Wallerstein 1974) was to transcend the nation state as the only unity of analysis and rather focus on the exploitative relationship between the capitalist core, including the developed countries, and the periphery, composed of the underdeveloped world regions.

Conceptualizing international relations as conflictual, critical IPE scholars agree with the realist approach, but they do not see the origin of conflicts in the division of the world into nation states. Instead, a major contribution of critical approaches is that they transcend the nation state. Neo-Marxist studies of transnational class formation go the furthest by claiming that a 'transnational capitalist class' (Sklair 2001) is emerging. This concept goes back to Kautsky's predictions (1914) of an emerging 'ultra imperialism' that would overcome conflicts between states through international cooperation to ensure the 'orderly' exploitation of colonies. While transnational class formation is an intriguing concept, in particular when one is trying to understand European integration-led capitalism and European integration in general (Apeldoorn 2002), it is, however, less useful for our endeavour to investigate international conflicts between different models of capitalism. Instead, the argument of this book is that part of the explanation for conflicts between countries is the competition between *different* dominant class factions in different models of capitalism at the global level. While in Europe transnational capitalism is becoming a reality, the global arena is still dominated by the classic competition of capitalisms, as pointed out by studies on imperialism. In this sense, this book can be read as a critic of neo-Marxists who highlight the importance of a rising transnational class.

Finally, the literature on financial globalization is a crucial foundation for this book, although the book does depart from the view that stresses financialization as a sign of either US global dominance (Schwartz 2009) or US decline (Arrighi 1994, 2005a,b, 2007). Instead, financial globalization is seen as one complementary aspect of global capitalism, equally important as export orientation and European integration. The study of financial globalization pays particular attention to the exponential growth of financial markets and international flows and the rise of 'casino capitalism' (Strange 1986) since the collapse of the BWS of fixed exchange rates in 1971 (Strange 1998; Lütz 2002). Financial globalization was accelerated by competitive deregulation, in which countries competed to become the most attractive base for financial services (Helleiner 1994). A process of 'financialization' (Epstein 2005;

Krippner 2005), defined as an 'increasing role of financial motives, financial markets, financial actors and financial institutions in the operation of the domestic and international economies' (Epstein 2005: 3), can be observed in most countries. In the US (and to some degree the UK), financialization has reached the stage of a new type of finance-led capitalism (Boyer 2000, 2011) in which finance has a privileged position in shaping domestic and foreign economic policies and institutions. Within the field of IPE, there is a strong focus on the US as the hegemonic or at least most powerful country in the global economy and its regulation. Financial globalization is often interpreted or criticized as a convergence towards Anglo-Saxon-style financial market capitalism and the result of US hegemony or a form of American neo-imperialism (Panitch and Gindin 2003). IPE scholars have devoted particular attention to the role of international organizations such as the International Monetary Fund (IMF), the World Bank, and the World Trade Organization (WTO) to disseminate US-style institutions and spread the gospel of a market-oriented growth model (Bullard et al. 1998; Woods 2006). The 'Wall Street, Treasury, IMF complex' (Bhagwati 1998; Veneroso and Wade, 1998) was seen as pushing through a specific set of neoliberal regulations often referred to as the 'Washington Consensus' (Williamson 1990). From this IPE perspective, international cooperation on regulating finance in the G20 since 2008 would constitute an at least partial departure from financialization. The importance of the financial industry for the UK and the US, as well as the opposition of the powerful financial lobby, can thus be seen as an important obstacle to international cooperation. Helleiner (2014) recently built on Strange's concept of structural power of the US to explain that the global financial crisis since 2008 has led not to fundamental changes but rather just to a tweak of the status quo. I generally agree with his argument; Helleiner, however, understands structural power only in its international dimension as a result of the US centrality for global finance and trade, its geopolitical dominance, and the role of the US dollar as the global currency (Helleiner 2014: 9). Consequently, Helleiner does not investigate the domestic institutional and structural developments that allow the US to play such a dominant role globally. This also means that he might underestimate the potential of change driven by domestic contradictions. Ultimately, structural power can be fully understood only if we take into account its domestic foundation as well (see the following section).

The cited critical IPE studies develop a comprehensive understanding of how international institutions are connected to domestic structural changes and developments. However, they tend to focus on the dominance of the US model of finance-led capitalism that is driving the dynamics of financial globalization as well as the spread of US-controlled international institutions around the world. To put it very simply, in most critical IPE accounts globalization is conceptualized as a process of Americanization, and either the resulting international conflicts are seen as the consequence of the expansion of US-style institutions around the world or, in the case of Arrighi and Gill, the crisis is seen as a symptom of the decline of US dominance. This US-centred view is problematic, because it overestimates US hegemonic power. The US is able to extend domestic institutions to the international level and has been more successful than others in shaping global rules. At the same time, as we know from studies of CPE and the diversity of capitalism, this hegemonic role has not led to a convergence towards a US-style finance-led capitalism. Different models of capitalisms remain path dependent and complement each other internationally.

1.2.4. Comparative Political Economy and the Path Dependency of Capitalist Models

From the CPE perspective, finance-led capitalism is not the institutional gravity centre towards which all national political economies converge but rather just one idiosyncratic model of capitalism. It was an important contribution of the French regulation school (Boyer and Saillard 2002; Amable 2003) and the debate on the varieties of capitalism (VoC) started by Hall and Soskice (2001) that challenged the hypothesis of a convergence to one 'best-practice' model of capitalism (Coates 2005; Hancké et al. 2007). These studies show that different models of capitalism do not primarily represent different 'stages of economic growth' (Rostow 1990), as the classics of modernization theory would argue, but that they are different institutional strategies to adapt to the process of economic globalization. The effectiveness of different models of capitalism to generate economic performance cannot be deducted from theories of development but only assessed empirically.

The strength of CPE studies of the diversity of capitalism is their elaborate understanding of the stability and dynamics of national political economies. Liberal market economies (LMEs) in the US transformed from the 'Fordist' model of mass consumption and mass production to a finance-led capitalism based on mass consumption and financialization. On the other hand, coordinated market economies (CMEs) in Europe and state-led capitalism in East Asia followed a very different trajectory (Yamamura and Streeck 2003; Vogel 2006). The strong path dependency of different variants of capitalism is explained by an 'institutional complementarily' that constitutes their 'comparative institutional advantage' (Hall and Soskice 2001: 52). Institutional complementarity means that institutions in different areas (financial regulation, labour regulation, industrial policies, and so on) complement and reinforce each other. For example, liberal 'hire-and-fire' labour markets correspond well with a weak welfare state, radical business innovations, market-oriented financial systems, and an education system based on universal skills. 'Inflexible' labour relations, on the other hand, correspond well with a strong welfare state, experience-based gradual innovations, a bank-based financial system, and an education system based on specific skill sets. Comparative institutional advantage means that national political economies follow not a 'best-practice approach' but an endogenous dynamics. That is the reason why different variations of capitalism tend to react differently to the same global challenges (Gourevitch 1986; Stallings 1995). Some VoC scholars, including Hall and Soskice, go further in claiming that countries achieving competitive advantages have an advantage in making institutional systems as complementary as possible and that pressure from globalization would lead to a divergence of capitalist models. In this book, however, we see institutional complementarity primarily as an explanation for path dependency of capitalist models and not so much as a cause for capitalist divergence. Indeed, as we will see in the historical account, there are phases of convergence and divergence within the broader trend of path dependency of capitalist models.

Since the 1970s, the capitalist world has faced the challenges of lower growth rates, saturated domestic markets, and economic globalization. Amid the collapse of the BWS, Anglo-Saxon liberal market economies, European coordinated market economies, and East Asian developmental states reacted with different strategies. The US revitalized growth through financialization and by providing financial services for the whole world. As we will see in detail in Chapter 3, this finance-led model of capitalism consists of a distinct institutional framework and class compromise that shape the global orientation of the US. European coordinated market economies have been trying to revitalize growth by following an integration-led growth model, building a European single market, and harmonizing rules and regulations, including the creation of a common currency. As we will see in detail in Chapter 4, European capitalism, and particularly euro-capitalism (Beckmann et al. 2003), have a regional framework concentrating on stability and convergence within the single market, which has a dominant influence on the preferences for shaping international institutions. Finally, East Asian developmental states have been improving their national competitiveness by pursuing an export-led growth model. As we will see in Chapter 5, East Asian state-led capitalism follows a national self-help strategy and tries to shape international institutions to support these policies rather than shaping a legalistic international framework that would bind them. As we will see in the empirical analysis in Chapters 2–5, this simple triangulation of models of capitalism is helpful for our purpose to investigate the domestic political underpinnings of international competition and institutional preferences. Of course, the three models of capitalism are ideal types that are useful abstractions and tools for our investigation, but not all countries fit neatly into them. In the EU, France and Germany differ substantially, just as China and Japan in East Asia do not always have the same interests when it comes to international economic institutions. In this context, the UK's exit from the EU seems logical, because structurally the UK resembles most closely the US model of capitalism, while its institutional framework was increasingly dominated by the EU. We will discuss the diversity within the models in the respective chapters. This book still maintains that consistency within the models and differences between the models are strong enough to justify the analytical categorization.

An important contribution of the CPE literature is the discovery of 'path dependencies' of different models of capitalism (Beyer 2006). The path dependency limits the options available to decision makers when negotiating and deciding about institutional changes. It is important to note that this book does not subscribe to a rigid interpretation of path dependency that sees path dependency only as given when it shows quantifiable 'increasing returns' (Beyer 2006). Rather, this book sees path dependency as a way to understand decisions by looking at decisions made in the past and the institutions and structures that emerged from these decisions. It is trivial to state that history matters, but, while it is probably impossible to quantify *how much* it matters exactly, the most interesting question that is touched upon here is in *which ways* it matters. Another too rigid interpretation of path dependency is that changes to path dependency can happen only due to external shocks. This position has rightly been criticized by Streeck and Thelen (2005). One of the defining features of capitalism is its dynamic development. While U-turns and radical path-breaking changes are rare, adjustments and partial convergence happen frequently without challenging the overall path. Each example of this model of capitalism has its own institutional regime, economic structure, and distinct balances of domestic social struggles, but these configurations are constantly changing, not just through the external shocks of a changing world economic structure, but also through the permanence of domestic interest struggles. This study highlights path dependency but at the same time acknowledges that capitalism remains a very dynamic system. Institutions are understood as the result of the solidification of a competition and struggle of interests, which means they are changing along with the relative balance of power within societies. At the same time, this change is path dependent, as the institutions in turn structure the struggles of interest, which brings us back to the critical tradition of IPE already outlined.

1.3. Investigating International Conflicts from a Comparative IPE Approach

In short, this book explores the usefulness of a Comparative International Political Economy approach and can be described as taking a second-image IPE perspective. Different from mainstream 'top-down' approaches of international political economy, this approach builds on studies of critical IPE and investigates the domestic origins of conflict, crisis, and cooperation. Unlike classic studies of second-image IR, in the political-economy perspective of this book domestic does not mean national but refers rather to domestic political economies and different models of capitalism. This second-image IPE perspective is substantiated by studies of comparative capitalism (CC) that highlight the path dependency of different models of capitalism. Studies of CC offer a sophisticated understanding of how domestic institutional complementarities are a good stepping-stone for our investigation of the competition to extend these complementarities to the international level. Our investigation starts with a classic IPE analysis of the conflicts on the international level about how to regulate economic globalization but follows these conflicts to their domestic origins. In other words, a second-image IPE approach investigates the connection between domestic, social, and economic conflicts and interstate conflicts about international economic institutions. These domestic struggles are intermediated through domestic institutions that, according to the tradition of critical political economy (or historical institutionalism), constitute the result or the solidification of the domestic social struggle (Figure 1.1). In Katzenstein's words (1978: 19), the 'governing coalitions of social forces in each of the advanced industrial states find their institutional expression in distinct policy networks which link the public and the private sector in the implementation of foreign economic policies'. As this quotation shows, this approach is not entirely new, but rather reconnects to a long tradition in IPE (see also the discussion in Nölke 2011). Unfortunately, this tradition has been marginalized by tendencies in international studies

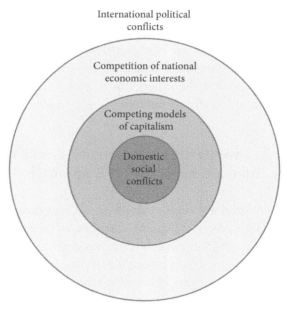

Figure 1.1. Research strategy of second-image IPE approach

for specialization and compartmentalization into IR, IPE, CPE, CC, and development studies. In addition, mainstream realist and institutionalist studies remain surprisingly dominant in our understanding of international relations, while critical approaches have drifted towards constructivism, focusing on identities and discourses but neglecting their foundation and the struggle of economic interests and power. In this sense, this book reconnects to the older materialistic traditions of critical approaches and could be called neo-structuralist as opposed to post-structuralist, constructivist, or neo-Gramscian studies that focus primarily on discourses and ideological struggles. While discourses matter, too, they are relevant primarily in the context of struggles over economic resources and political power.

Second-image IPE studies investigate how domestic political economies influence international institutions, taking into account the findings from studies of CPE that domestic political economies can differ substantially. Rebuking the convergence hypothesis, CPE studies analyse how distinct growth models or models of capitalism have reacted to the challenges of economic globalization in different ways (Figure 1.2). While international institutions like regulations of capital requirements for banks or IMF preferences of capital account liberalization did have an effect on the way

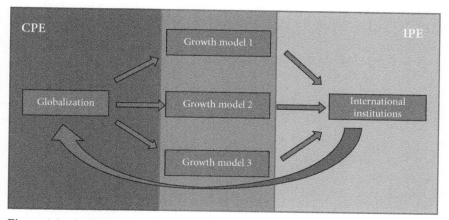

Figure 1.2. A CPE-inspired IPE approach

globalization and national political economies are evolving, they have not let to a general trend of convergence. In other words, while IPE studies offer a profound understanding of international conflicts over regulating the global economy, CPE studies offer a deeper understanding of how domestic struggles affect domestic institutions. Studies of CIPE connect the findings of the two approaches.

Within the field of CPE, studies of comparative capitalism highlight the fact that capitalist economies are dominated by business interests and the needs of companies (Hall and Soskice 2001: 28). As we will see in more detail throughout this book, this dominance of business takes very different shapes in different models. In all three main models of capitalism—US finance led, EU integration led, and East Asian export led—organized labour and progressive demand-side oriented policies have been on the retreat. When it comes to dominant capital factions, however, the three models are very different (Figure 1.3).

In the US, finance has become the gravity centre of the economy around which all rules and regulation are drawn to. In the EU, the creation of a European single economy has preserved manufacturing that is dominated by high-quality niche producers. In East Asia, the export-oriented business conglomerate emerged as the dominant capital faction around which rules and regulations are built. The result is three very different models of capitalisms with different 'embedded policy preferences' (Hiwatari 2003), rules, regulations, relative strength of societal forces, and ideologies. In many ways, this is an extension of the approach taken by Katzenstein and others before the European integration process gained its dynamics with the introduction of

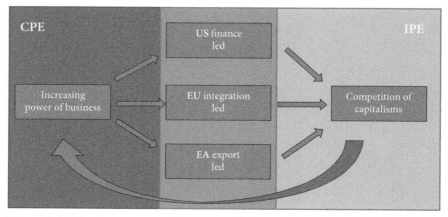

Figure 1.3. The dominance of business and the models of capitalism

the single market and the rise of the whole East Asian region.[4] The full scope of their distinct character will reveal itself throughout the book and Table 1.1 offers only a brief and an at this point necessarily abstract glimpse into what will unfold over the following chapters.

A Comparative IPE or second-image IPE approach views conflicts about international cooperation in regulating the global economy as the result of competing models of capitalism. Different models of capitalism react in distinct ways to the pressure of economic globalization. The evolving different models of capitalism depend on each other and exist only in the interdependence with each other. In order to regulate international economic relations, these different models of capitalism compete over the creation of international institutions, as we will see in more detail in Chapter 2. Table 1.2 briefly summarizes the main competing preferences of different models of capitalism in the G20 during the global financial crisis.

Following this approach, complementary institutional frameworks have the tendency to extend to the international level. Conflicts in international negotiations and regimes are thus the result not of national egoisms, but of a competition to extend different institutional frameworks to the international level. This tendency for institutional hegemony is not driven primarily by

---

[4] Already in the 1970s, Katzenstein (1978: 295) noted that 'an inventory of the objectives and instruments which characterize the differing political strategies of six advanced industrial states in the industrial political economy yields three groups of states: the two Anglo-Saxon countries, mercantilist Japan, and the states of the European continent. Corresponding differences exist in the distinctive elements of domestic structure: the coalition between business and state and the policy networks linking public and private sectors. An historical explanation of these differences is most appropriate. In the future, stresses in the relations between business and the state in contradiction between ruling coalitions and organized labor may lead to changes in political strategies.'

Table 1.1. Summary of the argument

	US	EU	East Asia
Growth model	Finance-led	Integration-led	Export-led
Institutional system	Market regulatory	Coordinated	State-led
Primary goal	Global hegemony	Regional stability	National development
Preferences for international regulation	Capital account liberalization	Monetary and fiscal stability	Sovereignty of economic policies, competitive currency exchange rates

Table 1.2. Summary of the positions within the G20

	Macroeconomic coordination	Financial regulation	Currencies
US	Initiative for strong stimulus	Open markets, regulation of products and institutions	Maintain global role of dollar
EU	Reluctant follower	Open markets but some regulation of flows and institutions	Stabilize euro
East Asia	Enthusiastic follower but with mercantilist twist	Regulation of flows and institutions, little regulation of products	Currencies used to achieve competitive advantages

national 'egoistic interests' but is the result of structural power and the extension of formal and informal institutions from the domestic to the international level. If we want to understand international institutions, we have to understand the conflict of interests on the international level. If we want to understand the conflict on the international level, we have to understand the different institutional complementarities of different varieties of capitalism. If we want to understand the varieties of capitalism, we also need to take into account the domestic interest struggles. This combination of critical IPE with CPE is the essence of the Comparative IPE (CIPE) approach.

1.3.1. Preferences for International Cooperation and the Trilemma of Economic Policies

After I have introduced the general approach of the book and presented the rational for focusing on three models of capitalism competing for extending their domestic institutional framework to the international level, it is now necessary to introduce an analytical focus. In our globalized world, everything is connected, but some connections matter more than others. A CIPE approach can be useful in understanding international relations in many different areas, but in this book I want to demonstrate its usefulness by looking at links between international conflicts on the regulation of finance and the competition of different models of capitalisms. To identify these crucial links between the international phenomena of financial globalization since the 1970s and the different reactions of distinct models of capitalism, it is first of all important to look at the different paths national political economies can take when faced with the challenges of financial globalization since the 1970s. The concept of the 'Mundell–Fleming trilemma' (Mundell 1963; Obstfeld et al. 2005) provides an excellent starting point for our investigation into international financial cooperation. It describes how the globalization of international finance is limiting the options of domestic economic policies. In the original version of the trilemma, Mundell and Fleming argue that, under capital mobility and fixed exchange rates, sovereign fiscal policies are effective and sovereign monetary policies ineffective, whereas the effectiveness is the other way round under flexible exchange rates (Mundell 1963). Departing from the original treatment of the trilemma by Mundell and Fleming, I collapse sovereign fiscal and monetary policies into sovereign macroeconomic policies targeted to achieve domestic goals such as achieving growth and reducing unemployment. In most cases, under the conditions of open capital accounts and stable exchange rates, sovereign fiscal policies have become ineffective as well, because governments fear that high public debt levels will create inflation and undermine the confidence of financial investors. This obsession with anti-inflationary policies is particularly dominant in Germany and the EU (see Chapter 4), but is also part of the Washington consensus that is recommended for or even imposed on developing countries by the IMF and the World Bank. On the other hand, countries with flexible exchange rates, such as the US and the UK, have been able to maintain sovereign fiscal policies (as seen in their obsession with tax cuts), partly because their role as 'bankers of the world' has allowed them hitherto to finance huge deficits (see Chapter 3).

According to this modified 'economic policy trilemma', there are clear trade-offs between desirable economic policies, such as stable exchange rates, sovereign macroeconomic policies, and open capital accounts (see Figure 1.4). Only two of these goals can be achieved at any one time. Originally, the concept of the trilemma was used to explain only the constraints

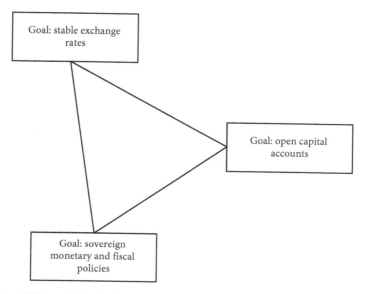

Figure 1.4. The modified trilemma triangle

imposed on the macroeconomic policies of small and open economies, but it has explanatory power with regard to all countries. As we will see in this book, even smaller economies such as Korea have some leeway within the triangle, while large economies such as the EU, the US, and China, too, have to accept trade-offs. This modified concept can help us to group countries according to the policy choices they made when faced with the trilemma. Under the BWS up until 1971, countries combined fixed exchange rates with controls on private capital account flows, while the IMF provided support to finance short-term current account deficits. This arrangement facilitated sovereign fiscal and monetary policies that would support rapid economic growth and ameliorate economic crises. Under the conditions of freely flowing capital, which proliferated from the end of the BWS in 1971 and became the ortho-doxy from the 1980s, governments had to move away from the 'Bretton Woods corner' of the 'trilemma triangle' (Figure 1.5) and choose either to stabilize their currencies or to maintain sovereign fiscal and monetary policies. In the former case, their monetary and fiscal policies merely react to the inflows and outflows of capital. In the latter case, they can use monetary and fiscal policies to govern the economy and allow the exchange rate to adjust to the inflows and outflows of capital.

The Mundell–Fleming trilemma is most often used as an economic model in the tradition of functionalist approaches of IPE. In this interpretation, it is

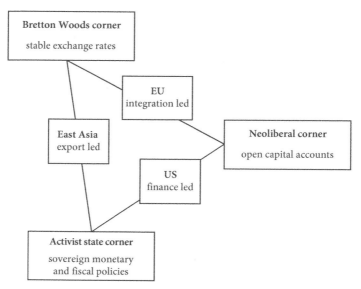

Figure 1.5. The trilemma triangle with different models of capitalism

implicitly assumed that governments are free to choose their 'two out of three' options. As we have seen, studies of CPE criticize such a view and highlight the role of institutional baggage and path dependency. Table 1.1 and Figure 1.5 indicate the differences of distinct models of capitalism and the interconnect- edness or complementarity of the different dimensions of each model. This argument will unfold throughout the book and I will return to it in Chapter 6. For example, the preference for an open capital account complements a finance-led growth model, which comes with certain institutional preferences such as a market-based financial system that corresponds with businesses models based on radical innovations and a flexible labour market. A market- based financial system thrives on expansive monetary policies and radical innovation corresponds with a universal-skill focused education system, quick labour turnover, weak labour unions, and weak welfare states. Weak welfare states increase the necessity for active fiscal policies to smooth business cycles, and so on. A focus on stable exchange regimes corresponds with a strong and export-oriented industrial sector based on incremental innovations and experience. Incremental innovations need a 'conservative' bank-based system and an education system based on specialized knowledge. Incremental innova- tion systems work best when complemented with strong labour unions and welfare states that in turn are often balanced by independent central banks to offset the inflationary tendency of wage increases and so on. The two different approaches differ substantially not just in relation to macroeconomic policies and exchange-rate regimes; they also need very different kinds of bank regulation, labour regulations, education systems, and so on. In short, choices within the trillemma triangle are connected to the domestic political economies in many different ways, as we will see in Chapters 3–5.

Different variants of capitalism have dealt with this challenge in different ways and in doing so have chosen different sides of the trilemma triangle.[5] Finance-led countries such as the US and the UK have been the most enthusiastic supporters of the free flow of capital, while maintaining an autonomous monetary policy to stimulate the domestic economy in the case of an economic downturn. On the other hand, the US and the UK have let their currencies float freely and have not intervened in the currency markets, although the US has used its international political power to pressure other countries to revalue their currencies against the dollar. The US and the UK are closest to what I call the 'neoliberal corner'[6] of the triangle; however, because of their ability to implement sovereign monetary and fiscal decisions, they also remain closer to what I call the 'activist state corner' of the triangle (see Figure 1.5).[7]

European countries that were part of the creation of the EU integration process have also opened their capital accounts, but at a much slower pace (Bakker and Chapple 2002). In contrast to the US, these integration-oriented countries established a regional system of fixed exchange rates within the European Union (European Exchange Rate Mechanism (ERM)) in 1979, which led to the introduction of a single currency, the euro, in 1999. Owing to the focus on stable exchange rates, the EU—with the exception of the UK— remains attached to the 'Bretton Woods corner' of the triangle, while moving in the direction of the neoliberal corner.[8] In contrast, East Asian countries

---

[5] The three different goals that make up the impossible trinity are ideal types. No country is completely sovereign in its monetary policies, and few have been able to maintain inflexible fixed exchange rates for long. Most importantly, all countries have some form of explicit or hidden capital controls, at least for the case of a capital account crisis. However, even though ideal types are idealized versions of existing phenomena, some countries come closer to the ideals than others. It is important to note that these ideal types are not created by deducing from any grand theory but that they evolve in Weber's spirit by distilling the essence and distinct character of each model of capitalism.

[6] I use the term 'Bretton Woods corner', 'neoliberal corner', and 'activist state corner' to highlight the first priority of a certain set of policies, even though I am aware that, for example, state activism means something very different in the USA with its Keynesian legacy and East Asia with its legacy of authoritarian developmental states.

[7] The ability of liberal market economies like that of the USA to implement more expansive macroeconomic policies than coordinated market economies such as Germany has also recently been described from a domestic political–economic perspective by Carlin and Soskice (Soskice 2007; Carlin and Soskice 2009).

[8] It could be argued that, since the introduction of the euro as a common currency, the euro area seems to have moved away from the Bretton Woods corner, because the external value of the euro is not among the goals of the European Central Bank (ECB). However, the priority of the internal

maintained a sovereign macroeconomic policy to revitalize the economy by running persistent fiscal deficits, accumulating the highest government debt level in the world.[9] At the same time, Japan, China, and Korea limit the volatility of exchange-rate fluctuation, while private capital flows remain restricted through a combination of regulations and cultural factors, as we will see in Chapter 5. The accumulation of foreign currency reserves in Japan and East Asian emerging markets also helped to protect their policy choices from the volatility of international financial markets, because currency reserves provide a buffer against erratic capital flows (Aizenman et al. 2008).

For the matter of completeness, I also want to mention that countries outside our focus have followed similar trajectories. Most developing countries and emerging markets, unable to afford a completely free exchange rate, have copied either the European model (stable exchange rates plus open capital accounts) or the East Asian model (limited exchange-rate volatility plus a higher degree of sovereignty in macroeconomic policies). Concerning general tendencies, we can say that small developing countries or emerging markets that are export dependent and/or have a strong financial sector—for example, Malaysia, Singapore, and Hong Kong—have preferred the 'European model'. Developing countries and emerging markets with large domestic markets and/or active industrial policies—for example, India and Brazil—however, have preferred the 'East Asian model,' including the tendency to use foreign-currency reserves as a buffer for erratic private capital flows.

1.4. The Argument of the Book in Brief

The main argument of the book can be summarized in six main theses, which will be investigated in the following empirical chapters.

1. Different models of capitalism have reacted in distinct ways to the challenges of financial globalization and declining growth rates since the collapse of the BWS in the 1970s. They took different sides within the trilemma of economic policies that limits the institutional and policy choices of countries when it comes to financial openness, macroeconomic sovereignty, and exchange-rate regimes.

---

stabilization of the euro area (plus the so-called ERM 2 countries) has left little room for more Keynesian sovereign macroeconomic policies. In effect, the euro area remains within the path dependency of the ERM.

[9] In 2006, the Japanese central government debt was 161% of GDP, nearly three times higher than what is considered 'excessive' under the Maastricht Treaty (OECD 2009).

The choices that different models took are shaped by the path dependency of their domestic political economies.

a. Finance-led countries like the US have opted for capital account openness and sovereign macroeconomic policies.

b. European integration-led countries ('euro capitalism') have opted for the introduction of a regional monetary system, the creation of a single market including the free flow of capital, and conservative macroeconomic policies mandated by the Maastricht Treaty.

c. East Asian state-led countries such as China, Japan, and Korea have opted for sovereign macroeconomic policies, national exchange-rate management, while restricting the free flow of capital.

2. Taking one side or another within the 'trilemma triangle' leads to distinct and partly conflicting preferences with regard to international economic cooperation. These conflicts shaped the discussion on the international regulation of finance since the 1970s and constituted a formidable obstacle to international agreements in this field. Since the beginning of the global economic crisis in 2008 and within the G20 we can observe such conflicts in three main areas.[10]

a. A conflict between the US and East Asia favouring large macroeconomic stimuli versus a stability-oriented European Union. This conflict can be particularly observed in the discussion about fiscal stimulus packages and the reduction of global imbalances.

b. A conflict largely between the US, which favours financial regulation based on stability of financial institutions, a European Union, which favours an approach to curb global market excesses, and an East Asian strategy to protect its national financial markets from global instability. This conflict can be exemplified by the discussions over Basel 3 regulations, a financial transaction tax, and national capital controls.

c. A conflict between the US, favouring a floating exchang-rate currency system with the dollar as the global currency, the European Union, favouring a new global monetary system such as a new BWS, and the East Asian strategy of national currency management through the accumulation of currency reserves.

---

[10] These are the broad categories of issues related to financial regulation discussed in the G20 summits of 2008–10 (G20 2008b, 2009b, c, 2010a, b).

3. It is not primarily the hegemony of the US and the convergence towards a US model but the competition between these different models of capitalism that have been shaping the dynamics, crisis, and conflict of global capitalism since the 1970s. Nor are the failures to regulate international finance and the conflicting regulatory preferences merely the result of competing national egoisms and disagreements on direction and degree of reforms. From the perspective of this book, the conflicts are much more deeply embedded in the competition of different models of capitalism that each have their own institutional path dependency.

4. At the global level, the three models of capitalism are not just interdependent but complement each other. In a nutshell, the US uses its position as 'banker of the world' to attract capital inflows and generate fees from global financial transactions while importing price competitive consumer goods from the East Asian 'factory of the world'. With its investment-driven growth model, East Asia also buys large amounts of capital goods and specialized products made in the integrated 'workshop EU'. Finally, the workshop EU produces the artisan and luxurious products fancied by the winners of globalization around the world. This global economic system is relatively stable but also creates massive economic imbalances and potential for crisis.

5. Path dependency of domestic institutional regimes and global economic complementarity does not mean that changes are impossible. On the contrary, global economic interdependence increases the possibilities of external shocks. In addition, domestic institutions are not just entities shaping the behaviour of actors; they are also the solidification of the conflicts and compromises generated by these actors. As the global economy changes and domestic balances of power change, institutions change, too.

6. For international cooperation this means that cooperation becomes both more difficult and easier. More difficult, because changes on the global level have to be accompanied by changes within the domestic political economies. Fortunately, these changes are not preconditions but can go hand in hand. In fact, all three models of capitalism are internally contested, and domestic changes might open up new avenues of international cooperation. International cooperation might also become easier, because in a multipolar world a new era of hegemonic stability has obviously become an illusion. A return to a global system that is underwritten by one global leader with one currency is neither possible nor desirable, and international cooperation is without a viable alternative.

1.5. Structure of the Book

The structure of the book is very straightforward. Chapter 2 introduces the empirical problem in more detail and in particular looks at the conflicts within the G20 on how to regulate international finance. The three chapters dealing with the three distinct models of capitalism (Chapters, 3, 4, and 5) follow the same structure, beginning with a historical political economic analysis of the respective variant of capitalism since the 1970s. This analysis is followed by an investigation of preferences related to international financial regulation based on the CIPE framework outlined in this chapter. Finally, each chapter concludes with the position of each country in the discussion in the G20 on regulating international finance since 2008.

Chapter 3 concerns finance-led capitalism in the US and to a lesser extent in the UK. The chapter builds on and updates the existing literature by Susan Strange, Eric Helleiner, and many other scholars, which highlights the role of the US in financial globalization and the competitive deregulation of finance driven by states. The chapter explains the US positions on the regulation of banks, financial flows, currency coordination, and macroeconomic policies, linking these positions to the domestic political economy of a finance-led growth model. For example, we can explain the US focus on macroeconomic coordination and bank regulation in the G20, while remaining opposed to regulations on international financial flows and the coordination of currency policies.

Chapter 4 presents a new perspective on Europe's role in financial globalization, which can be explained by the EU's regional integration-led growth model. A focus of the investigation is monetary integration leading to the introduction of the euro. Unlike the finance-led variant of capitalism, euro capitalism is not a major driving force of financial globalization but is instead focused on currency stability and regional economic and financial integration. This distinct variant of capitalism emerging in Europe leads to very different preferences in the G20 from the finance-led capitalism in the US. For example, in the G20 discussions, France and Germany were much more focused on budget consolidation and only reluctantly followed the lead of the US in macroeconomic coordination. These countries were also much more reserved with regard to tougher bank regulations, while they initiated measures to curb volatile international financial flows and erratic exchange rates.

Chapter 5 provides a major new contribution to the field, as it investigates the role of East Asian capitalism in the regulation of international finance.

State-led capitalism in the East Asian G20 members, Japan, Korea, and China, constitutes a distinct form of capitalism with distinct preferences regarding the international regulation of finance. Most importantly, an export orientation, a strong focus on national self-help solutions, and the vigorous economic competition in the region produce a reluctance to commit to global rules. For example, China, Japan, and Korea implemented some of the largest fiscal stimulus packages in the G20 and implemented measures to manage international financial flows and exchange rates, while being reluctant to support global standards on banks and financial products.

The final chapter connects the conclusions from the empirical analysis to the theoretical section of the book. It concludes that the failure to regulate international finance is not the simple outcome of financial globalization, the result of weak political leaders or the rivalry of national egoisms. The different, path-dependent variants of capitalism compete over the extension of their distinct institutional frameworks to the global level. These results have important practical ramifications, as comprehensive and effective international regulation of finance is linked to changes in domestic political economies. This interdependence does not mean that international financial regulation is impossible to achieve, but it questions the viability of the merely technocratic solutions that are now pursued in the G20. A reconfiguration of capitalist institutions on the domestic or regional level is not a precondition for comprehensive global financial regulation, but both developments can advance simultaneously.

2

The Problem in Detail

The Clash of Capitalisms and the Rules of International Finance

In Chapter 1, I outlined the general empirical problem and the argument of the book. A second-image IPE perspective was introduced, combining traditions from critical IPE and CPE studies. This chapter sets the stage for the empirical investigation of the domestic political economic sources of international conflicts and cooperation. Before we proceed to the details of how different models of capitalism have reacted to the collapse of BWS and investigate the domestic origins of foreign economic policies, it is necessary to illustrate the relevance and historical context of the issue and outline some of the problems and conflicts on the international level when it comes to the international regulation of finance. Most importantly, it is crucial to understand domestic capitalist development and the international regulation of finance from a historical perspective. All theories need to be checked in the light of historical facts. 'History, including economic history, is the essential corrective for intellectual hubris' (Strange 1998: 20). Ultimately, only a historical perspective can vindicate theoretical considerations because not only does it take into account empirical facts but it also puts them into a context that gives the facts a meaning by identifying patterns, structures, path dependencies, and critical junctures. This chapter consists of four parts. First there is a general brief historical overview of the problems of the international regulation of finance since nineteenth-century imperialism until the financial crisis that started in 2008. Second, this chapter introduces the G20 as the main forum for global economic cooperation. Third, it offers an overview of the different reactions to the global economic crisis since 2008. Fourth, it introduces the major conflicts in the G20 about the international regulation of finance in the three crucial areas identified in Chapter 1: global imbalances and macroeconomic coordination, financial globalization and financial regulation as well as currency competition and management.

Why International Cooperation Is Failing: How the Clash of Capitalisms Undermines the Regulation of Finance. Thomas Kalinowski, Oxford University Press (2019). © Thomas Kalinowski
DOI: 10.1093/oso/9780198714729.001.0001

2.1. An Historical Overview of International Finance and its Regulation

Conflicts over the regulation of international finance are not a recent phenomenon but rather have a long history. The same is true for international financial crises that were caused by failures to keep international finance under control. In fact, the development of modern capitalism has a long history of failures to deal with international financial relations, with some short-lived periods of smooth operation.

2.1.1. The Emergence of National Finance and Money

Over most of history, international financial relations were based on the circulation of objects with intrinsic value, most importantly gold and silver coins. Owing to their intrinsic value, they needed few institutional underpinnings to ensure the value of money. At the same time, the problem of unsustainable debt and crisis management have always been much more complex issues amid the absence of strong states to oversee the regulation of finance as part of their mandate. Such strong states emerged only with the formation of nation states and socialist concepts of economic planning in the nineteenth century and later with the rise of Keynesianism as well as fascism in the 1930s. In premodern times, debt settlement was organized in a simple way. If a creditor was not able to repay his or her debt, he would be punished drastically and directly—for example, by enslavement or by imprisonment in the 'debtor's tower'. Institutions like the biblical ban on interests (e.g. Deuteronomy 23:19–20)[1] provided a certain form of interest-rate regulation. Interestingly the Bible already distinguishes between 'domestic debt' to 'brothers', which should carry no interest, and credits to foreigners, where charging interest was allowed. The jubilee rule (Deuteronomy 15:1–23), which mandates a cancellation of all debt every seven years,[2] was an early attempt of debt restructuring, although it was never consequently implemented. In general,

---

[1] 'You shall not charge interest on loans to your brother, interest on money, interest on food, interest on anything that is lent for interest. You may charge a foreigner interest, but you may not charge your brother interest, that the Lord your God may bless you in all that you undertake in the land that you are entering to take possession of it.'

[2] 'At the end of every seven years you shall grant a release. And this is the manner of the release: every creditor shall release what he has lent to his neighbour. He shall not exact it of his neighbour, his brother, because the Lord's release has been proclaimed. Of a foreigner you may exact it, but whatever of yours is with your brother your hand shall release.'

matters of finance in premodern times were simple, brutal, and lacked a coherent implementation. Slightly stronger institutions regulating finance emerged only when in the Middle Ages private paper currencies (promissory notes) started to circulate alongside gold and silver coins. Paper currencies made trade easier because they were easier and safer to carry around. Private financial institutions such as the Medicis in Italy or the Fuggers in Germany facilitated trade by allowing these notes to be exchanged into cash in their vast network of branches throughout Europe (Ferguson 2008). Only in the nineteenth century did nation states start to monopolize the issuance of currencies and central banks gain the monopoly to issue a legal tender in which public and private debt could be repaid (Helleiner 2003). The nationalization of currencies became necessary with the rapid economic development in the nineteenth century, which required a reliable financial system based on easy-to-use paper currencies and a strict enforcement of regulations. This included the foundation of central banks monopolizing the issuance of money and legal bankruptcy procedures that would regulate debt restructuring. The nationalization and formalization of financial regulations were facilitated by numerous national and international financial crises that required governments to step in and improve regulations and oversight. The rise of the modern nation state in the nineteenth century established a national regulation of finance, and on the international level the gold standard emerged as the first international system governing finance.

2.1.2. The Gold Standard

The gold standard became the dominant international institution regulating international financial transactions from the 1870s until the First World War. It was the first global regime to govern finance, and for some time it was quite successful, at least from the perspective of imperialist countries. Even today, conservatives, particularly in the US Republican Party, still consider the gold standard as a 'golden age' and the reference point for good international governance.[3] The gold standard fixed all national currencies at a certain exchange rate to the gold, allowing the international convertibility and flow of national currencies. The gold standard contributed massively to the growth of international trade and the emergence of an international division of labour.

---

[3] Milton Friedman believed that a gold standard "would provide an excellent solution to the liberal's (i.e., classic liberal) dilemma: a stable monetary framework without danger of the irresponsible exercise of monetary powers.' Unlike some right wing politicians, however, Friedman did not believe that the gold standard would be *politically* feasible. (Friedman and Friedman 1982).

The UK, which had had a gold standard since 1844, was the leading trading power, and thus trading partners had a strong incentive to adopt the gold standard, too. When the US and Germany joined the gold camp in the 1870s, the three largest trading powers were on gold, which made it difficult and costly for others to stay outside. The gold standard had the great advantage that it was low maintenance and needed little international cooperation—at least in normal times. During times of crisis, however, the gold standard depended on the solidarity of central banks to reinforce the trust in the convertibility into gold. For example, when the Bank of England had to step in as a lender of last resort during the crisis that followed the collapse of Barings Brother in 1890, it depended on borrowed money from the French and the Russian central banks (Eichengreen 2008: 32–4).

The beauty of the gold standard was that, at least in theory, domestic adjustments to changes in international competitiveness were automatic, requiring little active political decision-making. Current-account deficits led to an outflow of gold, which shrank the monetary base and thus reduced prices. Deflation reduced imports and re-established export competiveness to balance the current account by reducing prices and wages. In surplus countries, the inflow of gold increased the monetary base and created inflation, which increased imports and undermined export competiveness, because prices and wages went up. In such a model, rebalancing is an automatic process and monetary decisions are completely depoliticized.

The problem of the gold standard was its inflexibility, its deflationary bias, and the resulting incompatibility with the increasing strength of the democracy movement and the success of democratic revolutions particularly in the aftermath of the First World War. The absolute priority of maintaining stability and convertibility of currencies into gold was a main feature of the gold standard. Monetary and fiscal policies were completely put on the backseat, which made the deflationary bias even worse. In other word, the 'automatic adjustment' of the economy was done on the back of employees and farmers, as their income shrank during periods of deflation. Farmers who had to repay fixed mortgages but were suffering from declining prices were hit the hardest. At that time, farmers were a very important political force, which made the US experiment with the introduction of a bimetallic system in 1890 (the Sherman Silver Purchase Act). The hope was that a bimetallic standard would increase the discretion of domestic monetary policies by adjusting the value of money and increasing liquidity backed by silver. The US even promoted an international bimetallic standard, which failed at the international monetary conferences of 1892 because Germany and particularly Britain as the main trading powers were the biggest beneficiary of the gold standard and objected to the transition. Without the two biggest trading powers on board, there were few incentives for other countries to adopt a bimetallic standard, because it would have created little additional international liquidity but would have led to a massive outflow of gold. In 1893, the US suffered exactly this fate when gold reserves reached a critical level and the Sherman Act had to be repealed (Eichengreen 2008: 37–41).

The gold standard facilitated international capital flows and investment, particularly from Europe and the US, to countries in the periphery, and thus allowed the imperialist expansion of European powers. These early international investments and the establishment of European businesses around the world immediately caused problems, because indigenous people in the colonies were rebelling against the occupation of their land and the exploitation of their labour. This triggered the intervention of imperialist governments, which used their military to protect the foreign investments of their national 'global players'.

2.1.3. The Era of Imperialism and Nationalism until 1945

At the international level, the defining development of the nineteenth and the first half of the twentieth centuries was imperialist expansion. This global economic expansion was dependent on support and protection from the emerging nation states in order to secure financial transactions, trade, and security. All imperialist countries had in common that they used the exploitation of colonies as a way to diffuse domestic, social, and political conflicts that emerged from the political rise of the working class. 'You are simply exporting the social question,' commented the German social democrat Wilhelm Liebknecht in the German parliament after Chancellor Bismarck had announced Germany's colonial ambitions in 1884 (*Der Spiegel*, 12 January 2004). In Europe, large national companies emerged, and, because returns on investments fell in their home markets, capital was recycled globally through foreign investments in underdeveloped regions of the world. Hobson (1975 [1902]) and later Lenin highlighted the role of international financial flows as one of the underlying economic forces of imperialism that distinguished imperialism as the first era of globalization from previous stages of capitalism. 'Typical of the old capitalism when free competition had undivided sway, was the export of goods. Typical of the latest stage of capitalism, when monopolies rule, is the export of capital' (Lenin 1933 [1917]). The imperialism of the nineteenth century was in effect the division of the world into competing spheres of influence within which trade, capital flows, and debt service were protected by the respective imperialist power. Companies from competing countries were excluded from this preferential trade area either by protectionist measures or by the structural advantages that companies from the imperial power had obtained over time.

In their internal structure, the competing imperialist powers differed substantially, and these differences expressed themselves in various international strategies. The UK, as the most developed country and established colonial power, could rely on its firm structural control within the empire and pursued a global liberal market approach based on free trade that focused on expanding market access beyond its colonies. In contrast, new rising powers such as Germany and Japan, with an expansionary neo-mercantilist model of capitalism, saw their colonial empires as preferential trade areas. As they saw themselves as latecomers, they followed a particularly aggressive colonial expansion that pitted them against established colonial powers such as France and Britain. The US remained largely outside this global competition, as it was preoccupied with its internal expansion to the 'Wild West', which provided more than enough opportunities for investment.

Countries in the periphery that had already became independent before the imperialist division of the world, most notably in Latin America, were affected differently by the inflow of capital from Europe and North America. In the nineteenth and early twentieth centuries, debt crises and sovereign default were common events. Because an international mechanism of debt settlement was missing, creditors asked their governments unilaterally to demand debt repayment. In order to enforce debt payment, governments of creditor nations frequently engaged in 'gun boat diplomacy', sending military and navy ships. In the context of the international regulation of finance, imperialism can be seen as a specific form of the international regulation of trade and finance characterized by military coercion and conflicts that emerged from a competition of different models of capitalisms. The tendency to solve problems through the use of force led to many conflicts and distrust between competing imperialist countries, which ultimately prepared the stage for the First World War.

The Age of Nationalism and War, 1914–1945

The First World War put an end to the 'long nineteenth century' (Hobsbawm 1962) and the first 'golden age of capitalism'. An era of liberal optimism that international trade and economic globalization would ultimately make war obsolete was replaced by a pessimistic view of imperialist conflict. Previously liberal and social-democratic scholars had believed that economic interaction would make war a 'great illusion' (Angell 1910). In Kautsky's words (1914), the emergence of an 'ultra imperialism' meant that imperialist countries would cooperate internationally to ensure the 'orderly' exploitation of the colonies. This corresponded with the presumed rise of a domestic 'organized capitalism' (Hilferding 1910) that ensured national economic stability and, at least from the perspective of a socialist like Hilferding, a smooth transformation towards a socialist planned economy. The war that broke out in 1914 made these theories obsolete and radically altered international economic relations.

With the First World War, the first era of globalization collapsed and with it the gold standard, which remained intact only in the US. The socialist and democratic revolutions that followed the war completely altered the political landscape in Europe, and in consequence also fundamentally changed international relations between states. The First World War transformed Europe deeply, and social revolutions achieved universal suffrage, social reforms like the eight-hour working day, freedom to form labour unions, as well as guaranteed civil liberties. The belief that economic exchange alone would lead to eternal peace was shattered, and the League of Nations was installed as an international organization to advance international cooperation and to prevent war. Unfortunately, the League of Nations remained weak and did not provide a framework to deal with the pressing issues of international economic relations. From an economic point of view, the reconstruction of the economy and the repayment of domestic and international war debts were the paramount issues. At the end of the war all European countries had large amounts of war debt towards their own population (war bonds) and other states (international war debt and reparation), with the US being the biggest creditor. To repay their domestic war debt, European countries printed money. This led to a period of high inflation rates between 1922 and 1924. In Germany, the hyperinflation was particularly severe, reaching an incredible 32,000 per cent per month in 1923. The inflation in Europe effectively rid governments and companies of their domestic debt but also wiped out the savings of the middle class. Once a currency reform had been undertaken, as in Germany in 1924, the economy quickly picked up, leading to a period of economic growth in Europe and the 'golden 20s' from 1924 to 1928. The international debt that was denominated in gold was far more difficult to repay, and thus the issue of international war debts and reparations became a major source of conflict on the international arena. The experience of hyperinflation and the issue of settling war debts and reparations led to a series of international conferences under the auspices of the League of Nations. The first conference was held in Genoa in 1922 and proposed the reintroduction of the gold standard in order to overcome currency instabilities created by hyperinflation and the insecurity connected with the ability of European countries to service their international war debts. Because a return to the gold coin standard of the past was seen as unfeasible, the gold exchange standard became the new reference point. Under such a standard, central banks would guarantee 30–40 per cent of circulating banknotes with its gold reserves and the rest with foreign currency reserves. Banknotes completely replaced gold in the circulation, and gold became solely a reserve kept by central banks. Not surprisingly, those countries suffering from worst hyperinflation were most eager to rejoin the gold standard, and this was achieved through radical currency reforms in Austria in 1923, in Germany and Poland in 1924, and in Hungary in 1925. Other countries with high inflation rates, such as France, Italy, and Belgium, joined later (Eichengreen 2008: 44–7). Because the new gold exchange standard replaced the circulation of gold with paper money, the gold exchange era also saw the rise of the independent central bank, which would guard gold reserves against access from the government and thus guarantee the stability of the currency.

From the beginning, the new gold standard was unstable and lacked credibility. With the democratic revolutions sweeping through Europe after the First World War and the challenge posed on capitalist countries by the Russian Revolution and the rise of the socialist movement, the self-regulatory system of the gold standard was no longer feasible. During deflationary restructuring, employees would lose their jobs or see their wages cut, and protests and resistance against this technocratic, supply-side-oriented growth model increased. It now became clear that it was only due to the lack of universal suffrage in most countries and the sometimes brutal suppression of the socialist movement that the gold standard had survived until the First World War. The political rise of the working class and universal suffrage made it extremely difficult for governments to concentrate all efforts on stabilizing their currency and to guarantee convertibility into gold. Other political goals, such as economic planning and later stimulating growth or reducing unemployment with the help of active macroeconomic policies and welfare policies, became new objectives that challenged the gold standard. In other words, with the rise of the working class, the technocratic gold standard was replaced by politicization of monetary policies. Ever since, the struggle for and against the 'independence' of monetary policies and the central bank has been a key political struggle.

The return to the gold standard also exacerbated the global economic imbalances at that time, particularly between the UK as a major deficit country and France as the main surplus country. The French and to a lesser extend the German central banks seemed to have little trust in the gold exchange standard, as they were keen to exchange their currency reserves into gold, which was a constant challenge to the stability of the system. An even bigger threat to the stability of the international monetary system was that Germany accumulated its gold reserves, not primarily through current account surpluses, but by massive inflows of capital, particularly from the US.

The Debacle of War Debt Management

The problem of war debts and the failure to manage them at the international level made the period between the wars economically unstable and politically toxic. Politically, the problem of the reparations was passed on by the winners of the First World War to Germany and Austria, which were singled out as the sole aggressors in the war.[4] The Versailles Treaty and the resulting German war debts were financially ruinous for Germany and politically fatal for the young German democracy that began to see the light with the November Revolution of 1918. The Treaty of Versailles forced Germany to pay 132 billion gold mark, almost three times the German GDP of 48 billion mark in 1913.[5] Between 1919 and 1923 Germany annually used 10 per cent of its GDP and 80 per cent of exports to service reparation demands, and consequently government spending exceeded revenues by about 50 per cent (Hetzel, 2002: 3). Many observers, including John Maynard Keynes (1988 [1919]), warned of the catastrophic economic consequences for Germany, but also for the global economic and monetary system, stemming from these huge debt flows. During the 1920s Germany remained internationally solvent only because of a constant stream of credits and foreign investments coming from the US. By that time, the US had already evolved as a global financial centre and the giant recycler of international credits (see Chapter 3). Wall Street had lend huge amounts of money to US allies such as France and the UK that were now repaying these debts with the reparation payments they received from Germany. Wall Street recycled these funds and lent them back to Germany or to US companies acquiring German assets such as GM, which bought the German carmaker Opel in 1929. When the stream of capital stopped because of the crisis in the US financial sector after 1929, a financial crisis in Germany was inevitable.

---

[4] Although there is little doubt that Germany and Austria had the biggest fault in the starting of World War 1, it is disputed until today if they were really the only ones responsible for it (see for example Clark 2013).

[5] BPB 2012.

There were attempts between the wars to cooperate internationally to manage the war debt. Owing to the inability (and unwillingness) of Germany to repay these debts, the Dawes plan of 1924, and the Young plan of 1929, restructured and reduced the war reparations substantially. In 1930, the Bank for International Settlements (BIS) was founded in Geneva to handle German war reparations and other war debts. For the first time it was acknowledged that an international organization would be necessary to deal with the international debt problem and to manage the emerging international crisis. However, it was too late, and the new international system could not be built up as fast as the old system failed. The most important signs of this failure were the collapse of the gold standard and the revival of nationalism and imperialism in Europe and East Asia.

With the benefit of hindsight, the return to the gold standard after the First World War was doomed from the beginning, but it was only when the world economic crisis struck in 1929 that governments slowly realized that the gold standard was a relic of the past that is incompatible with democratic governance. Owing to its rigid structure, the gold standard worsened deflationary tendencies, and, because the economic crisis was global in its dimension, declining wages did not increase competiveness but accelerated a deflationary race to the bottom. In 1931, the UK and its colonies abandoned the gold standard and reverted to a strategy of imperialist regionalism, focusing on stability at least within the empire by forming the 'Sterling-block'. The same year, Japan left the gold standard and started its colonial expansion into Manchuria in order to create a regional empire within East Asia. The US abandoned the guarantee to exchange dollars into gold in 1933, and most other countries followed suit. Attempts to reform the gold standard at the London Economic Conference in 1933 failed owing to the opposition of US President Roosevelt, who was concerned that the value of the dollar was too high, which was seen as a challenge to the prioritized domestic reforms. His focus shifted from currency stability to reviving growth and reducing unemployment with a 'New Deal', which included expansionary ('Keynesian') macroeconomic policies. As a consequence of the collapse of the gold standard, countries now tried to export their deflation and engaged in a competition to devalue their national currencies in a race to the bottom. Besides devaluing their currencies, they implemented strict capital controls and protected their national markets in order to achieve current-account surpluses. The nationalist attempt to snap larger pieces of the shrinking world market away from competitors further exacerbated the downward spiral of world trade. This period of economic 'currency wars' undermined any attempt for an international solution to the crisis (Rickards 2011: 56–77).

Like the UK, Germany, Austria, and most of Eastern Europe had already abandoned gold in 1931 when the outflow of foreign capital created a devastating banking crisis. They imposed strict capital controls that would prevent exports of gold and reserves. Unlike the UK and the US, this group of countries left their exchange rates nominally unchanged (Eichengreen 2008: 83), because a devaluation would have undermined their ability to repay their foreign debt. In Germany a devaluation of the German Reichsmark would have increased foreign debts and reparation payments, which had to be made in gold mark. Initially, Germany even shied away from stimulating the domestic economy through active macroeconomic policies, because it wanted to demonstrate that the cancellation of reparations was a precondition for German economic recovery. 'Hungerkanzler' Brüning (1930–2) pushed through extreme deflationary austerity measures that led to massive unemployment and political radicalization, which contributed to the rise to power of the Nazi party in 1933. When the Nazis took over, they immediately stopped reparation payments and implemented a form of military Keynesianism with a mandatory work service (*Arbeitsdienst*) and investments in the military and transport infrastructure (*Autobahn*). The Nazis also threw out central bank independency and Hjalmar Schacht became President of the Reichsbank and Minister of Economics in one person. Concerns of inflation were pushed aside owing to the control of the Nazi government over the economy, which would prevent wage and price increases alike through regulations or intimidation (Frieden 2007: ch. 9).

By 1932 the interwar gold standard was dead, and three regional currency zones emerged: countries that maintained the gold standard such as France and until 1933 the US; the sterling block of the British Empire; and the Reichsmark zone led by Germany and consisting of most East European countries. After 1937 Japan would add a fourth currency area with the yen block comprising Japan, Manchuria, and later its South-East Asian colonies. While the reactions to the world economic crisis are often correctly described as protectionist and nationalistic, there was a strong trend of regionalization as well. As world trade collapsed, major powers formed trade and currency blocks under their leadership. For the UK and France, this naturally meant deepening economic integration with their colonies. For Germany, which had lost its colonies in the First World War, this meant the formation of an East European sphere of influence that would trade through a clearing union (Fisher 1939; Kube 1984; Teichert 1984; Spaulding 1991). In 1938 a clearing union with twenty-five countries in Eastern Europe and Latin America accounted for more than half of Germany's trade (Neal 1979: 391). For Eastern Europe, the German share of its trade increased from an average of around 15 per cent in the 1920s to, on average, 40 per cent in the 1930s (Frieden 2007: ch. 9, p. 16). Within the clearing union, East European countries could use the *Sperrmark* they earned from exports to Germany just to purchase German imports. Because most countries in Eastern Europe were running a trade surplus with Germany, the clearing unions amounted to a provision of credits to Germany from Eastern Europe (Neal 1979: 401). Soon regionalization and economic domination of Eastern Europe in the so called *Grosswirtschaftsraum* (greater economic zone) was not enough for the German Nazi government. It longed for direct control over natural resources and wanted formally to integrate exporters of natural resources into the German currency system (Schacht 1937). The Nazi government saw Germany as the 'unsatisfied nation' and the only major power that had no colonial possessions. In 1938, Germany started an imperialist expansion into Eastern Europe, exploited its natural resources, and created '*Lebensraum*' ('living space') for Germans in Eastern Europe. The German attempt to achieve a brutal imperialist expansion by enslaving the people of Eastern Europe ultimately triggered the Second World War, which killed sixty million people, including the genocide of eleven million 'enemies' of the Nazi regime, the vast majority of them Eastern Europeans and more than half of them Jews.

Even before Germany, Japan had chosen an imperialistic solution to deal with the collapse of the world market by the occupation of Manchuria in 1931, war against China in 1937, and expansion into South-East Asia in 1941. The Japanese attempt to create an 'East Asian Co-Prosperity Sphere' was the East Asian version of creating a regional trading and monetary area that would be isolated from the collapse of the global currency system and the decline of world trade. This strategy pitted Japan directly against the US, which aimed to keep South-East Asia open for trade and to gain hegemonic control in the area. Japan believed it had only two choices: to give up its plans to build its own regional economic bloc or to risk war with the US. It chose the latter. In sum, until the Second World War, international economic relations were dominated by the competition between established and rising imperialist powers. International institutions like the rigid gold standard failed owing to the dynamics of the global economy, the rise of organized labour, and the establishment of democratic states with free elections.

2.1.4. The Bretton Woods System, 1944–1971

In 1944, the Bretton Woods conference was held to devise a new postwar global monetary system that would create an environment facilitating international trade and prevent a repetition of the catastrophic nationalist beggar-thy-neighbour policies of the 1930s. In order to prevent competitive devaluations and currency wars, Bretton Woods installed a new monetary system that would provide the stability of the gold standard but without its rigidity. John Maynard Keynes, who was the main architect of the Bretton Woods System (BWS) originally envisioned a new global accounting currency (the Bancor) to replace gold as the international unit of account. National currencies would be fixed to the Bancor, which could be used for all international currency transactions. An international clearing union would ensure that global economic imbalances would be limited, by penalizing countries running current-account deficits and surpluses alike (Kahler, in Andrews et al. 2002). Unfortunately, the US opposed this plan because in the 1940s it was running large current-account surpluses, and thus Keynes's plan was politically not feasible. Instead, the US took the lead and established the dollar as the new global currency, with a guarantee to exchange dollar into gold. In this gold–dollar standard, all other currencies would be fixed to the dollar, and the IMF was created to 'promote international monetary cooperation through a permanent institution which provides the machinery for consultation and collaboration on international monetary problems' (IMF Articles of Agreement of 1944, Art. 1, sect. 1). In particular, the IMF would ensure that 'each member undertakes to collaborate with the Fund to promote exchange stability, to maintain orderly exchange arrangements with other members, and to avoid competitive exchange alterations' (IMF 1944: art. IV, sect. 4). Changes of exchange rates could be made only after consultation with the IMF (1944: art. IV, sect. 5). In order to help countries financing short-term current- account deficits avoid devaluing their currencies, the IMF made 're-sources available to them under adequate safeguards, thus providing them with opportunity to correct maladjustments in their balance of payments without resorting to measures destructive of national or international prosperity' (IMF 1944: art. I, sect. 5). National capital controls sanctioned by the IMF allowed countries to implement expansionary ('Keynesian') macroeconomic policies that facilitated reconstruction after the war.

In order to prevent the repetition of the disaster of international debt management that had taken place between the wars, the victorious countries of the Second World War did not penalize the defeated countries with reparation payments. Instead, reparations were limited to the annexation of German territories east of the Oder/Neisse, the temporary occupation of the Saarland, and the transfer of German industrial assets. Western Germany was spared most reparations, when the Western Allies gave up the dismantling of German industrial assets in 1949 and instead supported reconstruction with the Marshall Plan. The International Bank for Reconstruction and Development (better known as the World Bank) was founded, together with the IMF, to provide war-destroyed countries with international credits. Instead of the losers of the war being punished through reparation payments, they would receive credits for reconstruction. With the US concerned about the expansion of communism in Europe and Asia, IMF and World Bank became important tools to achieve the goal of capitalist reconstruction in Western Europe. Not surprisingly, the Soviet Union (and its East European Allies), although originally part of the Bretton Woods conference, remained outside the BWS, which they (correctly) identified as an attempt by the US to exercise global economic hegemony.

The BWS worked very well as long as the US and the dollar were strong and provided the 'hegemonic stability' (Kindleberger 1986) needed for the system. The period from 1945 to 1971 is often referred to as the second golden age of capitalism in the Western world. In fact, the BWS is to liberal observers what the gold standard is for conservatives, a point of reference to evaluate any global monetary regime and sometimes even an object of nostalgia. Indeed, during the BWS, there were few international financial crises, the world economy and trade were growing at record rates, and international debt issues and exchange-rate adjustments were negotiated in a cooperative multilateral way.

Bretton Woods constituted a time of convergence not just internationally but also concerning the underlying domestic political economies. The hegemonic stability at the international level was embedded in strong Keynesian states that were willing and able to take charge and govern the economy through various means of macroeconomic policies, industrial policies, and welfare spending. This 'embedded liberalism' (Ruggie 1982) provided the domestic complementary of the BWS at the international level. This convergence towards a Keynesian best practice extended across the political isles, and even Milton Friedman declared in 1965 that in some way 'we are all Keynesians now' (*Time Magazine*, 31 December 1965). Free-market capitalism was discredited, and the vast majority believed that the economy and in particularly financial markets needed to be engineered to become more efficient and more stable. This convergence towards Keynesian thinking can be partly explained by the external threat of Soviet-style socialism as an alternative economic model. At that time the socialist countries were doing quite well economically, with growth rates above those of Western countries (albeit from a much lower starting point), and were thus seen as a credible economic threat. More importantly, strong labour unions in the West influenced the public debate far beyond the social democratic parties and achieved an ideological influence that politicians could not ignore. Despite the convergence towards an embedded liberalism and a strong state intervening in the economy, the embeddedness and the types of interventions differed substantially. While in the US macroeconomic and in particularly fiscal policies played the most important role, most countries in Europe focused on expanding the welfare state. In Japan, Korea, and later other East Asian countries, the focus of state interventions was on industrial polices. In the early 1970s, this specific complementarity between domestic Keynesianism and the BWS came increasingly under attack.

The major flaw of the BWS was that it was dependent on the leadership of the US and the dollar as the global currency. Right up to today, the dominance of the US in the IMF is enshrined in its veto power in all major decisions and the fact that the IMF headquarters is just a few blocks away from the US government district in Washington DC. As long as the US was willing to underwrite the system, it remained intact, but with the relative economic decline of the US because of the Vietnam War and the reconstruction of Europe and Japan, it was less and less willing to pay the costs of leadership. With the economic recovery of Europe and Japan in the 1950s and 1960s, more and more dollars were circulating outside the US, and in 1971 the US became a deficit country. Globalizing financial markets started to undermine capital controls, and speculators started to question the stability of the dollar. Initially, IMF member countries tried to solve the problem of a weaker US by strengthening the IMF. In 1961, the London gold pool, collectively to defend the value of the dollar against gold, was installed, and 'Roosa bonds' were created and sold to foreign central banks as an alternative to gold. In the general agreement to borrow of 1962, major IMF members agreed to extend additional credit to the IMF in case it would be needed. In 1969, the IMF even went back to Keynes's original proposal to create an artificial global currency within the IMF. These Special Drawing Rights (SDRs) would be used for IMF internal transaction and supplement the dollar as a global currency but not replace it (Eichengreen 2011: 53–7). The SDR would allow deficit countries such as Britain to borrow from the IMF to finance their current-account deficits without devaluing their currency. All attempts to rescue the BWS, however, were doomed when in 1971 President Nixon unilaterally declared that the US would abolish the guarantee to exchange US dollars into gold. With the Nixon Shock, the US effectively abandoned the BWS, while the US dollar remained by default the global currency (see Chapter 3).

European governments initially tried to save the BWS, and at a meeting at the Smithsonian Institution in December 1971 they succeeded in persuading the US to preserve multilateral currency management and retain some controls on capital exports (Helleiner 1994: 104). The French government was particularly active persuading others that, in order to maintain fixed exchange rates, it would be necessary internationally to coordinate capital flows and bring the pockets of deregulated finance, like the Eurodollar market in London, back under control. Ultimately all attempts failed, because the US opposed an international coordination of regulating financial flows, and in 1973 European countries abandoned the Smithsonian Agreement. The European Community switched to a regional approach exchange-rate system, in the form of first the 'currency snake', then the European Monetary System (EMS) in 1979, and finally the European Economic and Monetary Union (EMU) from 1999 (see Chapter 4). Japan and other East Asian countries opted for unilateral currency pegs and thus decided to maintain the link of their currencies to the US dollar but without the institutional framework and support of the BWS (see Chapter 5).

2.1.5. Financial Globalization and the Decline of National Keynesianism since 1971

The main characteristic of the post Bretton Woods era is that since 1971 a comprehensive international system to regulate monetary and financial relations has been missing. This 'non-system' (Gilpin 1987) has been an era of massive financial globalization and liberalization, and at the same time a period of financial crisis, with the tendency of crises to become more frequent and more severe. The US dollar remains the most widely used international currency, because no other currency is currently able to challenge its global role. Coordination of exchange rates has been given up, and international financial flows have been liberalized. The IMF changed its role from the manager of a global monetary system to a crisis manager, while monetary interventions since then have tended to be uncoordinated and ad hoc. Instead of clear rules for international cooperation, crisis management was now governed by an ideological 'Washington Consensus' that consisted of a set of neoliberal policies, placing the burden of all costs of crises on debtor countries.

Since the 1970s, financial markets have been growing much more quickly than the real economy, and growth has accelerated since the 1990s. For example, in the US, stock market capitalization more than tripled from less than 50 per cent of GDP in the early 1990s to more than 150 per cent at the end of the decade, just before the dot.com bubble burst (World Bank 2013). Chapter 3 will investigate the financialization of the US economy and its transformation into a finance-led capitalism in more detail. Growth of financial markets was far less explosive in other countries, but the increasing role of financial markets can be found in all major economies, with the exception of Japan, which saw its own financial bubble burst at the beginning of the 1990s. Even more impressive has been the growth of international financial transactions. For example, currency transactions not connected to trade and direct investments were negligible in the 1970s but increased to a market with a turnover of more than US$5 trillion in 2016. Growth has been particularly strong since 2002, despite the fact that the introduction of the euro in 1999 had considerably lowered the number of currencies (Figure 2.1). This currency turnover is more than one quarter of the *annual* world merchandized trade, which amounted to US$18 trillion in 2017. In other words, four days of currency trading would be enough to purchase all merchandised exports for one year, while the remaining transactions consist of pure financial transactions.

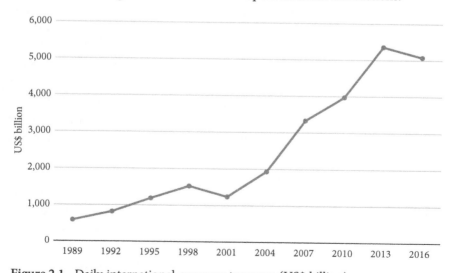

Figure 2.1. Daily international currency turnover (US$ billion)

Source: BIS. 2016. Triennial Central Bank Survey of foreign exchange and OTC derivatives markets in 2016 [Online]. Available: https://www.bis.org/publ/rpfx16.htm.

The growth of international finance had a massive impact on the ability and will of nation states to regulate financial activities. Nation states engaged in 'competitive deregulation' (Helleiner 1994: 12) to benefit from financial businesses conducted within their own territory and generally to attract capital from abroad. Interest-rate curbs and capital controls were abolished in Europe and the US, but not so much in East Asia, as we shall see in Chapter 5. Through this process, those people owning or managing capital gained the upper hand over national regulators and could twist the arms of governments to offer them better conditions and higher returns. The competitive deregulation became a competition for capital, the 'timid deer' that would flee at any hint of regulation or cuts of interest rates. In the US, as we will see in more detail in Chapter 3, the process has reached a level of 'financialization' in which financial transactions and motives increasingly dominate the economy.

From the beginning, financial globalization and liberalization went hand in hand and led to an increase of financial volatility as well as an increase in the number and severity of financial crisis. Financial crises (banking crises and/or currency crises) were substantially more numerous and more severe in the period between the wars and after the collapse of BWS in 1971. The increase in the number of crises since 1971 has been particularly acute for developing and newly industrializing countries (Bordo et al. 2001; Eichengreen and Bordo 2002). In the 1970s, money from the US, Europe, and the oil-exporting countries was flowing to the emerging market, mostly in Latin America, which led to the debt crisis of the 1980s (Altvater 1987). In the 1990s, it was the 'East Asian Economic Miracle' (World Bank 1993) that was attractive for international investors, leading to the Asian financial crisis of 1997–8, followed by the dot.com bubble that burst in 2001. Finally from 2001 until 2008 it was the US housing and in particularly the subprime mortgage market that was flooded with money and then collapsed in 2008, as we will see. Because of these boom-and-bust cycles, Susan Strange (1998: 1) likened financial markets to a manic depressive patient who is 'erratically manic at one moment, unreasonably depressive at others'.

Financial globalization and the liberalization of financial markets increasingly undermined not just the global rules of finance but also the national foundation on which the embedded liberal model of Bretton Woods had rested. Financial globalization meant that investors could move their money around more easily and threaten to invest elsewhere if governments did not implement investor-friendly policies. 'Competition states' (Hirsch 1995; Cerny 1997) would compete against each other to attract investments and create a regulatory race to the bottom. It is important to note that the state itself has not lost any of its importance. On the contrary, states have become more and more important, when it comes to both public spending as well as regulations. For example, welfare spending has increased since the 1970s as we will see in Chapter 4 (Figure 4.3). A good example for the bureaucratic character of 'free markets' is that just the GATT part (the part concerned with trade in goods) of the WTO consists of 30 agreements and 30,000 pages, which show just how much globalization depends on governments and detailed regulation. The growing power of the judiciary, which is dealing with disputes over an increasing number of social and economic regulations, is another aspect that has seen an increasing role of the state particularly in countries with a common-law tradition. The state itself is not losing power, but it is the limitation of the political choices about what kind of regulations and policies should be implemented that characterizes the era of globalization. Policies and regulation that are limiting the expansion and profitability of capital and businesses have little possibility of success on a national level. Narr and Schubert (1994) have summarized this dilemma in arguing that economic globalization creates not the crisis of the state but a 'misery of politics'. The German term *Sachzwang*, which literally means 'force of the objective circumstance', is the most concise way of describing this mentality of 'there is no alternative', which was hijacked by neoliberals like Margaret Thatcher and conservatives like Helmut Kohl in the 1980s. Alternative reactions to the pressure of globalization, like Mitterrand's attempt to radicalize Keynesian policies in the 1980s, failed (see Chapter 4).

2.2. The Global Financial Crisis and the G20

2.2.1. The Global Financial Crisis since 2008 and the Failure of Global Governance

The global financial and economic crisis since 2008 has been one of the most significant crises in the international political economy since the emergence of global capitalism in the nineteenth century. It is second only to the imperialist confrontations that led to the First World War and the World Economic crisis of the 1930s that brought about the disaster of fascism and the Second World War, as just described. Even the two oil crises of the 1970s arguably did not have the same severity and scope, although both crises contributed somewhat to the process of financialization in various ways, as we will see in Chapter 3. The developments since 2008 have many aspects, and there have been numerous studies on the causes of the crisis, its management, and its consequences.

Owing to the already vast amount of literature on the global financial crisis,[6] it is unnecessary to describe it in detail; rather, I will focus on what is essential as a foundation for a second-image IPE perspective. The potential for the crisis built after the collapse of the dot.com bubble in 2000, when banks and investors were looking for new investment opportunities. They decided that the real-estate market had potential for growth and extended their mortgage loans. This trend was particularly pronounced in the US, but also in fast-growing economies in East Asia (Korea, China) and Europe (Ireland, Spain, and other Southern European countries). A real-estate bubble started to build, and lenders advanced into more and more risky sectors of the market. In addition, amid increasing house prices, houseowners started to use their real estate as collateral for consumer credits. Over time, the real-estate market became increasingly saturated, and lenders extended their credit to previously uncreditworthy customers in the subprime mortgages sector. In the US in particular, the increasing risks in the market were reduced by the creation of new financial products that allowed for the reduction of individual risks for creditors. Lenders compensated for the increased risk by packaging loans into collaterized debt olbigations (CDOs) and selling them to investors around the world. They also purchased insurances in the form of credit default swaps (CDS) against the risk of falling prices. Since the mortgage market was relatively stable based on historical data, their models and the models of rating agencies considered products involving collateral in the real-estate market as very safe. These new financial products, in combination with the lightly regulated sector of non-bank financial institutions and investment banks, were the important domestic factors of the crisis. This unholy combination was made possible by a quarter century of financial liberalization, deregulation and a massive concentration of power in the financial sector. Financial in-stitutions did not just grow exponentially; they were also able to take on risks, because their massive economic power led to the assumption that the govern-ment would bail them out in the event of a crisis. When the historically unrepresented 'black swan' event of broad falling real-estate prices became reality in 2007, banks and financial investors ran for the exit at the same time, making the situation worse. When the first institutions, such as Bear Sterns, became insolvent in May 2008 and mortgage lenders Freddie Mac and Fannie Mae ran into financial difficulties in July, the government believed

---

[6] A good starting point is the excellent official inquiry report by the US Congress on the crisis (United States. Financial Crisis Inquiry Commission 2011). Other excellent accounts include: Shiller (2008); Albo et al. (2010); Helleiner et al. (2010); Stiglitz and United Nations (2010); Krippner (2011); Helleiner (2014); Gill (2015); and Piketty (2016).

it had no other choice but to rescue them. From the perspective of market fundamentalists in the Bush administration, these bailouts were against market discipline and would create a moral hazard. Consequently, the Bush administration believed it needed to set an example, and, when Lehman Brothers became insolvent in September 2008, the government did not intervene and let it fail. The already tense situation in the financial market evolved into a full-blown panic. Even the most stable markets, such as short-term interbank lending, froze as trust vaporized. The Bush government made another U-turn and provided $700 billion in bailout funds as part of the Troubled Asset Relief Program (TARP) to rescue financial institutions from collapse.

At that time, however, the crisis had already spread to the global financial markets and the real economy. Financial flows and international trade collapsed as consumers and companies cut down spending. Companies reduced wages and laid off employees, further worsening the downward spiral. East Asian countries, which are particularly dependent on trade, were among the worst hit by the collapse of international trade. Initially Europe seemed to be less affected by the crisis, but it was soon discovered that European banks were heavily engaged in risky US assets. More importantly, from 2009 it became increasingly clear that the Southern European real-estate and debt crisis was as least as serious as the one in the US (see Chapter 4).

When it comes to the causes of the crisis, most studies concentrate on regulatory failure in the financial market and particularly the subprime market (Shiller 2008) or focus on greedy bankers (Lewis 2010). While these interpretations have their merit, they are US-centric and underestimate the global scope of the crisis, concerning not just the effects but in particular the causes. Initially it seemed that the crisis of 2008 was primarily a product of the failure of domestic financial regulation, particularly in the US. As we will see, these domestic defects had extended to the international level, as financial globalization, global imbalances, and currency competition. Most of the often criticized deregulation of the US financial sector was not just a result of lobbying by the financial sector within the US but was equally a manifestation of the US being the undisputed centre for recycling global funds (see Chapter 3). In Europe, the euro crisis was not just the result of contagion from the US, but also the logical consequence of a decade-long attempt in the EU to find a regional solution for international monetary volatility (see Chapter 4). Finally, the global imbalances that resulted from East Asia's successful development contributed to the massive increase in global financial flows that led to the financial bubble in the US (see Chapter 5). The global financial crisis of 2008 was the result not just of regulatory failure on the national level but also of a failure of international cooperation and global economic governance.

2.2.2. The G20: From Hegemonic Instability towards a New Multilateralism?

At the international level, the causes of the crisis were rooted in the failure of the post Bretton-Woods 'non-system' of international financial governance. First, there was a failure of the proper international standards to regulate banks and 'financial innovations' in the Basel agreements and the Financial Stability Board (FSB). Second, there was the failure of basically all international organizations to acknowledge the problems of crisis-prone financial globalization and the obsession with open capital accounts, which prevented a sound international regulation of financial markets and sometimes even undermined national attempts to protect domestic financial markets. Third, there was the failure of the IMF to prevent countries from using the 'currency weapon' to become more competitive. Fourth, the G20 failed to coordinate efforts for improved financial stability from its foundation in 1999 up to the beginning of the crisis in 2008.

During the time of crisis management, from 2008 to 2012, the G20 became the main forum coordinating the crisis management and introducing institutional changes to avoid future crisis. The G20 had originally been founded in 1999 at the level of finance ministers and central bank chiefs, in the aftermath of the Asian financial crisis of 1997–8. Even then there were doubts about the benefits of two decades of financial globalization as the lack of international cooperation in monetary issues emerged (Stiglitz 2002). The 1990s, however, were shaped by the survival of the US as the sole remaining superpower, and the dominance of the US in international institutions was extremely strong. The neoliberal hegemony and the dominance of the US were strongest under President Clinton and during the relatively high economic growth in the US during his time in office. Although the period from 1997 to 2008 was haunted by massive global economic and financial turmoil, neoliberal hegemony remained strong, and financial globalization was seen as without an alternative within the G20. While there was a lack of alternatives, the decade of 'hegemonic instability' (Beeson and Broome 2010) fuelled the conviction that neither the G20 nor the US and the US-dominated IMF would be able to provide stability to the global monetary system and support countries in crisis. The Asian financial crisis was a particularly harsh blow to the notion that the

US would be able to establish global financial stability by globalizing US-style institutions. Although the Asian financial crisis had started in the periphery of the world economy in South-East Asia, it spread to the 'developed' financial markets, cumulating in the collapse of the US hedge fund LTCM (Blustein 2003). During the whole period, the US and the IMF seemed incapable of preventing the contagion effect, and their neoliberal austerity and structural adjustment reforms were criticized of deepening the crisis (Kalinowski 2005a, b, 2007). In 2003, even the IMF's own evaluation office presented a harsh critique of misguided IMF conditionality, particularly in the first months of the crisis (IEO/IMF 2003).

The minister level G20 was founded because it became clear that crisis in the 'periphery' could now spread to the financial centres of the West, and it was thus seen necessary to bring all 'systemically important' economies to the table. Besides the G8, these systemically important countries were China, Brazil, Argentina, Mexico, South Africa, Saudi Arabia, India, Australia, Indonesia, and South Korea, as well as the EU, reflecting the development towards a unified European economy. Unfortunately, during the first decade of the new millennium, multilateral institutions in general dramatically lost influence owing to the neoconservative turn in the US. The US under the Bush administration reverted to unilateralism and focused on the self-proclaimed 'war against terror'. At the same time, there was no major financial crisis between the burst of the dot.com bubble in 2000 and the collapse of Lehman Brothers in 2008. The G20, and the financial stability forum that was founded together with the G20 to coordinate work with other international organizations, lost influence dramatically. Under pressure from the US, the G20 focused on fighting terrorist finances. The IMF experienced a legitimacy crisis, owing to the dramatic decline in lending during the 2000s and the criticism that its crisis management strategy was flawed and its decision-making undemocratic (Seabrooke 2007). G20 meetings slipped into obscurity, and discussion centred around the expansion of the G8 to a G13 (to include the other BRIC countries, Mexico, and South Africa), initiated by Germany in the 'Heiligendamm process', which led to the summit in Germany in 2007 (Cooper 2008). The G13 was seen as a more flexible alternative to the G20. In addition, topics at the G8 summits shifted away from economic issues to topics such as terrorism, climate change, or the achievements of the Millennium Development Goals. Issues of financial stability were pushed into the background. For example, at the G8 summit in Heiligendamm in 2007, German Chancellor Merkel proposed a 'code of conduct' to curb the activities of largely unregulated hedge funds. Even this modest proposal on the eve of the global financial crisis was prevented by the US and the UK, because they strongly believed in the efficiency of deregulated financial markets.

The acceleration of the subprime crisis and the collapse of Lehman Brothers in September 2008 that triggered the global financial crisis dramatically changed the situation, and in the same year the G20 was upgraded to the level of leaders. The US preferred this upgrade to an expanded G8, because it would include close allies such as Australia and South Korea, while at the same time limiting the influence of China and Europe. Upon the initiative of the US, the first leaders' summit took place in Washington DC in November 2008. The second summit was held in London in April 2009, the third in Pittsburgh in September 2009, the fourth in Toronto in June 2010, the fifth in Seoul in November 2010, the sixth in Cannes in 2011, and the seventh in Los Cabos in 2012. Since 2011, the leaders' summits have been held annually in the country of the rotating chair. Owing to the global financial and economic crisis, since 2008 the G20 has returned to its origins of crisis management, financial regulation, and better global economic coordination.

As an informal discussion forum, the G20 has no direct power to make decisions or implement policies. There are no statutes of the G20 and no organization ensuring compliance or settling disputes. There is not even a secretariat, as meetings are organized by the rotating chair. However, when leaders in the G20 agree on an issue, their agreement often leads to working-level decisions in formal international organizations such as the IMF, the BIS, and the Financial Stability Board. This practice has been quite successful but has also been criticized as undemocratic and a further demotion of the United Nations (Kalinowski 2010; Vestergaard and Wade 2012). Indeed, even though the G20 represents about 80 per cent of the global GDP and world trade, it represents just two-thirds of the world population and excludes 174 of the 193 members of the UN (23 additional European countries are represented indirectly through the EU commission). At the same time, however, the G20 constitutes progress compared to the G7, which was even more exclusive and was the premier forum for monetary and economic cooperation before the G20. The G20 also is more inclusive by acknowledging a new global role for the EU, which at the time of writing represents twenty-eight states.

As regards the topics discussed, the G20 agenda has changed over the years (see Table 2.1). Working groups ensure a continuous discussion on the core topics. There are working groups on 'financial architecture' (chaired by Australia and Turkey), 'growth' (chaired by Canada and India), 'development' (chaired by South Africa, South Korea, and France), and 'energy' (chaired by the UK and Indonesia). Initially however, the agenda was clearly dominated by

Table 2.1. Priorities of leaders' G20 summits

Date	Place	Chair	Active macroeconomic policies	Financial regulation	Coordination of currencies	IMF reform	Reduce imbalances
14-15 November 2008	Washington	US	++	++	—	+	—
1–2 April 2009	London	UK	+++	++	+	++	—
24–5 September 2009	Pittsburgh	US	++	+++	—	++	+
26–7 June 2010	Toronto	Canada	+	++	—	++	++
11–12 November 2010	Seoul	Korea	+	++	+	++	++
3–4 November 2011	Cannes	France	—	+++	++	+	+
18–19 June 2012	Los Cabos	Mexico	—	++	+	+	+

Note: — not mentioned in official final communiqué, + mentioned, ++ commitment for coordination, +++ very strong emphasis on the topic.

Source: own assessment, based on G20 summit communiqués.

the immediate stabilization of the crisis in 2008. At the first three summits in Washington (2008), and London and Pittsburgh (both 2009), the coordination of fiscal stimulus packages as well as a commitment against protectionism dominated the agenda. After the 2009 Pittsburgh summit, issues of bank regulation became more important, and members agreed to make the G20 into a regular meeting and the 'premier forum for our international economic cooperation' (G20 2009c). Since 2010, the issues of currency competition and monetary policies have entered the discussion. Besides these core issues, the G20 has also dealt with diverse issues, such as development at the Seoul summit or food security in Cannes. Table 2.1 summarizes my assessment of changing priorities in the G20 from 2008 to 2012—that is, during the time when crisis management and financial regulation were at the centre of the G20 agenda.

2.3. The Competition of Models of Capitalism and the Global Financial Crisis since 2008

The historical perspective has revealed a very dynamic process of economic and financial globalization and the different forms that the international regulation of finance has taken. As we have seen, the dynamics of globalization and its regulation were shaped by the competition between established and rising powers. Established colonial powers defended their turf against aspiring imperialist countries trying to get their share of the pie. During the British-dominated gold standard and the US-dominated BWS there was a relatively stable international system in place, but it was not truly multilateral, as both systems relied on the ability and goodwill of the hegemonic power. It would be too simple, however, to limit the dynamics of international economic relations to the 'rise and fall of the great powers' (Kennedy 1987). Rather, it is necessary to look at the internal dynamics of the great powers and their challengers and the way they complement each other internationally. Ultimately, the dynamics of the global economy are driven by the competition of different economic systems. A liberal, British-dominated system was challenged by the rising neo-mercantilist nations of Germany and Japan. Between the wars, conflicts between international creditor countries like the US and countries struggling to repay their war debts shaped international economic relations. This competition took very confrontational forms under imperialism and between the wars, but a more cooperative form under the BWS. In fact the BWS was the only time when there was some sort of convergence of domestic political economies under a consensus of a Keynesian and embedded liberalism. Even during the cooperative times under the BWS, global economic relations were not a harmonious affair but were driven by the interdependence between the US as the hegemonic power and exporter of capital and Europe and Japan trying to catch up during reconstruction. Ultimately, it was this dynamic that destroyed the BWS. Since the collapse of the BWS, relationships have become more competitive, as the three very distinct models of capitalism emerged from the challenges of intensified globalization and crisis after the 1970s. Until the 1960s, the US model of capitalism was widely considered the most advanced model towards which all others would converge. In this modernization theory, capitalist development was conceptualized as a ladder with US mass consumer capitalism at the top; all other models were seen as underdeveloped, following the US in the 'stages of economic growth' (Rostow 1959). Since the 1970s, however, European varieties of capitalism and the Japanese developmental state have emerged as formidable competitors that could not simply be dismissed as being at a lower stage of development.

2.3.1. International Economic Relations as Competition of Models of Capitalism

Despite the dominance of the US and the hegemony of US-style neoliberal ideology, there was not a convergence of models of capitalism. Rather, as we shall see in Chapters 3, 4, and 5 the US, Europe, and East Asia have responded differently to the challenges of economic globalization. The dynamics of global capitalism does not derive from a convergence towards one superior model of capitalism but rather emerges from the interdependence and competition between different models of capitalism. Finance-led and export-led varieties of capitalism depend on each other, just as domestic, export-oriented, and financial capital depend on each other at the domestic level. A completely financialized global economy is not possible, because finance does not produce any values itself, and financial centres always need a real economy producing values that it can redistribute. The same is true for an export-oriented model of capitalism, which always depends on regions running trade deficits. Only the relatively balanced European integration-led model seems to have at least the theoretical possibility of being applied to the global level. Indeed, the EU likes to see itself as a 'laboratory for global governance' (Manners 2010). Given the problems of the European integration process, which will be discussed in more detail in Chapter 4, it seems unlikely that a project like the EU could be the stepping stone for a global system at least in the short or medium term.

Economic and particularly financial globalization has altered the relationship between state, business, and labour, but it has also altered the way states or different national and regional institutional systems compete with each other. The dynamics of globalization is not the convergence towards one type of capitalist institutional system but the competition between them. The different models of capitalism globally complement each other but are also in a state of constant imbalance, tension, and conflict, as was indicated in Chapter 1. It is now time briefly to explain the three most important conflicts: the struggle about international financial regulations, the problem of global economic imbalances, and currency competition.

2.3.2. The (De-)Regulation of International Finance since the 1970s and the Rise of Neoliberalism

From the perspective of the critical school of IPE, financial globalization has often been described as a process of Americanization driven by US imperialism (Panitch and Gindin 2003). Indeed, there can be little doubt that international rules and organizations have been dominated by the US, even after the formal dollar-based global currency system was abandoned and despite the fact that the US economy has lost its dominant role in world markets. Since the 1970s, the US has used bilateral pressure and its position in international organizations to build a global economy that suits its interests (Strange 1986). The most important element of this hegemony is the pressure for open capital accounts and the free flow of international capital. As we will see in more detail in Chapter 3, the US strategy to declining growth rates at home was to open international markets for US capital and to develop the US as the main financial centre for recycling global financial funds. Through its privileged role in global financial markets, the US could profit from the global need for financial services and the higher growth potential particularly in the East Asian emerging economies.

In the 1980s, the US used bilateral pressure to push partners to open their capital accounts and liberalize their economies, most prominently in the case of Japan (Ito 1993). It also used its position in international organizations such as the IMF and the World Bank to force creditor countries to implement structural adjustment measures, which often included financial liberalization, deregulation, and privatization, in particular during the debt crisis in Latin

America during the 1980s. When the Soviet Union collapsed in 1991 and Eastern Europe was freed from Soviet domination, the IMF and the World Bank extended their mission to transform Eastern Europe 'from plan to market' (World Bank 1996) in the early 1990s. Finally, when Japanese growth rates declined in the 1990s and the other East Asian miracle economies fell into crisis in 1997, the IMF declared that East Asian state-led 'crony capitalism' was finished and more or less tried to force East Asian countries to implement US-style institutions. The 'Wall Street–Treasury–IMF complex' (Veneroso and Wade 1998) was at the peak of its influence, and global finance seemed to be unstoppable. Since the mid-1990s, the US economy has also performed better than other advanced countries, and thus US neoliberalism gained the intellectual hegemony as a 'best-practice' strategy amid the 'fact' of economic and financial globalization. Figure 2.2 shows the IMF's 'financial reform index' up to the global financial crisis. Characteristically for this time and the dominance of US finance-led capitalism, reform is to a large degree defined by liberalization and openness. It can be seen that the US (and the UK) were the frontrunner(s) in financial liberalization after the 1980s, with other countries moving in the same direction but starting later and moving much more slowly.

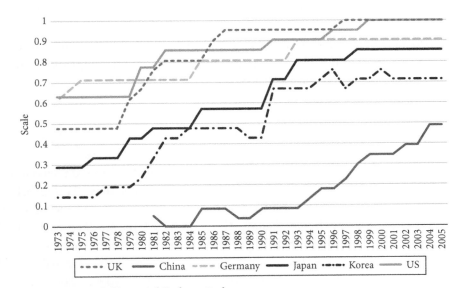

Figure 2.2. IMF Financial Reform Index

Note: Scale 0–1, A higher score reflects a larger degree of financial reform.

Source: Abiad, A., Detragiache, E. & Tressel, T. 2008. A new database of financial reforms. IMF Working Papers, 08.

Despite the dominance of the US and the hegemony of US-style neoliberalism demanding financial deregulation and liberalization, there has been little convergence towards common rules for the financial sector. While a broad trend of deregulation and increasing financial volatility can be observed everywhere, it took different trajectories in different countries. For example, as we will see in Chapter 4 the EU has prioritized the harmonization of rules within the Union rather than simply following US standards. While harmonization did become a code for deregulation, rules in Europe reflected the specific organization of the largely bank-based European financial sector. In East Asia, the state-led financial system was not so much abandoned as maintained in China and 'remodelled' (Vogel 2006) in Japan and Korea (see Chapter 5).

The combination and mutual reinforcement of global economic imbalances and financial globalization and deregulation are important factors setting the stage for a potential crisis. Current-account imbalances have to be compensated for by capital flows from surplus to deficit countries. This adds to the flow of capital and increases the potential for financial crisis. It creates an ever-increasing divide between international creditors in East Asia and Northern Europe as well as international debtors such as the US and South European countries. This development leads to the question of whether and how countries that run consistent deficits will be able to repay their international debt. Within a single currency, like the euro area, this problem can be observed, as, for example, in the case of the euro crisis (see Chapter 4), while an imbalance between East Asia and the US brings up the issue of currency competition and the role of the US dollar as the global reserve currency.

2.3.3. Global Imbalances

Financial globalization and deregulation are connected to a second phenomenon shaping international financial and economic relations. The global economic imbalances that emerged in the late 1960 have become more accentuated since the 1990s (Figure 2.3). In a nutshell, the US (and the UK) are constantly running large deficits, while East Asian countries are running surpluses. Deficits in the US and surpluses in East Asia are interconnected and depend on each other. Financial globalization and the dynamics of global capitalism are thus as much a result of US financial-led capitalism as the result of the economic rise of export-led East Asian capitalism. The European Union as such was relatively balanced from the outside until 2008, but suffered from

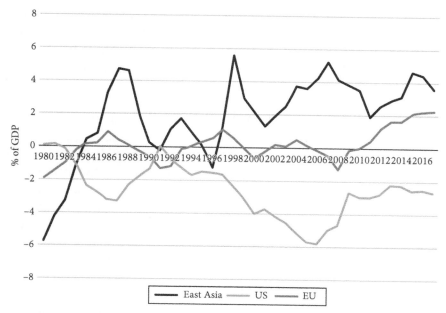

Figure 2.3. Current-account balance (% of GDP)

Note: East Asia is the unweighted average of China, Japan and Korea (until 1996 without China)
Source: IMF, WEO Oct 2016

internal imbalances between the north and the south, which became more problematic with the introduction of the euro in 1999 (see Chapter 4). After the global economic crisis spread to the euro crisis, the internal imbalances declined, but instead the EU became a net surplus economy. Although this trend is probably just temporary, it seems that the EU is partially converging with an export-led model of growth rather than a finance-led one.

The changing structure of the world economy (and in particular the global economic rise of East Asian countries (see Chapter 5) is one cause of the increasing global imbalances. This global trend is connected to changes within domestic political economies and the divergence of different models of capitalism. Most importantly, as we shall see in Chapter 3, finance-led countries are able to run long-term deficits because of their ability to recycle global capital based on a specific finance-led model of capitalism. At the same time, export-oriented countries depend on permanent surpluses, because their growth model is based on a corporatist model of capitalism, as we shall see in Chapter 5. The EU is a specific case, as its integration-led growth model is externally balanced but internally problematic, as we will discuss in Chapter 4.

Global imbalances go hand in hand with a dual development. At the domestic level they are driven by the competition of finance-led and export-oriented growth models, and at the international level they are connected to the trend of financial globalization as well as currency competition.

2.3.4. Currency Competition and Currency Wars

The third element of the international financial and economic dynamics and potential conflict is the problem of currency competition and exchange-rate volatility. As we can see in Figure 2.4, with the exemption of the Chinese yuan, exchange rates have been very volatile, both when it comes to daily changes as well as long-term fluctuations. Volatility and large adjustments in currency values have been particularly accentuated since the beginning of the global economic crisis in 2007. To some degree, the short-term volatility is a consequence of the growth of international financial transactions, while long-term adjustment is connected to global economic imbalances. At the same time, it is important to note that the international currency regime is not just dominated by market forces in the financial and the real economy, as the currency market is an arena of international relations structured by power.

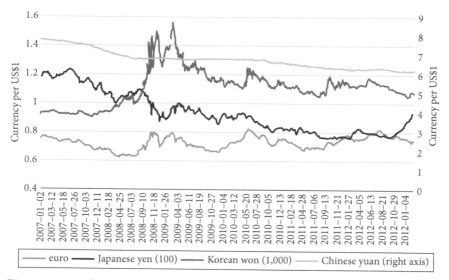

Figure 2.4. Exchange rates per US$

Source: FED 2013. Data Download Program [Online]. Available: http://www.federalreserve.gov/datadownload/.

First of all, not all currencies are equal. De facto, the neoliberal 'non-system' of monetary coordination is based on the role of the US dollar as the global currency. This 'exorbitant privilege' (Eichengreen 2011) allowed the US to run sustained deficits, because it was able to export dollars to finance them. This was possible only because most of the rest of the world needs US dollars for its international trade and to insure itself against the volatility of the global system by holding dollar reserves. While the US was able to enjoy this privilege, the central role of the dollar has created many problems for East Asia and Europe. Both regions are concerned that the US will print more and more dollars to finance its deficits and repay its debt through inflation, which would reduce the value of dollar assets of international creditors. A sharp decline in the value of the dollar also undermines export profits, particularly for East Asian exports, which are predominantly accounted for in dollars. For East Asia, the expansive monetary policies in the US have also led to a massive inflow of capital into the region, pushing East Asian currencies up and making exports from the region less competitive. As we shall see in detail in Chapter 5, East Asian countries have reacted by introducing capital controls and managing their currencies, as can be observed in the case of China, but also in South Korean and Japanese attempts to prevent a more pronounced and rapid appreciation of their currencies since 2009.

2.4. Conflicts on the International Regulation of Finance in the G20 since 2008

After having described the three arenas of potential international conflicts— global imbalances, financial regulation, and currency competition—in general terms, it is time to investigate how these potential conflicts have played out in the G20 since 2008. From the perspective of international relations, the conflicts emerging from global economic imbalances, financial globalization, and currency competition are problems of a lack of international cooperation and coordination in these areas. Before we investigate the domestic origins of these conflicts of interest in the following chapters, we look at some concrete and timely examples of conflicts on regulating finance that have occurred since 2008. We look at these conflicts through the lens of the trilemma triangle introduced in Chapter 1. The preferences for international rules are situated at three different corners of the triangle.

2.4.1. Global Imbalances and the International Coordination of Macroeconomic Policies

Conflicts over global economic imbalances have many aspects, including regulations on financial markets and currencies. However, the different approaches to crisis management and facilitating economic growth are most apparent in the field of macroeconomic policies. Likewise, the failure of international cooperation in crisis management becomes most obvious in the failure to coordinate macroeconomic policies owing to a conflict between expansionist preferences in the US and East Asia and a conservative macroeconomic stance in Europe.

Fiscal Policies

In 2008, the initial priority in the G20, promoted in particular by the US, was to coordinate large macroeconomic stimulus packages. This can partly be explained by the fact that the crisis originated in the US, but, as we will see in Chapter 3, active macroeconomic policy is the US-style of economic governance, which fits well into the political economy of finance-led economies. When the crisis started in the US in 2007, the US implemented a large stimulus package with a net effect of 5.6 per cent of GDP from 2008 to 2010 (see Figure 2.5). A large share of 64 per cent, or 2.6 per cent of GDP, was going into stimulating domestic demand through tax reduction for households and consumption, transfers to households, and direct government consumption. Fiscal stimulation of domestic consumption is a good way to revive the economy, because it can be implemented very quickly. Tax credits to private households can be sent out rapidly, and subsidies—for example, for scrapping old cars and purchasing new ones ('cash for clunkers')—have an almost immediate effect. Unfortunately, for national governments these forms of stimuli have downsides, because consumers will use some of the stimulus to buy imported products. The economic effects of the nationally financed stimulus is thus dispersed globally. This is why the US had a strong interest to prevent free riding and to persuade other countries to implement similar stimulus packages.

In the first G20 documents in 2008 and 2009, the urge to implement fiscal stimulus packages was very strong. For a short period of time during the height of the crisis and with contagion effects in full swing, international macroeconomic coordination became a reality, and there was talk of a return to Keynesianism and even of the possibilities of 'global Keynesianism' (Patomäki 2009). In the Washington communiqué of 2008, leaders agreed to 'use

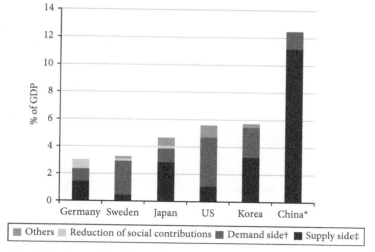

Figure 2.5. Direction of fiscal stimulus spending, 2008–10 (% of GDP)

Notes:

* Spending for public investment, transfers to businesses, and tax reduction for businesses.
† Spending for public consumption, transfers to private households, tax reductions for private households, consumption.
‡ Data for China is based on estimates by different studies (see for example IMF 2009:10; Zhang and Zhang 2009:9; Cova, Pisani, and Rebucci 2010:2).

Source: OECD 2010, OECD Factbook 2010, Paris.

fiscal measures to stimulate domestic demand to rapid effect, as appropriate, while maintaining a policy framework conducive to fiscal sustainability' (G20 2008b). Initially, the US was successful in persuading Europe and East Asia to follow its lead. Stimuli in China and Korea were even larger than the one in the US, amounting to 12.5 per cent and 6.1 per cent of their respective GDP (see Figure 2.5). Japan implemented a respectable stimulus of 4.7 per cent, while stimuli in Europe were much lower, with Germany and France at 3.2 per cent and 0.73 per cent respectively. As we shall see in Chapter 4, the low level of discretionary fiscal stimuli in Europe can be explained by features of integration in the European Union, such as the Maastricht criteria that govern the euro as the common European currency. In addition, automatic stabilizers, such as the comparatively well-developed unemployment insurance in the European model of capitalism, made direct, discretionary government interventions less urgent.

The willingness of East Asia to follow the US lead of macroeconomic expansion can be partly explained by the fact that, as export-oriented countries, governments in the region wanted to prevent the impression that they were free riding on US fiscal expansion. At the same time, the East Asian stimuli (and to a lesser degree the smaller European ones) differed quite substantially from their US counterparts, as large portions were directed not at stimulating consumption but at supporting businesses and infrastructure investments. In Germany, only 28.5 per cent of the stimuli were directly supporting consumption, in Korea the share was 36.2 per cent, and in Japan it was 21 per cent (Kalinowski 2013a).[7] In other words, while the US stimulated consumption, East Asian countries supported their companies to invest and become internationally more competitive.

The fiscal stimulus packages were thus not part of a unified strategy of global Keynesianism, but they were the expression of competing national strategies. For global economic governance, this means that the stimuli were not designed in a way to reduce global economic imbalances but rather to perpetuate them. Countries like the US that already had a large trade deficit increased their support for consumption, while countries with trade surpluses invested the stimulus in improving their global competitiveness. To achieve a global rebalancing in the long run the policies should have been the other way around. Once again, path dependency of domestic political economies beat effective international cooperation.

At the 2009 London summit, which was much better prepared than the ad hoc meeting in Washington, macroeconomic policies to stimulate the global economy played an even bigger role (see Table 2.1). The communiqué of the summit states that the G20 countries

> are undertaking an unprecedented and concerted fiscal expansion, which will save or create millions of jobs which would otherwise have been destroyed, and that will, by the end of next year, amount to $5 trillion, raise output by 4 per cent, and accelerate the transition to a green economy. We are committed to deliver the scale of sustained fiscal effort necessary to restore growth. (G20 2009a)

While fiscal sustainability appears in the final document, it is mentioned only as a long-term goal. At the same time, European countries started emphasizing the need to shift the agenda from a focus on fiscal stimulus to one on institutional reform and tougher regulations on financial markets (Beattie 2009).

The Pittsburgh summit communiqué of 2009 saw a changing focus. While leaders pledged to 'avoid any premature withdrawal of stimulus', much more

---

[7] This excludes reductions in social-security contributions, which benefit both businesses and employees.

emphasis was put on exit strategies and on finding the right timing to 'with-draw our extraordinary policy support in a cooperative and coordinated way, maintaining our commitment to fiscal responsibility' (G20 2009c). The divergence between the US, on the one hand, and East Asia and Europe, on the other, became even more pronounced after the first stimulus packages had ended in 2010. The Toronto summit in June 2010 was already strongly highlighting the importance of an exit strategy to

> avoid leaving future generations with a legacy of deficits and debt. The path of adjustment must be carefully calibrated to sustain the recovery in private demand. There is a risk that synchronized fiscal adjustment across several major economies could adversely impact the recovery. There is also a risk that the failure to implement consolidation where necessary would undermine confidence and hamper growth. Reflecting this balance, advanced economies have committed to fiscal plans that will at least halve deficits by 2013 and stabilize or reduce government debt-to-GDP ratios by 2016.
>
> (G20 2010b)

The whole Toronto communiqué breathes the language of compromise between those who wanted to continue expansive macroeconomic policies and those trying to step on the brake.

The Seoul summit in November 2010 was the tipping point when European scepticism on fiscal expansion prevailed—now joined by the UK under the new conservative government led by Prime Minister Cameron. The G20 abandoned language supporting fiscal stimuli and clearly highlighted fiscal consolidation as the new goal. The Seoul communiqué states that

> advanced economies will formulate and implement clear, credible, ambitious and growth-friendly medium-term fiscal consolidation plans in line with the Toronto commitment, differentiated according to national circumstances. We are mindful of the risk of synchronized adjustment on the global recovery and of the risk that failure to implement consolidation, where immediately necessary, would undermine confidence and growth.
>
> (G20 2010a)

After less than two years, G20 Keynesianism came to an end without even a discussion on how active fiscal policies could contribute to a more stable global economy beyond the immediate crisis recovery. Instead of relying on government initiatives, the Korean organizers invited business leaders to a 'B20 summit' in order to highlight the central role of the private sector in an economic recovery.

The Cannes summit of 2011 was held in the context of the worsening crisis in Southern Europe that is often referred to as the 'euro crisis'. However, instead of returning to calls for fiscal stimuli, the language shifted towards fostering employment and social protection through structural reforms and consolidation of government activities (G20 2011). Following such a European model of crisis management focusing on institutional reform, the G20 set up a task force for employment and highlighted the role of social dialogue between government, business, and labour. For this purpose, the G20 Business Forum (B20) was supplemented with the G20 Labour Forum (L20), which took place in Cannes for the first time. The US remained the only major supporter of stimulus, and, in September 2011, the Obama administration announced a new round of stimuli of $450 billion (Kirchgaessner et al. 2011). At the same time, East Asia and Europe reversed course and refocused on budget consolidation. Germany was particularly drastic in returning to its '"Swabian" habit' (Peel 2011) of frugality and fiscal conservatism and even implemented a 'debt break' into the constitution, limiting annual structural fiscal deficits to 0.35 per cent of GDP from 2011 on. The Los Cabos summit in 2012 continued with the rather vague language on strong, sustainable, and balanced growth, as well as giving a very clear message for 'appropriate' fiscal consolidation (G20 2012a).

The brief convergence on a consensus of active fiscal policies brought about by the massive shock of the global financial crisis lasted for less than two years and can best be observed at the G20 summits in Washington and London. After the Pittsburgh summit, the diverging positions on fiscal policies became more obvious, and with the Seoul summit active fiscal policies were excluded from the agenda, signalling the strong disagreement particularly between the US, on the one hand, and Europe and East Asia, on the other. The conflict concerning fiscal policies in the G20 is summarized in Figure 2.6. As we will see in Chapter 3, the US prefers large stimulus packages with a focus on tax breaks and encouraging consumption. In contrast, European countries are reluctant to implement active fiscal policies, as will be more closely investigated in Chapter 4. Finally, East Asian nations are very open to fiscal activism, but they prefer a neo-mercantilist strategy to fund infrastructure, R&D, and domestic industries, which have mostly domestical effects with very little global diffusion. We uncover the origins of this East Asian version of fiscal policies in more detail in Chapter 5.

Monetary Policies

Similar to fiscal policies, the agreement to implement expansive monetary policies played an important role in the initial G20 meetings, and there was

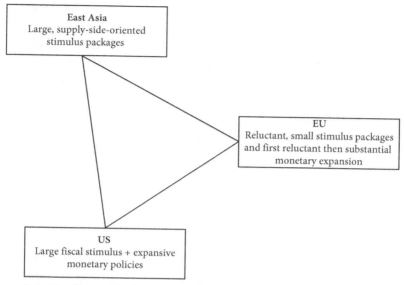

Figure 2.6. Conflicts in the international coordination of macroeconomic policies

also a similar tipping point at which European conservatism triumphed over the US preference for expansionary monetary policies. Originally the G20 was a rather 'technocratic' forum in which finance ministers and central bank chiefs met without much public attention. The upgrade to the leaders' level in 2008 changed that and politicized the G20, putting central banks under more political pressure. Monetary policies are a delicate issue in the G20, because most countries in the club have (at least formally) independent central banks that are not subject to decisions made by political leaders. The G20 offers a good opportunity for governments to put international pressure on central banks to support their fiscal policies without being accused of interfering with central bank independence. Instead of directly influencing central bank decisions, governments have the opportunity to influence the international discourse and to create a climate for more supportive monetary policies. In the first summits, the communiqué states rather vaguely that the leaders 'recognize the importance of monetary policy support, as deemed appropriate to domestic conditions' (G20 2008b). By the London summit the communiqué states more urgently that 'our central banks have pledged to maintain expansionary policies for as long as needed and to use the full range of monetary policy instruments, including unconventional instruments, consistent with price stability' (G20 2009a). By the Pittsburgh summit in September 2009, the mood in the G20 had switched to an exit strategy, as the leaders concluded that 'we also need to develop a transparent and credible process for withdrawing our extraordinary fiscal, monetary and financial sector support, to be implemented when recovery becomes fully secured' (G20 2009c). At the Seoul summit a year later sentiment had already swung completely towards concern about the negative aspects of expansionary monetary policies. For the first time, the US Fed's policy of quantitative easing came under criticism from emerging economies in East Asia and Latin America, because they suffered from a massive inflow of capital. The G20 (2010a) stated that 'advanced economies, including those with reserve currencies, will be vigilant against excess volatility and disorderly movements in exchange rates. Together these actions will help mitigate the risk of excessive volatility in capital flows facing some emerging market economies.'

Support for the US position for expansive monetary policies further eroded over the years as the initial urgency of the crisis subsided. Amid the changing global sentiment, the US continued with expansive monetary policies, including 'unorthodox measures' such as quantitative easing, which includes the Federal Reserve System (Fed) purchasing large amounts of US treasuries and other financial assets in the market. In the G20, proponents of conservative monetary policies in Asia and particularly in Europe gained the upper hand at Pittsburgh and then in particular at the Seoul summit. In stark contrast to fiscal policies, which remained conservative, however, monetary policies took another turn after the beginning of the euro crisis in 2010. Now leaders again highlighted the importance of monetary policies for supporting recovery and not just price stability. The Cannes communiqué explicitly highlighted price stability only as a medium-term goal (G20 2011). At the summit in Los Cabos, this expansionary stance was expanded with the argument that supportive monetary policies are needed to improve the financial situation of banks (G20 2012a). The Growth and Jobs Action Plan announced at the summit in Mexico also highlights the renewed priority on growth amid darkening expectations for global growth (G20 2012b). The changing attitude towards monetary policies can largely be explained by the weakening influence of ultra-conservative European central banks and particularly the German Bundesbank. While the ECB remains formally governed by a sole focus on price stability, the interpretation of its mandate has changed, and the ECB gradually became more open to considering unorthodox expansionary measures such as quantitative easing. The signs of change came at the G20 finance ministers' meeting in Moscow in February 2013: an expected harsh critique of Japanese expansionary central bank interventions from Europe turned out to be very mild, signalling that the return to looser monetary policies might continue. The communiqué states that

> monetary policy should be directed toward domestic price stability and continuing to support economic recovery according to the respective mandates. We commit to monitor and minimize the negative spill overs on other countries of policies implemented for domestic purposes. We look forward to the results of the ongoing work on spillovers in the Framework Working Group.   (G20 2013)

On the monetary front, we see a certain weakening of the classic and notorious Bundesbank-dominated extreme conservative bias. Although the ECB institutionalized rules ensuring price stability as its sole goal, it also introduced a system of central banks in which the Bundesbank has only one vote, just like any other member. As we will discuss in more detail in Chapter 4, Before the foundation of the ECB, European central banks usually had to follow the lead of the Bundesbank without having a say in their decisions. Now in the ECB, they have a say in the decision-making process and can actively balance the Bundesbank's hawkish stance.

2.4.2. Regulating Financial Markets and Capital Flows

Financial regulation, in a more narrow sense of governing financial markets and regulating financial institutions and products, has been the second priority of the G20 since 2008. It played a role in the summits from the beginning, but was initially overshadowed by the coordination of macroeconomic policies. It gained a higher priority from the London summit on, with the establishment of the FSB and the agreement in Pittsburgh in 2009 to work towards new capital standards for banks. There was consensus on including all sectors of the financial market under regulatory control, strengthening macroprudential regulation, and improving the stability of banks. However, conflicts soon re-emerged on how to achieve these goals. The main conflict in the G20 on the regulation of financial institutions was between financial-market-led countries such as the US and the UK (Chapter 3) and the bank-based system in Europe and East Asia (Chapters 4 and 5). In a nutshell, as we see in Figure 2.7, European countries favour a legalistic approach to governing finance—for example, by regulating financial products such as derivatives that have been inflating markets, curbing speculation through a financial transaction tax (FTT), or capping bonuses for financial managers in order to

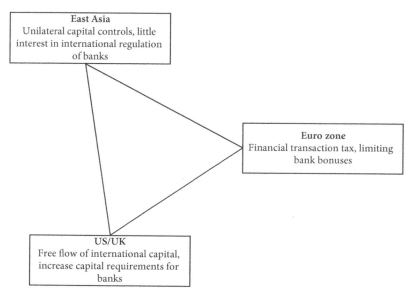

Figure 2.7. Conflicts in the international regulation of banks and financial transactions

limit incentives for risky behaviour. On the other hand, the US follows a more systemic approach, which aims not to regulate products and curb markets as such but rather to put a strong regulatory framework in place that provides incentives for market actors to behave in ways that will not destabilize the market. Such an approach leaves a certain amount of financial transaction and the volatility of the financial market untouched, but forces market actors to play by the rules and banks to hold reserves in preparation for a potential crisis situation. Unlike in the fields of macroeconomic coordination and currency policies, the formulation of bank regulations remains a bipolar, transatlantic affair (Mügge 2014). East Asian countries have shown little interest in global rule setting and have rather preferred to protect their national capital markets through (formal and informal) capital controls (see Chapter 5).

During the first summit in Washington, the agenda on financial regulation was discussed, but remained on a general level, and formulations on international coordination remained vague.

Regulation is first and foremost the responsibility of national regulators who constitute the first line of defense against market instability. However, our financial markets are global in scope, therefore, intensified international cooperation among regulators and strengthening of international standards, where necessary, and their consistent implementation is necessary to protect against adverse cross-border, regional and global developments affecting international financial stability.   (G20 2008b)

The outcome of the summit was important, because, as a result of the massive shock of the Lehman collapse, even the conservative Bush administration was forced to acknowledge the problems of unregulated financial markets. On substance, however, the first G20 leaders' meeting remained relatively weak, owing to the ad hoc character of the summit and particularly the weakness of the Bush administration, which at the time of the summit was about to be replaced by a democratic administration under President-elect Obama. The London summit added substance to the vague formulations of the first summit. It saw the establishment of the FSB and a pledge to strengthen macro-prudential risks and extend regulation to all important financial institutions including 'systemically important hedge funds' (G20 2009a). At the Pittsburgh summit, leaders agreed on more concrete measures, including a commitment to implement and improve Basel 2 in order to make sure that in the future banks would have enough core capital to absorb losses. Bankruptcy procedures for internationally operating banks were also agreed upon (G20 2009c). The leader's statement also for the first time highlighted the issue of restricting bonuses for bankers, which was particularly favoured by European G20 members.

At the Toronto and Seoul summits, the Basel 3 process was agreed upon, including a peer review process to monitor progress (G20 2010a). Generally, however, the drive for international financial rules lost steam, owing to the relatively fast recovery, particularly in the US, and the regained self-confidence of the Wall Street lobby (see Chapter 3). Under the French presidency, financial regulation regained importance, reaffirming many of the core commitments, including a full implementation of Basel 3 until 2019. New elements were introduced, such as the expansion of regulatory measures to the shadow banking system and a tougher stance against tax havens and 'uncooperative jurisdictions' (G20 2011). In other words, there was an agreement that all relevant financial actors, no matter whether they were deposit taking or not and where they had their corporate headquarters, would need to follow a common set of rules.

At the G20 summit in Mexico the leaders largely drew a positive conclusion.

In particular, we recognize the substantial progress to date in the priority reform areas identified by the FSB's Coordination Framework for Implementation Monitoring (CFIM): the Basel capital and liquidity framework;

the framework for global systemically important financial institutions (G-SIFIs), resolution regimes, over-the-counter (OTC) derivatives reforms, shadow banking, and compensation practices. We commit to complete work in these important areas to achieve full implementation of reforms.

(G20 2012a)

The need to bring all OTC contracts under the regulatory framework to make sure they are transparent and can be cleared without major disruption was highlighted as a particular success.

In short, the large initial shock of the Lehmann collapse and the election of US President Obama led to a brief convergence on the issue of financial reform. Over time, however, the different preferences for international rules once again became more pronounced. This can be seen particularly in the discussion on Basel 3 and the controversy over a financial transaction tax and other forms of limits on international financial flows.

Controversy about Basel 3

The controversy about new capital requirements for banks in the new Basel 3 framework is a good illustration of the conflicts between different models of capitalism on regulating finance within the G20. This conflict is not primarily on the general direction of tougher bank regulations but rather on how to achieve it. Finance-led countries such as the US and the UK favoured an approach that would simply increase the capital requirement for banks. This would mean that they would have to have a greater buffer in case of losses from their credit business and lessen the burden on taxpayers in case of a bank collapse. This systemic approach has the advantage that one regulation curbs the amount of risk banks can take while leaving the details of how banks achieve this goal to the market actors. Most importantly, there would be no regulation or taxation of transactions that could undermine the US role as the main recycler of global capital. As we shall see in Chapter 3, this strategy fits quite well with the market-oriented financial system, which profits from a large number of transactions, and makes it relatively easy to raise capital.

The US had already proposed strengthening the international regulatory framework and increasing the capital requirements for banks in the first G20 summit in Washington. In later summits, these general goals were further specified. At the Pittsburgh summit, leaders agreed fully to implement the old Basel 2 standards until 2011 and supplement them with stricter capital requirement rules. These stricter rules were decided upon as Basel 3 in 2010 (for a comparison of Basel 1, 2, and 3 see Table 2.2). Capital adequacy ratios

Table 2.2. Bank for International Settlements (BIS) Standards from Basel 1 to Basel 3

	Basel 1	Basel 2	Basel 3
Decision passed	1988	2004	2010
Capital requirements	Total 8%	Total 8% Common equity 2% Tier one 4%	Total 8%, 10.5% from 2019 Common equity 4.5% (2015) Tier one 6% (2015)
Additional information	Very general risk assessment based on asset class	Complex risk assessment based on rating agencies	Additional countercyclical buffer, 0–2.5%, additional rules for SIFIs

Source: BIS. 2010. International regulatory framework for banks (Basel III) [Online]. Available: http://www.bis.org/bcbs/basel3.htm?m=3%7C14%7C572 .

determine the amount of capital that banks have to hold to guarantee their (risk-weighted) assets. Capital requirements make banks safer by requiring them to have more reserves, but they do not limit the business of banks per se by reducing the number of transactions. On the contrary, the need for financial institutions to raise more capital increases investment opportunities in stocks and 'hybrid bonds', which would be swapped into equity if the capital ratio of a bank drops below a certain level. Increasing the capital adequacy ratio is a very simple way of improving the stability of the financial sector, because banks can take more losses before they become insolvent. In this sense, this measure is particularly suitable for financialized countries where banks are transaction oriented. In finance-led countries with deep financial markets, it is relatively easy to raise new capital by issuing stocks. Capital requirements constitute a buffer in case of a crisis in order to insulate taxpayers' money from risky private business activities. Countries in Europe and East Asia, on the other hand, have far smaller stock-market capitalization or have a tradition of public and cooperative banks, which find it much more difficult to raise new capital. France, Germany, and Japan were particularly active in weakening this part of the regulatory reform (Admati and Hellwig, 2013: 192–3). In these countries, raising capital largely depends on retained earnings, a process that impedes the banks' ability to lend money. Euro-area countries were, thus, reluctant for much stronger international standards for capital requirements and focused rather on issues such as curbing bonuses, although they largely failed to influence the discussion in the G20 in that matter. In other words, as we shall see, they are in favour of reducing instability by deflating the business transactions of banks and not by increasing the buffer for the event of a crisis. In the end, as we can see in Table 2.2, the G20 agreed on Basel 3 standards, which included a relatively small increase of the capital ratio from 4 per cent of tier 1 capital (mostly common shares and retained earnings) to 6 per cent (BIS 2010). An additional capital buffer will have to be built up only until 2019.

Regulating Financial Flows and Bankers' Compensation

While countries of the EU (and, as we shall see in chapter 5, East Asia) generally subscribed to the Basel 3 framework, they tried to limit its impact and thus its effectiveness. This does not mean that financial instability was not seen as a problem, but, unlike in the US, from the European and East Asian perspective financial stability is not seen primarily as a problem of weak capital requirements. In Europe and East Asia, banks are considered quasi-public institutions that provide a necessary infrastructure for the economy. Consequently, the goal is not to insulate banks from the public sector and ensure an orderly crisis management but to prevent crises from the beginning and to ensure that the market in which banks operate is stable. Two very distinctively European reform proposals were the introduction of an FTT in order to reduce market instability and the curbing of bankers' bonuses in order to prevent excessive risk-taking.

The European strategy was to tackle market volatility directly by demanding an FTT and reducing incentives for speculative behaviour by regulating bankers' bonuses. While national capital controls experienced increasing acceptance, European countries were unsuccessful in persuading others in the G20 to implement multilateral controls on international financial flows. Unlike East Asia, the EU joined the US in its opposition against unilateral capital controls, but instead proposed an FTT. This is essentially a very mild form of capital control, because it puts a very low tax on all financial transactions. As an academic concept, the FTT goes back to economist James Tobin, who proposed a tax of about 0.5 per cent on all currency transactions in a lecture in 1972 (Tobin 2015 [1974]). His concept was a solution for the problem of currency volatility arising amid the erosion of the Bretton Woods process. For a long time the concept remained purely academic, but in the 1990s civil society groups in Europe started promoting the concept amid an increasing number of financial crises. This civil society activism cumulated in the foundation of ATTAC (Association pour la Taxation des Transactions financières et pour l'Action Citoyenne or Association for the Taxation of Financial Transactions and Citizens' Action) in 1998 in France. ATTAC grew quickly into a global NGO network, with a worldwide membership of about 90,000, but remained a

Table 2.3. Tobin, Spahn, and the financial transaction tax

	Tobin tax	Spahn tax	European FTT
Coverage	Currency transactions	Currency transactions	All securities and derivative transactions
Tax rate	0.5%	0.01% Up to 100% for transactions outside exchange-rate corridor	0.1% for securities 0.01% for derivatives
Additional aspects	Originally proposed by James Tobin in 1972	Two-tier tax including an exchange-rate corridor	Needs to be paid by buyer and seller

Sources: SPAHN, P. B. 2002. On the Feasibility of a Tax on Foreign Exchange Transactions [Online]. Bonn: Report commissioned by the Federal Ministry for Economic Cooperation and Development. Available: http://www.wiwi.uni-frankfurt.de/Professoren/spahn/tobintax/index.html; European Commission, <http://ec.europa.eu/taxation_customs/taxation-financial-sector_en> (accessed April 2009).

largely European institution with most of its members in (Western) Europe. The German and French ATTAC organizations, with almost 30,000 and 10,000 members respectively, are the most influential groups. On the academic level, the Tobin tax was further developed—for example, by Paul-Bernd Spahn (2002), who proposed a two-tier currency transaction tax with a very low tax on all transactions and a punitive one on transactions in which currencies would leave a certain exchange-rate band (see Table 2.3).

Lobbying for an FTT initially showed little success, as large parts of the public and many political leaders believed in the concept but thought it would be unrealistic without the participation of the US. Support for the idea was politically quite broad, including not just left-of-centre political organizations such as ATTAC, labour unions, and social democratic parties, but also French Gaullists and German conservatives. It seems that France and Germany, with their long tradition in using taxes to steer the economy and finance relatively generous welfare states, provided a much more fertile ground for the debate than the low-tax, low-welfare compromise in the US and East Asia.[8] Naturally, the finance lobby in Europe successfully lobbied against the idea, but the crisis situation after 2008 suddenly changed the situation, as supporters gained the upper hand and became braver in showing international leadership over the issue.

Not surprisingly, the US and the UK were the biggest opponents of the tax. Opposition was largely independent of political leaning, as even Democrats were opposed to an FTT that conservatives such as French President Sarkozy and German Chancellor Merkel would support. Supported by a strong financial

[8] The German word for tax, *Steuern*, literally means 'to steer'.

lobby, the US and the UK fear that an FTT will reduce financial transactions, which would hurt revenues in their financial centres. Less volatility on international financial markets would also mean that market actors would buy fewer hedging products and other insurances against volatility, further undermining business opportunities for the financial industry. Even in the US, however, the crisis shifted the discussion, as President Obama proposed a national alternative with a 'financial crisis responsibility fee' in 2010. This fee (to avoid the word tax) would have been implemented in the US to recover some of the money used for bank bailouts. In 2012, Obama renewed his intention to introduce such a fee, but failed to gather support for the proposal.

Despite East Asian concerns about unsustainable capital inflows and volatility on financial markets, they remained uncommitted to an FTT. This has partly to do with the general East Asian scepticism for global solutions but also more importantly with the fact that the FTT is a very mild instrument that is designed to curb financial market volatility and speculation. The main East Asian problem is, however, the sustained inflow of capital into the region betting on high growth and exchange-rate appreciation. A bet on a currency appreciation of 10 per cent, 20 per cent, or even more is hardly prevented by a tax of 0.1 per cent. For East Asian countries, unilateral capital controls and the accumulation of national currency reserves seem to be a better way to protect themselves against the volatility of global financial markets. For them, the G20 and global coordination is seen not as a path for global solutions, but as a means to create leeway for their national solutions—for example, by allowing national capital controls and currency management. East Asian countries did not even try to frame the global agenda in the field of capital controls but rather acted unilaterally. In 2009, China and Korea implemented new national capital controls in order to insulate their own financial markets from global volatility (Gallagher 2015). Even Japan, which shuns direct capital controls, strengthened its management of international financial transaction by intervening in currency markets (see Chapter 5). Initially this East Asian strategy was strictly opposed by the US, which saw capital controls as part of a dangerous protectionism. This US priority for the free flow of capital has found its way into the G20, although the US position has been gradually eroded. The communiqué of the G20 finance ministers' meeting in 2008 urged 'all countries to resist protectionist pressures, whether in respect of trade or investment, and reiterate our strong support for a prompt and ambitious conclusion of the Doha Development Round of trade negotiations' (G20 2008a). At the leaders' meeting in Pittsburgh, the communiqué stated: 'We will keep markets open and free and reaffirm the commitments made in Washington and London: to refrain from raising barriers or imposing new barriers to investment or to trade in goods and services' (G20 2009c).

The Seoul summit in 2010 highlighted the role of strengthening 'financial stability nets' to support countries suffering from volatile capital (out-)flows (G20 2010a). The Seoul communiqué also includes the first implicit and cryptic acknowledgement that capital controls can be necessary. It states that, 'in circumstances where countries are facing undue burden of adjustment, policy responses in emerging market economies with adequate reserves and increasingly overvalued flexible exchange rates may also include carefully designed macro-prudential measures' (G20 2010a). The time was ripe, as the US switched its strategy from a principled objection to capital controls to the argument that they do not work and would be a slippery slope to even more controls. Ted Truman, Senior Fellow with the Peterson Institute for International Economics and an advisor to US Treasury Secretary Geithner, was quoted in 2010 as saying that 'I'm not against capital controls, but if you put them in and they don't work, you have to keep going further' (Beattie and Jung 2010). Geithner himself was careful to limit his criticism to 'very extensive capital controls' and not capital controls in general (Anderlini 2011). With the Cannes meeting in 2011, the gradual change continued and became more explicit. The Cannes communiqué states: '

> We have agreed on actions and principles that will help reap the benefits from financial integration and increase the resilience against volatile capital flows. This includes coherent conclusions to guide us in the management of capital flows, common principles for cooperation between the IMF and Regional Financial Arrangements, and an action plan for local currency bond markets.   (G20 2011)

For the first time, the management of capital flows was explicitly acknowledged and the US strategy changed from preventing capital controls altogether to creating rules for them. Ironically, through its unilateral action of implementing capital controls, East Asia has been far more successful in influencing the international debate than Europe's attempt to persuade the US and East Asia to join the initiative for an FTT.

Another European failed initiative in the G20 was the attempt to put the issue of curbing bankers' bonuses on the G20 agenda. This initiative was even less successful than the FTT and gained little traction outside Europe. Instead, the EU decided to move ahead alone, and in February 2013 the European Parliament and member countries agreed to restrict bonuses exceeding the amount of the actual salary (Barker 2013). Again, the division between an approach aimed directly at limiting the number of transactions, as pursued by the EU, and the US preference for a pure Basel 3 strategy, focusing on increasing reserves for risky transactions, made it difficult for an agreement to be reached on comprehensive rules for governing finance.

2.4.3. Regulating Currencies

The international regulation of currencies, which was at the centre of the BWS until 1971, remained the most underdeveloped area of cooperation within the G20. From the beginning, currency issues were part of the G20 agenda, but, despite the strong interest of Europe and East Asia in stable currencies, none of the G20 documents mentions stable exchange rates as a goal. A new comprehensive system of multilaterally coordinated exchange-rate coordination that would be similar to the old BWS was never promoted. This does not mean that there was no coordination of currency policies, but cooperation in this field was not geared towards reducing global imbalances or volatility of exchange rates. Rather any cooperation was ad hoc and coordinated outside the G20. For example, in the Plaza and Louvre accords of the 1980s, the US forced Japan, Germany, and others to adjust their domestic currencies in order first to devalue and then to stabilize the value of the US dollar. More recently, after the earthquake and tsunami in Japan in March 2011, it was the G7 and not the G20 that coordinated a massive intervention to curb the soaring Japanese currency (Milmo 2011).

As we shall see in Chapter 4, the EU is stuck in the contradictions between the global role of supporting the euro as an international currency and maintaining the internal stability of the eurozone. So far, the EU has always prioritized stability over a more global role for the euro. EU member countries and particularly France, but also the UK under Prime Minister Brown until 2010, wanted the G20 to have an ambitious agenda of installing a new comprehensive global monetary system. Such a 'new Bretton Woods system' would have provided a comprehensive regulation of capital account imbalances and currencies. While not openly stated, an obvious goal was also to reduce dependence on the dollar, which was increasingly seen as unreliable as the main global currency (Tett and Hall 2010). Global monetary cooperation was seen in Europe as the logical continuation of monetary cooperation in Europe. Unlike the US and East Asian countries, the euro area has broken the link between nation state and currency, which makes it easier to discuss international regulation because currencies are not seen as a core function of national sovereignty anymore. As we shall see in detail in Chapter 4, the political economy of continental European countries matches international monetary cooperation well, because it is based on specialized manufactured production. Unlike financialized countries, Europe benefits from predictable exchange rates, and there are fewer vested interests benefiting from financial volatility and selling hedging products.

The main goal of the US is to maintain the global role of the dollar and benefit from the 'exorbitant privilege' of paying its deficits by printing money. In addition, US financial companies benefit from currency instability, which increases demand for the dollar and 'financial innovations' that can help economic actors to hedge currency risks (see Chapter 3). Because of opposition from the US and the priority to prevent the collapse of the global economy in 2008–9, ambitious plans concerning a new global monetary system were shelved. G20 statements such as in the London summit were limited to a pledge to 'refrain from competitive devaluation of our currencies and promote a stable and well-functioning international monetary system' (G20 2009a). Currency issues dropped from the agenda completely at the Pittsburgh and Toronto summits and re-emerged only at the Seoul summit. In Seoul, the declaration referred to market-determined exchange rates and 'enhancing exchange rate flexibility to reflect underlying economic fundamentals' and included a direct criticism of countries like China that were managing their exchange rates. At the same time, it included a pledge that 'advanced economies, including those with reserve currencies, will be vigilant against excess volatility and disorderly movements in exchange rates' (G20 2010a). This was an acknowledgement of particularly East Asian criticism that expansionary monetary policies in the US flooded their countries with capital and put their currencies under massive upwards pressure.

In 2011, the Cannes summit, under the leadership of French President Sarkozy, was the only summit that explicitly set the goal of 'building a more stable and resilient International Monetary System' (G20 2011). While clearly being the most ambitious summit in this respect the final communique remained weak on details and without any concrete steps on monetary cooperation. On the contrary, the Cannes summit document also includes contradictory goals by repeating the pledge for market based exchange rates from the earlier communiques. The Cannes communique states that 'We reaffirm our commitment to move more rapidly toward market-determined exchange rate systems and enhance exchange rate flexibility to reflect underlying fundamentals, avoid persistent exchange rate misalignments, and refrain from competitive devaluation of currencies.' (G20, 2012a) The development of local bond markets was also on the agenda. Local bond markets are important, because they reduce the necessity to import capital and borrow in foreign currencies. Not surprisingly, the call for a new international monetary system was completely dropped from the G20 at the Los Cabos summit, and leaders returned to the unquestioned 'commitment to move more rapidly toward market-determined exchange rate systems' (G20 2012a). Apart from France's European partners, China also supported the French initiative for a new international monetary system (Wei Li, in Li 2012: 120), but its highest priority was not a global system as such but rather the strengthening of the IMF's SDR and the inclusion of the Chinese yuan into this club of global reserve currencies (Wei Li, in Li 2012: 119). An important new aspect was the pledge to broaden the SDR basket and facilitate the rise of new international currencies. The IMF board followed up on this and discussed the issue at its executive board meeting in November 2011; it came to the conclusion, however, that the then current SDR basket, based on the dollar (41.9 per cent), euro (37.4 per cent), pound sterling (11.3 per cent) and Japanese Yen (9.4 per cent), was still suitable (IMF 2011). The discussion about the inclusion of the Chinese yuan was postponed to the next SDR revision in 2015, in which the IMF finally decided to accept the Chinese yuan as the fifth currency in addition to the US dollar, the euro, the Japanese yen, and the British pound sterling (IMF 2018).

Despite the importance of currency issues for East Asian countries, they have little interest in multilateral solutions and prefer national solutions, as we shall see in Chapter 5. Instead, East Asian G20 members, together with emerging countries, strongly pushed for IMF reform and a stronger voice for them in the Bretton Woods institutions. The reform of the International Financial Institutions was one of the important topics at the G20 summit in Pittsburgh in 2009, and the IMF quota reform was decided upon at the G20 finance ministers' meeting in Gyeongju, Korea, in 2010. While most non-G8 members (except for Saudi Arabia and Indonesia) gained, the new North-East Asian members were the biggest beneficiaries. China increased its voting share by 3.1 percentage points to 6 per cent and Korea more than doubled its share to 1.7 per cent (IMF 2010). Even Japan, despite its weak economic performance since the early 1990s, was able very slightly to increase its share in the IMF. As the share of (North-)East Asian G20 members increased, it was the European G20 members that particularly lost influence, while the US share declined only slightly (Figure 2.8). Even this modest reform met fierce resistance in the US Congress. East Asia is still underrepresented in many other areas. For example, 23 per cent of the IMF staff are American (with 17 per cent voting shares) and 32 per cent are European (voting share 41 per cent) but

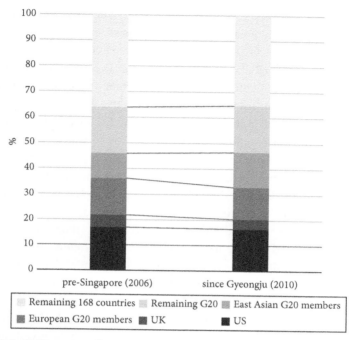

Figure 2.8. IMF quota reform

Source: IMF. 2010. New quota tables [Online]. Available: http://www.imf.org/external/np/sec/pr/2010/pdfs/pr10418_table.pdf [Accessed 10 November 2010].

only 9 per cent are East Asian (voting share 15 per cent) (Diversity Office 2009: 22). In addition, even among the non-Western staff, the majority of them were trained at US or British universities and are thus more likely to subscribe to economic theories shaped in the West.

In sum, the US has clearly got its way concerning discussions on currencies in the G20, insisting on a market-based 'non-system', in which central banks and governments should refrain from intervening in the currency market. This system is beneficial for the US, not just because a free-floating currency system is compatible with its primary goals of the free flow of capital and expansive macroeconomic policies. In fact, the non-system supports the efforts of macroeconomic stimuli, because it drives down the exchange rate of the dollar. At the same time, as US monetary policies reduced the international value of the dollar, the US used the G20 arena to criticize countries with trade surpluses to limit the appreciation of their currencies against the dollar. This goal entered the G20 agenda as 'global rebalancing' and aimed at reducing trade imbalances between surplus and deficit countries by adjusting exchange rates. The US criticized East Asian countries for intervening in currency markets to keep their currencies undervalued and thus partly offset the devaluation of the dollar caused by expansive macroeconomic policies. 'In the parlance of the G20, "rebalancing" became code for doing what the United States wanted' (Rickards 2011: 131). After the failure of the French in 2011 to revive the momentum for a global currency system, the EU is once again dominated by an inward-looking perspective focused on the stability of the euro and the integration of the remaining EU members into the euro area.[9] This inward orientation was exasperated by the euro crisis after 2010 and the BREXIT decision in 2016. At the same time, the external value of the euro has been comparably stable even during the so-called euro crisis (see Figure 2.4), and neither the ECB nor the EU as such is concerned with the external value of the euro.

East Asian countries were far less able to neglect their exchange rates, because they depend on exports for growth. Indeed, since 2008 there has been massive volatility, as well as numerous interventions, in the currency market in East Asia to prevent the appreciation of currencies (Chapter 5). Among East Asian currencies, the Japanese yen, as the only international currency in the region, is very different from the others. Unlike China and Korea, investors considered Japan a safe haven for their investment and transferred or repatriated money to Japan. Initially, the pressure on countries such as China, and to a lesser extend Korea, which manage their currencies through central bank interventions, was high. While disagreeing on the necessity for a new global monetary system, Europe and the US both agreed on the problems of unilateral currency interventions.

In sum, the US position clearly dominates the area of currency policies. Except for the modest strengthening of SDR, there is little evidence to suggest that the G20 is planning for a post-dollar global monetary system, not to mention a new global BWS. At the same time, the US has lost the ability to prevent unilateral paths in the case of East Asia, as well as the establishment of the euro as a potential rival in the mid to long-term future.

2.4.4. An Utopian Excursion

For the purpose of putting conflicts within the G20 in perspective, let us finally just for one moment imagine an ideal global financial system that is stable and

---

[9] Besides the UK, Denmark is the only other country within the EU that has also opted out of the euro, but it remains part of the ERM. All other EU countries have committed themselves to introduce the euro, although not all of them have set a schedule for membership.

supports all world regions to prosper. In such a well-regulated global financial system, exchange rates are stable but at the same time adjustable to reflect changes in real economic developments. A global (accounting) currency has replaced the US dollar as the means to account for and facilitate international trade and investment. Speculative global financial flows are curbed by a financial transaction tax and all countries and currency areas are allowed to prevent excessive in- and outflow of capital through targeted capital controls. In the case of an imbalance or a conflict, international organizations facilitate solutions that address the problem on both ends while limiting national free riding. A reformed IMF ensures that global economic imbalances are reduced by supporting surplus countries to increase consumption and deficit countries to invest in improving their competiveness. At the same time, World Bank and IMF do not impose structural and institutional reforms on developing or crisis countries but support good governance and civil society groups to develop a deliberative process in endogenous changes. The World Bank provides developing countries with low-interest loans and grants to fund public investments. A strengthened UN Economic and Social Council would coordinate the work of all international organizations in the economic area and would be the coordinating actor, including all countries and not just those organized in the G20 or other forums.

While this optimistic scenario seems unrealistic and like a distant utopian world, all elements of this utopia have already been discussed at the Bretton Woods conference in 1944 or the G20 meetings since 1999. More importantly, most of these elements of a new global system have already been implemented at a national or regional level. From 1944 until the 1970s, capital controls and strong national regulations of financial markets limited the number and severity of financial crises. In today's European Union, the euro as a transnational currency has broken the dependence on the US dollar and on other national anchor currencies (in the European case the German mark) at the regional level. In addition, the EU parliament has passed a resolution for a financial transaction tax in the euro area (although the motion remains stuck in the European Council). East Asia has been successful in stimulating development through national strategies and remains protected from volatile financial inflows through formal and informal capital controls. Finally, the US has proven that, even within a global economy, active monetary and fiscal policies that effectively stimulate the economy and create economic growth and employment are possible. The problem of implementing sound global financial rules in the form of a 'new Bretton Woods' is thus not the lack of good concepts and not even their general practicability. The problem is that this is politically difficult because, from a national perspective, international regulations on the global level are used as tools in a much broader competition of models of capitalism within the international division of labour. Particularly dominant national capital factions use their influence and structural power to shape the agenda of national governments and their role in negotiating international institutions to receive a competitive advantage over their competitors from other regions. A well-regulated global financial system is not a distant dream but rather a 'concrete utopia' in Ernst Bloch's sense (1986) of 'not yet realized objective and real possibilities' (see chapter 6).

2.5. Preferences of Different Models of Capitalism in the International Regulation of Money

Historically, international finance has been a major troublemaker, and it has always been regulated and governed in one way or another. Different ways of regulating finance, from the biblical ban on interest payments, the gold standard, and the BWS to the G20, have attempted to regulate inherently instable financial relationships. Since the beginning of the global financial crisis in 2008, the G20 has set itself the target to build a more stable global financial system. From the first G20 meeting there have been competing interests and conflict on the interpretation of the crisis, on how to manage the crisis, and on how to reform the global financial system to prevent such crises in the future. The results are mixed. Most successful was the coordination of monetary and fiscal policies when the acute crisis situation in 2008–9 created a short-lived convergence of interest to pull back the global economy from the brink. When it comes to financial regulation, limited agreements were made in the context of the Basel agreement on bank capital requirements. G20 countries have also partly retracted from their obsession with capital account liberalization and accepted the necessity of implementing capital controls in the event of a crisis situation. At the same time, the G20 has been reluctant to accept measures such as an international financial transaction tax that would help stabilize markets as such. The G20 has completely failed to come up with any discussion about a transition from a global monetary system dominated by the dollar to a multipolar monetary system based on a variety of international currencies that besides the dollar would at least include the euro, the Japanese yen, the British pound, and the Chinese yuan.

So far, we have approached the topic quite traditionally from an international relations perspective of which government, country, or group of countries has which position within the international negotiations. The following chapters will go beneath the surface of these 'national egoisms'. The investigation in this book into the origins of the conflicts, originating in the competition between different models of capitalism, offers value added to the study of these conflicts. I summarize the positions described in this chapter in Figure 2.9.

For finance-led countries, the most important goal when it comes to the international regulation of money is to allow the free flow of capital or, in technical terms, capital account liberalization. Countries like the US, but also the UK and some smaller financial centres such as Singapore and Hong Kong, thus moved closest to what I call the 'neoliberal corner' of the trilemma triangle. At the same time, the US chose to combine free capital accounts with sovereign macroeconomic policies, focusing on stimulating the domestic economy. This can be particularly well observed in the US obsession with tax-cut-driven deficit spending, as we shall see in Chapter 3 in more detail. Consequently, the US had to compromise the ability to maintain stable exchange rates. Indeed, the US abandoned exchange-rate management and coordination with other countries. It was allowed to swing to the inflow and outflow of capital without any direct intervention. Rather it found another mechanism to 'square the triangle'. As the hegemonic power in

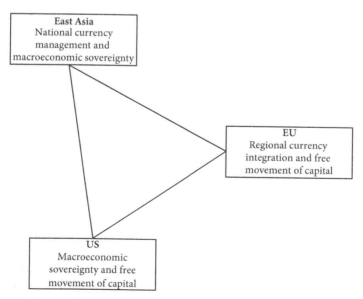

Figure 2.9. Competing priorities in the G20

the G20, the US largely imposed the costs of exchange-rate adjustment onto its economic partners.

As we shall see in Chapter 3 in more detail, the US position is embedded in a domestic institutional framework solidifying a specific compromise between competing interests. For example, the preference for capital account liberalization is compatible with the market-led financial system. The strong interest in active macroeconomic policies corresponds with a weak welfare system and a central bank with a broad mandate. The lack of interest in stable exchange rates corresponds with the function of the dollar and the hegemonic position of the US in the global monetary system, which makes it possible to externalize costs of exchange-rate volatility. Financial innovations like currency hedges also allow a market-oriented insurance against volatility, which in itself becomes a new form of financial revenues. This dense domestic web of institutions is relatively stable and the institutional complementarity reinforces path dependency. At the same time, domestic institutions are always the expression of an underlying class compromise that is the result of a certain balance of power—for example, the dominance of financial capital interested in financial globalization and the weakness of the export industry interested in stable exchange rates. The dominance of international debtors over international savers further strengthens the preference for inflationary currency policies. The weakness of organized labour in the US further exacerbates the dominance of finance by allowing a massive increase of social inequality. On the other hand, the weakness of organized labour and the limited welfare state in the US makes necessary a more active and Keynesian macroeconomic policy in order to maintain growth and win elections.

As we shall see in Chapter 4, the integration-oriented growth model in Europe positioned itself closer to the 'Bretton Woods corner', focusing on (regional) currency stability. Because of the establishment of the single market and the free flow of capital, the EU combined this stability approach with neoliberal reforms and the free flow of capital. Consequently, it surrendered sovereign macroeconomic policies, particularly with the establishment of the European Monetary Union in the Maastricht Treaty. As we shall see in detail in Chapter 4, this solution to global challenges rests on an economic structure based on the occupation of high-quality niche markets as well as the deepening and widening of the European single market, particularly since the 1990s. In Europe, there is a class compromise in which a strong neo-corporatist coalition between government and businesses is partly balanced by relatively influential labour unions. This class compromise is institutionalized by collective bargaining agreements, a bank-based financial system, a strong welfare state, and an independent central bank.

In Chapter 5 we investigate the export-oriented growth model in East Asia, which also maintains stable exchange rates through national currency management. Unlike Europe, however, the East Asian state-led model of capitalism is more inclined to keeping macroeconomic sovereignty by limiting exposure to the global financial markets. As we shall see, this position is practically tailor-made for the East Asian focus on mass production of final consumer goods and a dominant export industry. Unlike in Europe's corporatist system, export interests are organized with a very limited number of very large conglomerates, which have direct access to the government. Their power is barely limited, owing to weak labour unions organized at the company level. This authoritarian corporatism excludes organized labour and is characterized by a state guided bank-based financial system, strong government institutions engaged in micro management, as well as politicized central banks.

3

Finance-Led Capitalism in the US

The Globalization of Finance, and the Quest for Global Neoliberal Hegemony

This chapter on US finance-led capitalism is the first of the three chapters to investigate the domestic origins of international economic cooperation and conflicts. First it builds on the 'trilemma triangle' introduced in Chapter 2 and explains the US position. The chapter then investigates the historical origin of the US finance-led model of capitalism. It then turns to investigating the economic foundation of this model, before turning to the political economy of the US-specific neoliberal class compromise. As we shall see, the UK is also mentioned frequently as another finance-led country that has similar preferences to the US, and, with the British exit from the EU, the UK will probably align even more closely with the US.

3.1. The US Position in the Trilemma Triangle

In the previous chapters, we have already introduced the general position of the US in the trilemma triangle (see Figure 1.5). We have seen that the US and other finance-led countries put the free movement of capital as their first priority, while at the same time preferring expansionary macroeconomic policies. In order to achieve this goal, finance-led countries sacrifice control over their exchange rate. This specific position of the US in the trilemma triangle corresponds with a specific set of foreign economic policy preferences. Most importantly, the priority put on the free flow of capital makes the US opposed to capital controls, a financial transaction tax, and any kind of measures that would slow down global financial flows and thus the ability of the US to sell financial services globally. On the other hand, this does not mean that the US is opposed to any kind of financial regulation. On the contrary, the importance of a highly developed financial sector for the US economy means that the US favours clear international rules for banks such as capital adequacy

Why International Cooperation Is Failing: How the Clash of Capitalisms Undermines the Regulation of Finance. Thomas Kalinowski, Oxford University Press (2019). © Thomas Kalinowski
DOI: 10.1093/oso/9780198714729.001.0001

ratios. This has to do not just with previous experiences of financial crisis but also with the fact that international rules applied equally to all players tend to favour the most developed ones.

The second priority of the US is to maintain sovereign macroeconomic policies in order to steer the economy, particularly in times of economic downturn. As we shall see in this chapter, the US needs this ability, because it has relatively few automatic stabilizers, such as a strong welfare system. At the same time, the dominance of the US financial sector makes it easy to finance government deficits through government bond issues, which in turn perpetuate the liquidity and strength of the US financial sector.

In order to achieve these two priorities, the US has to sacrifice control over the external value of its currency. This is not a big problem for the country, because its debt is almost exclusively in its own currency, which remains in demand, owing to its unique position in international trade and finance. At the same time, the volatility of the US dollar creates conflicts within the international community, as the US tries to externalize costs of adjustment and to pressure other countries to adjust the value of their currency to the US dollar. However, this hegemonic position of the US is increasingly precarious. Ultimately, US finance-led capitalism depends on its attractiveness as a financial centre and on the demand of international actors for its financial services. In Schartz's words, 'US economic power derives from the willingness of other private and public actors to buy and hold US assets' (Schwartz 2009: 227). We have to add that, even more importantly, it rests on the ability of the US to produce the assets that the world wants to purchase and the infrastructure ('the market') to trade these assets and recycle capital around the world. Both aspects are far from trivial. The role of the US as the financial service centre of the world requires a specific form of finance-led capitalism and the corresponding policies, institutions, structures, and ideologies. In short, as we shall see in this chapter, its place in the triangle is the result of a distinct model of finance-led capitalism and its specific position in the international division of labour.

3.2. The Emergence of US Finance-Led Capitalism and the Globalization of Finance

As introduced in Chapters 1 and 2, we seek to trace the origins of the preferences just described to the political economy of distinct models of capitalism. These models have evolved in a long process of path-dependent development and change. In the case of US finance-led capitalism, the origins can be traced back to the first wave of financial globalization associated with the age of imperialism, and it reached its current form after the neoliberal restructuring of the 1980s and 1990s.

3.2.1. The History of the Finance-Led Growth Model

The observation of a finance-led model of capitalism and the dominance of financial over manufacturing ('real') capital is not new and has been discussed at least since Rudolf Hilferding described the first wave of financialization before the First World War. In his seminal work *Das Finanzkapital*, Rudolf Hilferding (1910) analysed the increasing role of finance in the capitalism of the early twentieth century. He showed that the increasing role of finance had created a new stage of capitalist development that was quite different from the version brought about by the Industrial Revolution, and that this transformation had far-reaching consequences for the way capitalism was structured. Hilferding believed that banks would become more and more important and that they would help to organize a previously chaotic capitalism based on competition. Through credit allocation and direct capital investments, banks would gradually take control of industries. Financial capitalism would thus provide stability and allow an orderly exploitation of employees as well as resource-rich colonies (see Chapter 2). From such a Marxist perspective, finance represents the commanding heights of capitalism and a stabilizing factor while at the same time being the Achilles heel of capitalism (a theme also used by Lenin 1933 [1917])).

Imperialist competition and ultimately the First World War ended the illusion of a neatly organized and stable global capitalism. The short-sighted solution to put all the blame for the war onto Germany in the Treaty of Versailles, however, prevented a more comprehensive approach to overcoming imperialist competition and dealing with the destabilizing forces of the financial sector. Thus finance enjoyed a revival during the stock-market bubble and the profitable but ultimately disastrous management of war debts in the 1920s that led to the Great Crash of 1929 and the banking crisis of the early 1930s (Galbraith 1997: 191–232; Chancellor 1999). Financialization was pushed back during the New Deal of the 1930s and remained subordinate to industrial capital during the Keynesian era of the 'new industrial state' (Galbraith 1967) from the 1930s until the 1970s. In the US, the 'New Deal coalition' of big business, labour unions, and the Roosevelt administration singled out the financial sector as the main culprit with regard to the Great

Depression of the 1930s.[1] The US government limited the influence and power of Wall Street through the Glass-Steagall Act of 1933, which required the separation of commercial and investment banking, thereby mandating the breakup of previously untouchable banks, such as J. P. Morgan (Chernow 2001). Many other regulations that limited banking activities and competition were implemented, while, at the same time, the banking system was given a safety net against bank runs through the newly introduced deposit insurance systems. The 'financial innovations' of the 1920s—including stock-market pools, insider trading, market manipulation, and short selling in falling markets—were forbidden by the Security Exchange Act, and the Security and Exchange Commission was established to police financial markets (Chancellor 1999: 220–2; Kroszner and Strahan 2007).

During the New Deal, stricter regulation of finance went hand in hand with a generally more active role of the government and the central bank, a Keynesian revolution championing active macroeconomic policies, and an active public sector providing jobs and training. Until today, the New Deal and the Roosevelt administration in general remain an important reference point, particularly for the more progressive side of the political aisle. An even stronger collective memory that is bipartisan and not limited to political progressives is the negative evaluation of the previous Hoover administration, which followed an austerity-oriented crisis management and in particular the protectionist tendencies under the Smoot Hawley Tariff Act of 1930. Until today, this collective memory has helped to rationalize a consensus on combining economic globalization with active macroeconomic policies.

It is important to note that the New Deal was not the only strategy to revive the economy and push back the influence of finance. Unlike the rational Keynesian management in the US, Europe and particularly Germany witnessed the rise of an authoritarian and racist variety of state activism in the form of fascism. In Germany, the Nazi government that came to power in 1933 also blamed the financial sector for the economic crisis and promised the end of 'interest slavery'. The Nazis applied their pseudo-scientific 'race theory' to the economy and blamed Jews—who were strongly represented in the financial community—for the 'parasitic' character of the financial industry

---

[1] In his inauguration address, Roosevelt (1933) stated that 'practices of the unscrupulous money changers stand indicted in the court of public opinion, rejected by the hearts and minds of men. [...] In our progress toward a resumption of work we require two safeguards against a return of the evils of the old order; there must be a strict supervision of all banking and credits and investments; there must be an end to speculation with other people's money, and there must be provision for an adequate but sound currency.'

(Neumann 1981: 186–97). The racist separation between 'parasitic Jewish financial capital' and 'productive German capital' provided a pretext for expropriating Jewish bankers and utilizing the financial industry for the military Keynesianism of the Nazis. Fortunately the Nazi regime and its ideology were defeated, and after the Second World War the social democratic variant of Keynesianism prevailed over its militaristic rival in Europe as well.

The Second World War and the subsequent efforts of reconstruction under the leadership of the US led to a revival of industry and weakened the role of finance in the economy. In the US, the Keynesian revolution strengthened the role of the state as a redistributive intermediary agency and limited the financial sector's role as the command centre of the economy. At the international level, the BWS facilitated trade of goods with strict controls on financial flows and allowed destroyed and underdeveloped countries to reconstruct and develop their national industries. As we have seen in Chapter 2, the BWS was a clear break from the liberal pre-1929 tradition (Helleiner 1994). In many ways, the BWS was the second image of domestic national Keynesianism. 'Much of the way policy makers envisaged international economic reconstruction derived from the ambivalent way in which domestic economic conflict had been resolved before and during the New Deal' (Maier, in Katzenstein 1978: 23) The cold-war confrontation with the USSR further strengthened the importance of the state as a protector of the capitalist economic system. The US as the hegemonic country representing about half the global economy had a huge interest in promoting international trade to facilitate the transformation from a war to a peace economy.

3.2.2. US Hegemony in the BWS

The BWS established at the Bretton Woods conference in 1944 was dominated by the US, and the BWS institutions largely followed the US agenda for a US-centred post-Second World War world. The more far-reaching proposals for a truly multilateral international order by Keynes and the British delegation were rejected (see Chapter 2). During the time of US hegemony in the capitalist world, the US had a strong interest to boost international trade and install a liberal world order. The stability of currencies provided by the BWS and the reduction of tariffs and trade restrictions under the GATT trade rounds facilitated the massive increase of world trade. This development was reinforced by the historical narrative of the Smoot–Hawley Tariff Act of 1930 as a reason for the collapse of the world economy, although protectionism around the world was more likely a reaction to the crisis rather than a cause. The 'embedded liberalism' (Ruggie 1982) of the post-war economic order promoted international trade, while an active Keynesian state ensured domestic welfare and curbed international financial flows. The BWS was designed to curtail the power of international finance and bankers and was an extension of 'a New Deal in international economics' (Helleiner 1994: 31).

As we have seen in Chapter 2, the BWS was shaped, dominated, and underwritten by the US, but at the same time it provided a 'hegemonic stability' that gave war-destroyed Europe and developing Asia a framework that facilitated their economic catch-up. The US explicitly tolerated the introduction of capital controls in other countries and allowed some leeway for national economic development strategies (Helleiner 1994). The US was also a strong supporter of the European regional integration process, although this meant a weakening of its bilateral leverage with its European allies. For a period of time, the interest of the hegemonic power for stability matched the interest of those countries that were catching up. While the US enjoyed the exorbitant privilege of issuing the world currency, the dynamic countries enjoyed access to credit and currency stability (see Chapters 4 and 5). For the US, the BWS was a way to institutionalize the global role of the dollar, thus facilitating US trade and private investment abroad, which in turn strengthened the global dominance of the dollar. At the same time, the BWS enabled the US to recycle US capital globally through international public institutions such as the Marshall Fund and the World Bank.

The BWS was stable as long as the US was dominant and willing to guarantee the fixed exchange-rate system with the convertibility of dollars into gold. When the dominance of the US weakened, owing to the economic re-emergence of Europe and Japan, as well as the disastrous and expensive Vietnam War, the star of the BWS descended. Instead of running trade surpluses and exporting capital, the US became a deficit country in need of importing capital. Already in the early 1960s Robert Triffin (1978) had predicted that the dual role of the dollar as a national and an international currency would mean trouble, because both functions would require different priorities. According to the Triffin dilemma, an international currency needs to provide a global supply of money and thus requires a constant outflow of money. Because of its exorbitant privilege, the US can print money to buy foreign products in US dollars and finance trade deficits. These sustained trade deficits had the tendency to undermine the credibility of the dollar as a reserve currency that was 'as good as gold'. As more and more dollars circulated outside the US, the credibility of an exchange guarantee into gold diminished.

For this new situation the BWS was less advantageous for the US, and in 1971 the Nixon administration came to the conclusion that the US could keep the privilege of having the dollar as the global currency, but without taking over the responsibility of guaranteeing the stability of the dollar.

3.2.3. Abandoning the BWS and the Finance-Led Solution to the Challenges of Globalization

When the Nixon administration abandoned the convertibility of the US dollar into gold in 1971, the decision was a huge shock for the world, but it was a liberation for US economic policies. Abandoning the BWS allowed the US to follow expansionary Keynesian macroeconomic policies and devalue the dollar to increase exports. At the same time, the belief that a liberal framework for trade needed a restriction of volatile and disruptive financial flows was replaced by the view that trade in goods and trade in finance are essentially the same, and both should be as free as possible. Initially a post-war liberal world order meant current-account liberalization, but since the 1970s it extended to capital-account liberalization. In fact, already in the 1960s pockets of financial deregulation had emerged with the support of the US, such as the 'eurodollar market' in London (Helleiner 1994: 81–100). While memories of financial crisis and Roosevelt's warning of unfettered finance faded, memories of the perils of Smoot–Hawley and protectionism remained an important element in the collective memory. Embedded liberalism that included restrictions on capital flows was replaced by neoliberalism, in which the state became active in freeing market actors from regulatory burdens. Economic liberalization was not a process of liberalizing a 'naturally' free market but rather a deliberate process of constructing a specific form of a liberal market economy that would benefit in particularly the financial sector, and was heavily regulated in its favour. While the Keynesian revolution and even the BWS were an uncharted and relatively spontaneous reaction to the world economic crisis, the neoliberal 'counter-revolution' (Friedman 1970) of the 1970s was planned. As Polanyi (2001: 147) once noted: 'Laissez- faire was planned; planning was not'.

Dismantling embedded liberalism and creating a new business- and finance-industry-friendly institutional framework were planned in many countries, but the way they were implemented differed quite substantially, as we shall see in Chapters 4 and 5. In the US, the changes were most radical. Already in the 1960s, the old 'New Deal' coalition supporting an embedded liberal system with strictly regulated financial markets had started to disintegrate. In the 1960s, industrialists in the US became increasingly concerned that capital controls would interfere with their businesses, particularly when President Johnson introduced the first controls on foreign direct investments in 1968 (Helleiner 1994: 119). The globalization of production and the connected need for international financial transactions meant that interest in the free movement of capital gained importance over the interest in stable financial markets and predictable exchange rates.

Capital-account liberalization, which created a global financial market, was the most prominent reform, but the deregulation of interest rates was equally important, because it allowed banks and other financial institutions to compete against each other in order to attract customers (Krippner 2011). It was this competition that transformed the dull job of a banking bureaucrat into the highly paid and competitive position of financial innovator and broker, where the salary to a large degree depended on how many deals were made. In 1974, the Nixon administration abolished all temporarily introduced capital controls. The competition between financial centres that had started within the very limited deregulated pocket of the London Eurodollar market, became the driving forces of financial (de-)regulation. Through the process of competitive deregulation, all other major countries followed the US lead. Some followed quickly and enthusiastically, such as the UK under Thatcher, and some more slowly and reluctantly, such as continental Europe and East Asia (see Chapters 4 and 5). The IMF financial reform index can act as an indicator for financial liberalization as well as for accompanying regulatory reforms. As Figure 2.3 shows, it was the US that first liberalized its financial markets, while other countries lacked behind. Within the non-liberal camp, Germany was an exception, as it was slow in liberalizing but did begin from a more liberal starting point compared to other European countries and even the US.

From the beginning, financial reform was not just an insulated policy change but was part of a general reaction to falling economic growth rates and increasing social conflicts. Initially, financial liberalization was not promoted primarily by the financial sector, because the first phases of financialization were a political project to deal with social problems arising from the high inflation and low interest rates of the 1970s (Krippner 2011). Through financial liberalization, increasing competition, and particularly the abolishment of interest-rate caps, the Nixon administration hoped to mitigate inflation and offer savers more opportunities to invest their money. Another initial effect of financial liberalization was that it allowed more active Keynesian macroeconomic policies (Helleiner 1994: 114). The inflow of capital allowed the US to continue expansive Keynesian macroeconomic policies stimulating the economy. This meant that the growth of financial markets initially remained embedded in an expanding real economy. Indeed, Keynesian stimulus programmes became increasingly important in the 1970s, as growth rates (and profit rates) in advanced capitalist countries started to decline. In the US, as the most advanced country, growth rates started to decline first. The 'long boom' of the post-war period in the US until the 1970s came to an end and was followed by a period of low interest rates or a 'long downturn' from 1973 to 1993 (Brenner 2002, 2006). The economic problems were amplified by the two oil crises, which depressed growth and led to a massive accumulation of capital in the oil-exporting countries. As investment opportunities in the West declined, these funds had to be recycled globally through the financial markets. Consequently, inflow of petrodollars and capital from Western Europe and Japan enabled US policy autonomy. The competition between the main financial centres and particularly New York and London to channel more and more financial services through their markets became another important motive for liberalizing financial markets. Competitive deregulation became the new driving force behind financial liberalization and globalization (Helleiner 1994).

It was only gradually that financial liberalization undermined the effectiveness of the national Keynesian policies that it had initially supported, because expansionary fiscal policies did not stimulate domestic investment and consumption but instead led to inflation and outflow of capital. Instead of investing domestically, businesses limited domestic expansion amid lower growth rates and rather raised prices while investing abroad. The oil shock further contributed to inflation, and the combination of low growth and inflation was quickly dubbed 'stagflation'. Stagflation was a new phenomenon and showed the limits of classic Keynesian macroeconomic policies under the condition of capital-account liberalization. Neoliberal monetary policies focusing on price stability were one possible solution to stagflation. When the Fed, under its president Volcker raised interest rates to a peak of 20 per cent in 1981 to starve inflation, the unemployment rate hiked to more than 10 per cent. The combination of high interest rates and the liberalization of financial markets in the US led to a massive inflow of capital from around the world. For the US, this facilitated a radical supply-side-oriented turn in economic policies. Under the label of 'Reagonomics', the Reagan administration dramatically lowered taxes and increased defence spending to defeat the Soviet Union and its 'evil empire' through an arms race. Fiscal policies dramatically diverged between the expansive policies in the US and austerity in Japan and

Europe, with the brief exception of France under Mitterrand (Chapter 4). The ability of the US to run a dual deficit of the national and current accounts meant that US government and consumers could spend much more than their income, but at the same time the US was accumulating external debt, which was soon exceeding its international assets.

During the Clinton administration of 1993–2001, the neoliberal hegemony reached its peak. The financial sector, which had been freed from regulations in the 1980s but had been limited by a sluggish economy, took off during the 'roaring nineties' (Stiglitz 2003) of the Clinton years, from 1993 until the collapse of the dot.com bubble in 2000 (Brenner 2002: 48–93). After the collapse of the Soviet Union, free market capitalism seemed to be without alternative and was seen as 'the end of history' (Fukuyama 1992). Even the most moderate attempts to strengthen market regulations would be accused of ignoring the 'realities' of a globalized competition and had little chance of being implemented. In 1997, the US led an attempt to change the IMF statutes to include capital-account liberalization as an official goal of the IMF. This complete reversal of the original IMF purpose failed only because the Asian financial crisis that broke out in June 1997 highlighted the problems of volatile global financial markets and premature financial liberalization (see Chapter 5). Nevertheless, the US continued on its liberalization course, and the repeal of the Glass Steagall Act in 1999 marked the peak of the neoliberal or monetarist 'counterrevolution' (Friedman 1970) that Friedrich Hayek, Milton Friedman, and the Mont Pelerin Society had been preparing intellectually since the 1950s (Mirowski and Plehwe 2009).

Within the two decades from 1980 to 2000 the US evolved from the largest creditor country to the largest debtor country in the world (Kindleberger and Aliber 2005: 237). This was due to persistent trade deficits and the large demand for US assets on the global market. A huge share of these assets were accumulated as official currency reserves by countries that wanted to insure themselves against increasingly volatile financial markets. Initially, public debt was the most important instrument absorbing the massive inflows of foreign credit, but since the 1990s, more and more capital imports have been channelled into venture capital and the housing market. A positive side effect of the massive inflow of capital was that there was abundant capital to invest in innovate new industries, in particular in the IT sector. This venture capital was willing to take high risks but also reap huge profits in the case of success. This led to the emergence of a start-up company culture in areas such as Silicon Valley, where most companies failed but the very few successes created billions in wealth and created completely new industries from Internet platforms to social media and media streaming. When the dot.com bubble burst in 2000, a large part of these investments was lost, but some of the start-up companies, such as Amazon (founded in 1994) or Google (1998), became multibillion dollar multinational corporations (MNCs), while others, like Facebook (2004), followed in their footsteps after the stock market had recovered.

In the 2000s, the housing market became another target for abundant capital, and new subprime mortgage markets thrived (Schwartz 2009). The abundant capital flowing into housing finance not only opened up house ownership for ('subprime') households that previously had no access to credit; it also allowed those who had a house to take out loans and use them to buy consumer products they could not otherwise afford. The next step of financialization further fuelled the housing credit boom, when the massive amount of debt accumulated in the US housing market was made internationally tradable with the 'securitization' of debt in collaterized debt obligations (CDO). These CDOs were sold on the international markets, and as they had very high ratings, they carried relatively low interest rates. They attracted investors from around the world who were looking for safe alternatives to even lower-yielding US treasury bonds.

Finally, from the 1990s, capital inflows were recycled through US financial markets and reinvested abroad—for example, by purchasing foreign companies or in order to move domestic production offshore. These foreign investments were much more profitable investments than the investments made by foreigners in US treasuries or CDOs, which resulted in a net income on capital, despite the fact that foreign debts were much higher than foreign assets. This 'global financial arbitrage' (Schwartz 2009: 1) allowed the US to grow more quickly than other developed countries in the 1990s and 2000s, but also contributed to the outbreak of the crisis when more and more subprime mortgages were packaged into CDOs.

3.2.4. US Global Hegemony in the Post-Bretton Woods World

Much has been written about the dominance of the US in pushing for the free flow of capital and spreading the gospel of capital-account liberalization after the 1970s. This dominance was particularly strong when the US was able to utilize its power to support its economic interest freely after the collapse of the Soviet Union in 1991. During the cold war, US foreign policies were concentrated on containing 'real existing socialism' through strong multilateral cooperation with its allies. The US assumed a 'benevolent' form of hegemony (Helleiner 1994: 5) in which leadership also meant underwriting international institutions and giving weaker partners leeway in their domestic development strategies as long as they remained firmly in the US camp. This started to change under the Nixon administration, when the US abolished capital controls and started to push for a more liberal financial world order. Initially, in the early 1970s, it was largely isolated in the world (Helleiner 1994: 109) and pursued its neoliberal agenda not primarily by changing global rules but through unilateral action. In 1976, the US achieved its first international victory, when IMF members agreed to add a provision to article 4 that the 'essential purpose of the international monetary system' would be to facilitate not just the exchange of goods and services among countries but also the exchange of capital (Helleiner 1994: 110).

After the end of the BWS, the US used its remaining hegemonic position in a less benevolent way and concentrated on putting US growth first, even when this was at the expense of allies. Instead of internalizing and solving global problems, the US started to externalize its domestic problems of low growth rates by forcing economic adjustment on others. For example, the Volcker Shock of high interest rates in the early 1980s helped stave off inflation in the US by bringing about a massive inflow of capital and consequently a massive appreciation of the US dollar. The costs of combatting inflation in the US were paid by developing countries that had borrowed massively in US dollars in the 1970s. The debt crisis in the developing world and particularly in Latin America also allowed the US to use its dominant position within the IMF to force crisis countries under IMF structural adjustment programmes to implement major reforms that would benefit US foreign investors. The US pressured its partners to liberalize capital accounts and influenced the IMF and the World Bank to make liberalization the conditional for financial support (Altvater 1991; Schydlowsky 1995; SAPRIN 2004). Through this strategy the US could open up foreign markets and allow US-based financial companies to expand globally. With this kind of political support, US financial companies evolved as bankers of the world, recycling international funds. The 1980s were also the time when the US used its international power bilaterally to negotiate 'voluntary' export quotas with trading partners and to pressure trade-surplus countries to appreciate their currencies instead of devaluing the dollar. For example, in the Plaza Accord of 1985, it forced European countries and Japan to allow their own currencies to appreciate in order to reverse the appreciation of the US dollar.

The forum for global economic coordination at that time was the G5, consisting of the US, the UK, Japan, (West) Germany, and France. In an acknowledgement of Japanese economic power, the US chose a G2 approach to deal with global economic imbalances. It first negotiated with Japan and only later included the other G5 countries (Grimes 2001: 108–35). In the Plaza Accord of 1985, Japan agreed that its currency could appreciate, and as a consequence the value of the yen increased from 264 yen per dollar in February 1985 to 154 yen at the time of the Louvre Accord two years later. In the Louvre Accord, the G5 countries acknowledged that ad hoc interventions into exchange rates like the Plaza Accord were not sufficient and called for a systematic coordination of major currencies within an exchange-rate band of 2.5 per cent with an obligation to intervene (Grimes 2001: 124). However, the Louvre Accord failed, because the US was not willing to reduce its deficit, and nor was Japan willing to loosen fiscal policies in a way that would allow such currency stabilization.

When the Soviet Union collapsed in 1991, the US intensified its efforts and took off the gloves in international negotiations. Financial account liberalization, neoliberal reforms, and the whole 'Washington Consensus' were presented as the sole solution in a US-dominated world. From the 1990s, foreign policies of the sole remaining superpower could focus on exporting its economic model without the fear of alienating allies. In the 'Reverse Plaza Accord' of 1995, the US aimed to reverse the decline of the dollar initiated by the Plaza Accord one decade earlier in order to curb inflation (Brenner 2002). A rising dollar helped to keep prices in the US down without requiring the US Fed to raise interest rates substantially, which would have endangered economic recovery and particularly the massive growth of financial markets. The US skilfully used bilateral pressure and international organizations such as the IMF, World Bank, WTO, and OECD to spread US-style institutions around the world (Bullard et al. 1998; Gowan 1999; Wade 2002; Peet 2003; Harvey 2005; Woods 2006). The Wall Street–Treasury–IMF-complex (Bhagwati 1998; Veneroso and Wade 1998) was particularly pronounced during the Clinton administration. Criticism increased after the mishandling of the Asian financial crisis (see Chapter 5) by the IMF in 1997–8 (Stiglitz 2002), and the attractiveness of the US economic model declined, a trend that was aggravated by the burst of the dot.com bubble in 2000.

Under the Bush administration of 2001–9, the US took a more unilateral approach based less on international organization and more on bilateral pressure and even military power. Ultimately, this strategy failed (Arrighi 2005a, b) and undermined the ability of the US to demonstrate global leadership (de Graaff and van Apeldoorn 2011). President Obama partly abandoned Bush-style unilateralism, but the irreversible weakening of the US and the rise of competitors in East Asia (see Chapter 5) meant he was unable to restore US hegemony to the level reached during the Clinton administration (de Graaff and van Apeldoorn 2011). The global crisis since 2008 has further questioned the credibility of US finance-led capitalism and the US's capacity to lead, as we shall see.

3.2.5. Alternatives to Financial Globalization

At any time of history since the 1970s, there were alternatives to the path of financial liberalization and globalization just described. For example, in 1971, the French government started an initiative to tighten capital controls to make sure that controls took place on 'both ends', meaning not just in countries experiencing an outflow of capital but also in countries experiencing an inflow of capital. While France succeeded in getting Germany as another capital exporter on its side, it failed to persuade the US as the main importer of capital. Without the US on board, tightened capital controls would be limited to capital exports, which would undermine the effectiveness of controls and leave France and Germany at a massive competitive disadvantage. Another continental European initiative, to get the offshore eurodollar market in London under control, was slightly more successful, although the central bankers of the G10 agreed only to limit their own placement of funds in the market and could not agree on stricter controls in general (Helleiner 1994: 104). In a clear break with the principles of the BWS, which had prioritized the expansion of trade at the expense of free-flowing capital, the US now considered trade and capital-account liberalization as equally important. Unlike during the BWS, when restrictions on the free movement of capital were seen as a necessity for a liberal trading system, capital controls were now seen as equally distorting as protectionism (Helleiner 1994: 106–7). In December 1971, the Smithsonian Agreement was an attempt to save the BWS and create a more flexible but stable exchange-rate system. The dollar was devalued by 8 per cent but remained the reference point of the new global system around which all other currencies would fluctuate within an exchange-rate band of ±2.25 per cent. US President Nixon called the Smithsonian Agreement 'the most significant monetary agreement in the history of the world' (Argy 2013: 65), but after just fifteen months the agreement collapsed, as excessive exchange-rate fluctuation forced European countries to stop defending the exchange-rate bands. Instead, they opted for regional exchange-rate cooperation in the form of the European 'currency snake' and later the European Monetary System (see Chapter 4).

Another initiative proposed by IMF Managing Director Witteveen aimed at channelling expanding global financial flows through the IMF. The plan was to use the IMF to recycle abundant 'petrodollars' earned by oil exporters amid increasing oil prices since the oil crises of 1973. The additional funds at the IMF would be used to finance development in the Third World through a special 'Witteveen Fund' within the IMF (Helleiner 1994: 112–14). The US opposed this new role of the IMF as a major recycler of international capital, because it believed that the US would benefit more if financial markets in the US provided services to recycle these funds for a fee. Not only would Wall Street become the global financial centre, but the inflow of capital would also help to offset the increasing trade deficit and generate service income from abroad. US financial centres benefited from a market-oriented global financial system, because the size and liquidity of the US market automatically drew most of the international financial deals to the US. This additional business further increased the clout of US financial markets and reinforced the dollar as the global currency. This strengthened 'structural power' (Strange 1994) also allowed the US to make external adjustment processes amid trade deficits by letting the value of the dollar slip ('dollar weapon'), which left European countries with the options either to stabilize their currencies and purchase US assets or to accept an appreciation of their currency and implement expansive macroeconomic policies that would increase US exports (Helleiner 1994: 113).

3.2.6. The 2008–2009 Crisis from a US Perspective: Subprime Mortgages and Global Imbalances

The crisis of 2008–9 was a logical outcome of this process of financial globalization and national competitive deregulation with the emergence of a US finance-led model of capitalism without a proper international institution to prevent or to manage crises. Consequently, the global financial crisis that started in the US subprime mortgage market in 2008 was not just a crisis of the US finance-led model of capitalism but, from the beginning, a global financial crisis. Nevertheless, the course it took and the way it was interpreted in the US were specific in the sense that the crisis highlighted not just the regulatory flaws of a deregulated financial sector but also the role of global economic imbalances. In sum, from the US mainstream perspective, the crisis was a combination of human error, greed, and global imbalances, but not a flaw of finance-led capitalism as such. Of all the interpretations of the crisis, the US version is the one with the most global perspective, in the sense that global economic imbalances were seen as an important factor contributing to the crisis and not just as a mechanism of contagion.

The general story of the US subprime mortgage crisis and how it spread to a global financial crisis has been told many times and need not be repeated here in detail. For example, the Financial Crisis Inquiry Report of the US National Commission on the Causes of the Financial and Economic Crisis in the United States provides an excellent overview of the process and causes of the crisis (United States. Financial Crisis Inquiry Commission 2011). The crisis started locally in 2007 with an increase in the defaults of subprime mortgage loans, which had been extended to households with little ability to repay. The financial engineering that drove US economic growth despite a dual deficit and increasing social inequality during the 2000s now became the amplifier of the financial crisis. Subprime mortgages were not just one sector of the financial markets; they were the economic engine of the 'subprime nation' (Schwartz 2009) as well as the most fragile link of the global financial system. When the subprime mortgage market broke, it dragged first the global financial system with it and then the whole global economy.

In the US, the subprime crisis spread to the general financial sector, because these mortgages were traded as asset-backed securities, allowing the extender of the mortgage to sell the mortgages, and with it the risk of default, to an investor. These collaterized debt obligations (CDOs) were divided in tranches into different financial instruments with different credit rankings catering to low-risk investors and speculative investors alike. Unfortunately, as the mortgage crisis deepened, even the most highly rated tranches defaulted. Banks started to worry about the liquidity of the banking sector. When Lehman Brothers went bankrupt and was allowed to fail by the US government, the credit market and even the interbanking money market froze. At this point, another financial innovation—credit default swaps (CDS), which had been created to reduce risks—made matters worse. CDS were created as insurances against defaults of assets, but they were also traded widely for investment reasons by players that did not hold the underlying assets. AIG, one of the world's largest insurance companies, was the biggest player issuing CDS. When many of the CDS came due, AIG was unable to honour them and had to be bailed out by the government. Through the global interconnectedness of the financial sector, the crisis quickly spread to other regions, although mechanisms of contagion were different in Europe and East Asia, as we shall see in Chapters 4 and 5.

The flaws of the finance-led models were analysed by the National Commission on the Causes of the Financial and Economic Crisis in the United States. In its final report, the commission does not challenge the finance-led growth model in general, but rather focuses on the wrong choices made by decision-makers in financial companies and regulatory agencies. It does, however, name numerous aspects of finance-led capitalism itself that set the stage for the crisis, including the emergence of shadow banking, securitization, and derivatives, an ideology of deregulation, and the emergence of subprime lending (United States. Financial Crisis Inquiry Commission 2011). In essence, from the perspective of the US, a combination of three domestic and one international set of factors led to the crisis. First and foremost, the crisis is seen as a regulatory failure of mostly national regulations and in particular their enforcement within the US. While the political decision already described to deregulate and globalize finance is criticized, the commission does 'not accept the view that regulators lacked the power to protect the financial system. They had ample power in many arenas and they chose not to use it' (United States. Financial Crisis Inquiry Commission 2011: p. xviii) In its view, it was not the system itself that was disabled through deregulation but the lack of correct actions and political will by decision-makers. When the crisis came, the government was 'ill prepared for the crisis, and its inconsistent response added to the uncertainty and panic in the financial markets' (United States. Financial Crisis Inquiry Commission 2011: p. xxi) The relationship between public regulators and private financial companies is seen as one full of conflict in which the regulators failed to do their work. As we shall see in Chapters 4 and 5, this contrasts with a European view of finance as a quasi-public service sector and the East Asian notion of banks as mere tools of the state and industries. In hindsight, the causes of the crisis are seen in a government failure through regulatory capture by financial-sector interest.

Second, the crisis commission highlights the failure of corporate governance, risk management, and a 'systemic breakdown in accountability and ethics' in the financial sector and credit-rating agencies. The report does not generally question the important role of financial innovations, but it sees ill-informed and unethical decisions by agents in the financial sector as the main cause of the crisis in the financial sector. These failures were characterized as systemic, not because financial innovations or the financial system based on brokering deals are seen as problematic but because the failures of assessments and ethics were made 'from the ground level to the corporate suites' (United States. Financial Crisis Inquiry Commission 2011: p. xxii). Unlike in Europe or Asia, the typical US view sees finance as a business sector driven by self-interest and short-term profit maximization. The main emphasis is thus not on the quality of service that financial institutions provide for the economy but on their profitability. The analysis of mistakes made by financial institutions in the US crisis takes up the major part of the financial report. The report describes in detail how subprime borrowers were lured into risky mortgages that brokers knew they could not repay. Then investment banks bundled these risky subprime mortgages into asset-backed securities and CDOs and sold them to investors around the world. Rating agencies facilitated this trade by giving these securities very high investment ratings based on flawed risk-assessment models. Finally, investors and banks around the world failed to question these ratings and instead relied on CDS to reduce their individual risks in the case of default. Because of the flawed risk management, financial players took on many more risks, were much more leveraged, and thus were much more vulnerable to a financial crisis than before. Most importantly, while hedges like CDS lowered the individual risk of investors, they increased the systemic risk of a general financial crisis.

Third, when the crisis began, the crisis management was massively hindered by the complexity of financial products and the interconnectedness of financial players without any central clearing mechanism. Financial innovations and the lack of transparency in the market meant that regulators had little chance rapidly to determine which financial institutions could be allowed to fail and which would be too big to fail. The international connectedness of financial markets further complicated the situation and made it difficult to develop a comprehensive crisis management strategy.

Fourth, when it comes to external factors, the report deals with the global economic imbalances and in particular with the massive inflow of capital especially from East Asian current-account-surplus countries. The combination of expansive monetary policy by Fed chairman Greenspan, who had a strong track record of monetary expansion during crisis times ('Greenspan put'), interest rates were kept at a low level. While this factor is seen as contributing to the increasing leverage by the commission, it features most prominently in the report of the dissenting conservative minority in the commission (United States. Financial Crisis Inquiry Commission 2011: 411–39). The commission makes clear that global imbalances are not the main cause of the crisis and that, in general, 'excess liquidity did not need to cause a crisis' (United States. Financial Crisis Inquiry Commission 2011: p. xxvi).

3.2.7. US Reaction to the Crisis

The specific reaction of the US to the crisis is characterized by an emphasis on four policy areas. First, the immediate bailout of banks and other systemically important financial institutes such as AIG, as well as the facilitation of acquisitions of insolvent financial institutions by more healthy competitors, such as the government-arranged and government-supported acquisition of Bear Stearns by J. P. Morgan Chase. Unlike European and East Asian governments, the US government was prepared to intervene directly in the financial sector and to restructure banks by injecting capital or facilitating private-sector solutions through government guarantees. The collapse of Lehman Brothers was the important exemption. The refusal to bail out Lehman was a political decision to counter the threat of moral hazard, but ultimately the disastrous effects of the collapse had the opposite effect and made the bailout of other major financial institutions almost inevitable.

Second, the most decisive action involved the kickstarting of the economy through macroeconomic stimuli, as we have seen in Figure 2.5. This strategy can be explained by the legacy of strong macroeconomic interventions in the US, as already described, in combination with the interpretation that the crisis was caused not by a fundamental flaw in the system but rather by regulatory failure. The understanding was thus that such a crisis could be overcome with some institutional readjustments and a kick-start from some expansive monetary policies and by priming the economy through some fiscal stimulus packages. Across the political aisles, it was seen as a lesson from the deep crisis of the 1930s that it is the responsibility of the central bank and the government to intervene through substantial macroeconomic stimuli. The political dispute between Democrats and Republican was only whether these stimuli should be primarily through an increase in government spending or through tax reduction. Consequently, as we have seen in Chapter 2, the US was the first to lower interest rates and it has been the main international force behind pushing for internationally coordinated fiscal stimulus packages. Indeed the great advantage of the US finance-led growth model is that it knows few constraints when it comes to active macroeconomic policies, as we shall see.

Third, a stricter regulation of financial markets and banks, which was pursued by the newly elected Obama administration, was a consequence of the analysis of the crisis as a regulatory failure. The Dodd Frank Act can be seen as the direct reaction to the US analysis of the causes of the crisis. The Dodd Frank Act introduced a comprehensive regulation of previously less regulated non-bank financial institutions and forced banks to separate their deposit-taking businesses from their trading activities (Acharya et al. 2010). Proprietary trading—meaning trading not on behalf of customers but on their own account—was completely forbidden with the 'Volcker rule' (sect. 619). To mitigate the problem of an institution being 'too big to fail' and to prevent future bailouts, stricter anti-cyclical capital requirements are mandated (sect. 171) and clear procedures are listed on how to liquidate insolvent banks and prevent the issue of 'too big to fail' (sects 201–17). Capital requirements and thus limits on banks' ability to create money are central elements of financial reforms in financial market-oriented countries. It is thus not surprising that the most radical proposals about the 'end of banking' (McMillan 2014) came from the US and the UK, where financial markets and peer-to-peer finance are most developed. Not only did the US push for Basel 3 standards (see Table 2.2); there were also several initiatives further to increase capital requirements of large banks above the Basel 3 standards. For example, the Brown–Vitter bill introduced to Congress in 2013 would have required large banks with assets of more than $500 billion to increase capital reserves to 15 per cent (*New York Times*, 2 May 2013).

Acknowledging the fact that the liquidation authority applies only to US banks and that international banks can still threaten financial stability, the Dodd Frank Act asks the president to extend domestic rules to the international level. Section 175 states:

> The President, or a designee of the President, may coordinate through all available international policy channels, similar policies as those found in United States law relating to limiting the scope, nature, size, scale, concentration, and interconnectedness of financial companies, in order to protect financial stability and the global economy.

Fourth, on the global level, global economic imbalances and in particular the trade deficit with China, which led to capital inflow from the East Asian region, were blamed as contributing to the US crisis. This position was highlighted by Republicans and conservative commentators (see, e.g., Paulson 2010; and minority opinion in: United States. Financial Crisis Inquiry Commission 2011: 413–39). The fact that financial flows from East Asia kept interest rates low in the US and facilitated the housing bubble became a powerful narrative, although there was little agreement whether this inflow of capital reflected the strength of the US (Schwartz 2009) or its weakness (Paulson 2010).

3.2.8. Conclusions: US Global Dominance
and Financial Globalization

We can conclude that the US is guided by a global orientation that means it is aware of its hegemonic position and leadership in shaping global international institutions. Initially, under the BWS, this meant that the US would exploit its exorbitant privilege of issuing the dollar as the world currency but at the same time providing the global economy with the necessary stability. After the Nixon Shock, the US decided to take advantage of the privilege while outsourcing the responsibility for global stability to relatively weak institutions such as the IMF and more recently the G20.

Unlike Europe and East Asia, historically, the US has had little interest in the external value of its currency and stable exchange rates in general. On the contrary, the US has used its international influence to pressure *other* countries—such as Japan in the 1980s (the Plaza and Louvre accords) and China today—to adjust their currencies in order to reduce global economic imbalances. While the influence of US monetary policies on the value of the US dollar is seen as conforming with market principles, the US accuses particularly East Asian countries to directly intervene into currency markets and 'manipulate' their exchange rates. The neglect of the external value of the US dollar is not just the result of the hegemonic position of the US, because volatility of exchange rates (and financial markets in general) are of little concern to financialized countries. Volatility even constitutes a business opportunity for the financial service industry, because investors and export-oriented firms alike have to hedge against risks by purchasing financial products such as options or currency swaps from financial firms. Consequently, the US (and other financialized countries like the UK) are not interested in international or regional institutions that would coordinate exchange rates or regulate the flow of capital, because this would limit business opportunities and diminish their competitive advantage. This explains why the discussions in the G20 and the FSB largely disregard the very issues that were at the core of the BWS: fixed exchange rates and capital controls. While the US is strictly opposed to limitations of capital flows, it is much more aggressive than Europe or East Asia when it comes to the regulation of banks and financial products.

Now that we have described the emergence of a finance-led solution to low growth and the impasse of national Keynesianism in the 1970s, it is now necessary to look beneath the surface of this model. The 'finance-led solution' should not be understood as a technocratic choice between different options based on a cool cost–benefit analysis. Instead, we know from comparative political economic studies that institutional path dependency is an important factor in limiting the options for change.

3.3. The Finance-Led Growth Model

The finance-led model of capitalism is not just the result of a set of certain policy decisions made by political actors, as described; these decisions are embedded in an institutional system and political economic structure. This section seeks to look in more detail at these actors and the policies they represent. In a finance-led country, financial markets and anonymous arm's-length interactions are the main principles interconnecting the different sectors of the economy. This political economy is characterized by structured or institutionalized relationships between finance and the (production) industry, finance and consumer as well as finance and the state. These institutional connections are relatively stable, as they reinforce each other, and change in one institution leads to change in other institutions. In the terminology of the varieties of capitalism approach, they constitute a system of complementary institutions. As we shall see in this and the following section, the complementarity goes much deeper than just institutions. In the finance-led model, relationships between state, business, finance, and labour are institutionalized in a specific way that is different from other models of capitalism, as we shall see in later chapters.

3.3.1. Financialization and the Dominance of Financial Motives

The main characteristic of finance-led capitalism is that the financial industry is transformed from a service industry facilitating real economic activities to the centre of gravity of the economy. It is not investments in the real economy or the accumulation of capital but the global reallocation of capital through financial markets that accounts for the economic dynamism of financialized countries. Financial firms in finance-led countries are very advanced and offer an increasing number of 'financial innovations' that allow investors to increase their share of the profits distributed by the financial markets. This path of development offers a specific solution to the problem of weak domestic growth by providing financial services to countries around the world that have faster-growing real economies. In short, finance-led countries such as the UK and the US have become the financial centres of the world. Financial globalization is, thus, an international development that is interconnected with structural changes and social struggles embedded in domestic political economies and particularly in the dominance of neoliberalism in the US.

Finance, like other service industries, differs from the production sector in that it does not produce a tangible product but rather facilitates real economic activities. A credit allows a consumer to purchase a car or a house now and pay it off over a long period of time. Issuing stocks or bonds allows a company to invest now and repay its creditors and shareholders through interest and dividend payments over time. Finance plays a crucial role in any advanced economy by providing the service of reallocating capital from those who have it (savers) to those who need it (investors, consumers). An efficient financial system can be compared to other infrastructural services, such as public transport or sewage systems, which also do not produce a tangible product but have the potential to increase the productivity of the real economy.

International finance is driven by and facilitates economic globalization, as it allows corporations to manage international production chains and creates what Saskia Sassen (2001: 11) calls 'global control ability'. Despite its central role, the financial sector always depends on a functioning real economy that creates savings and requires investment. Some financial centres provide their services primarily to the domestic economy (for example, Frankfurt for Germany and Tokyo for Japan). Finance-led countries, however, are character-ized by the fact that their financial sectors provide these services globally (for example, Wall Street in New York and 'the City' in London) or at least regionally (for example, Hong Kong and Singapore for China and South-East Asia). It is hard to measure the degree of financialization, but the scale and scope of financial markets, the growth of the banking industry, the share of bank profits in overall corporate profits, and, more generally, the share of rentier income (income derived from financial activities) all underline the same trend.[2] While all countries have been affected by financialization, the trend was parti-cularly accentuated in the US. In the US between 1975 and 1990, the share of GDP of the FIRE industries (finance, insurance, and real estate) doubled from about 12 per cent to almost 25 per cent (Krippner 2011: 32), while their share

---

[2] For a discussion of rentier income and its development, see Epstein (2005: 46–74).

of plant and equipment investment also doubled from 12–13 per cent to 25–6 per cent (Brenner 2002: 81). Financial-sector profits increased from 10–15 percent in the 1950s and 1960s to more than 40 per cent in the early 2000s (Krippner 2011: 28). This massive increase probably still understates the role of finance in the economy, because it does not account for the increasing role that financial motives play within traditional industrial companies, as we shall see.

At the international level, a couple of finance-led countries dominate the global market of financial services. In 2012, the US provided 24 per cent of all cross-border financial trades (excluding insurances), the UK 19 per cent, and Luxemburg 13 per cent (own calculations, from WTO 2013). Switzerland, Hong Kong, and Singapore occupy about 15 per cent of the market, which means that six finance-led economies control almost three-quarters of all international financial services. The role of major East Asian and central European economies such as Germany, France, China, and Japan in recycling global capital is very limited (Figure 3.1). Other economic data also support the financialization thesis. Stock-market capitalization in financialized countries such as the US are substantially higher than in other countries with the exception of occasional financial bubbles in non-finance-led economies, such as Japan in the 1980s and China in 2007 (see Figure 3.2). In the US in 2007, the financial industry accounted for 31.3 per cent of corporate profits (own calculations, from US Department of Commerce 2008), compared with 13 per cent in 1980 (Lahart 2008). If we take the share of rentier income (income from financial activities plus interest incomes) in all incomes as a

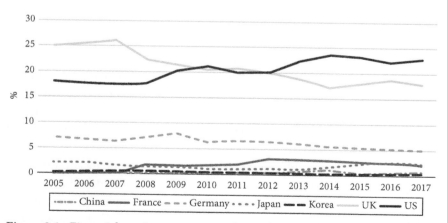

Figure 3.1. Financial service exports as a share of world exports (%)

Source: Own calculations from WTO, Statistics Database, timeline, http://stat.wto.org/StatisticalProgram/WSDBStatProgramHome.aspx?Language=E

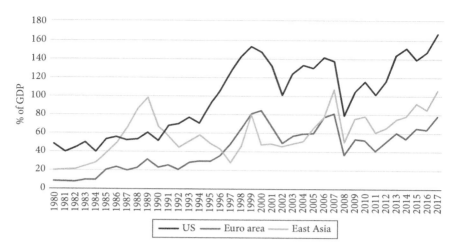

Figure 3.2. Stock-market capitalization (% of GDP)

Note: The East Asian value is the unweighted average of China, Japan and Korea.

Source: World Bank, WDI, http://data.worldbank.org/indicator/CM.MKT.LCAP.GD.ZS?page=6

rough estimate of financialization, we find that Germany, Japan, Korea, Mexico, the Scandinavian countries, and Turkey have the lowest share, whereas the US and the UK have among the highest (Epstein and Power 2003). Surprisingly, France and Italy also have a high share of rentier income, which can be explained less by the importance of the financial sector and more by the high level of public debt held by citizens.

Financial Oligarchy and Financial Deal-Making

The strongest preferences of finance-led countries are open capital accounts and the free flow of international capital. This affinity is often simply explained by the influence and lobbying power of banks and financial institutions. In this view, a 'financial regulatory complex' (Kahler and Lake 2013) has gained power and is shaping institutions in its favour. Since the collapse of the BWS and the financial market liberalization of the following decades, the political influence of the financial industry has increased dramatically, although to differing degrees in different world regions. The trend towards financialization was stronger in the UK and the US, where the 'military industrial complex' that President Eisenhower had warned about in 1961 was supplemented, from the 1970s onwards, by a 'Wall Street–Treasury–IMF Complex' (Bhagwati 1998; Veneroso and Wade 1998). The power of the 'financial oligarchy' (Johnson 2009; Johnson and Kwak 2011) is personalized by the revolving door between

Wall Street and the US administration. For example, about half of the US Treasury Secretaries since the 1970s worked at financial firms before and/or after their public service.[3] Similar power-resource arguments as to why the government fails efficiently to regulate Wall Street are made, for example, by Wilmarth (2013).

Such a power-resource argument is very persuasive, but it cannot explain why lobbyists in the financial industry seem to be much more successful than those in other industries. Wall Street has a powerful lobby, but so do manufacturing companies such as General Motors or IT firms such as Microsoft and Apple. The power-resource argument also offers few explanations about what kind of regulation the financial oligarchy opposes most strongly and what kind it prefers. Why is the financial oligarchy particularly opposed to limits on capital flows but less resistant to other forms of financial regulation such as capital requirements? To answer that, it is necessary to investigate how institutions governing finance interact with institutions governing businesses, labour, and innovation. First of all, in order to understand what drives finance-led economies, it is important to differentiate between the power of money and the power of the financial industry. In any capitalist economy, those who have more money tend to be more powerful than those with less money, because they can command more material resources. These material resources always have the tendency to be translated into ideological hegemony and political power. For example, economic resources can be used for lobbying, donations, hiring the best lawyers, influencing newspaper coverage, and funding academic research. The difference between non-financialized and financialized economies is thus not primarily the power of those owning financial assets but the power of the financial sector that is managing those assets. In financialized economies, it is the financial industry itself that wields influence. The differentiation is important, because those owning capital have very different interests from those managing it. Those owning the capital are interested in the security of their investment and the return on their investment. Those managing capital are interested in the number and the amounts of fee-generating transactions. For the financial industry, the return on invested capital is important only as a measure for competition with others over clients. They thus have few problems with rules on stricter capital requirements and on how financial products are structured. While these regulations reduce

---

[3] More precisely, six of the thirteen Treasury Secretaries since 1972 came from or went into the financial industry: William Simon (Salomon Brothers), Donald Regan (Merrill Lynch), Nicholas Brady (William E. Simon), Lloyd Benson (Lincoln Consolidated), Robert Rubin (Goldman Sachs, Citigroup), and Henry Paulson (Goldman Sachs).

leverage and thus profits, they do not matter as long as they are applied to all market players. With its superior know-how, the US financial service industry can even expect to improve its position, because it would be faster and better to adopt to new regulations. Every new regulation is a challenge to the financial industry, but those players that are fastest to adjust can be expected to have a competitive advantage and thus attract more fee-generating activities.

On the other hand, capital controls or taxes on financial transactions on financial flows limit the volatility of the market by reducing size and the velocity of the market and thus the number of fee-generating transactions. Smaller markets will mean fewer transactions and less volatility means less demand for insurances and hedging products built to insure against market volatility. In other words, regulation focusing on reducing market volatility will have a much bigger negative effect on the profitability of the financial industry than improved regulation of actors and products alone. While in general financial institutions might be in favour of less regulation altogether, when tougher financial regulation is inevitable, the financial industry prefers those regulations that reduce risks without reducing the number of transaction. For example, higher capital ratios under Basel 3 mean that banks have to raise capital and their profitability declines, but this does not reduce the number of fee-generating transactions. In addition, banks specializing on 'financial innovation' can hope to outwit regulations of financial products and competitors by creating new financial products. In this sense, new regulations might actually increase fee generation, because they benefit those market actors with the most experience and with the skills to create new products that take most advantage of the existing regulatory framework.

3.3.2. The Market-Based Financial System and the Relationship between Finance and Business

One of the core aspects of a comparative political economy—and a major contribution of the varieties of capitalism school—is to highlight the relationships between different sectors of the political economy. In particular, institutions in different sectors do not simply work side by side; they are interdependent and complement each other. In a finance-led country, the changes in the financial sector just described thus led to changes in other sectors that needed to adopt to the new reality of finance-led capitalism. Indeed, the gravity of the financial sector and its way of doing business have drawn other sectors of the political economy, such as business, into its orbit.

Shareholder Capitalism and the Financialization of Industries

When it comes to considering the relationship between finance and businesses, at least two aspects are important from a political economic perspective: financialization of industries and shareholder capitalism. With the rise of shareholder capitalism, traditional bank lending became less important. Companies increasingly issued bonds and shares to get capital for investments. More importantly, in a slow-growing economy, companies use the stock market to acquire or merge with other companies to grow instead of investing in the 'green field' to build new production capacities. Shareholder capitalism was thus a logical reaction of traditional businesses to declining growth rates and thus a reduction of investment in production facilities. In 1981, Jack Welch, the CEO of General Electric, outlined the principles of shareholder capitalism in his speech on 'Growing Fast in a Slow-Growth Economy' (*Financial Times*, 12 March 2009). Over time, 'shareholder value' became one of the important criteria in evaluating companies and most importantly the performance and pay of managers (Stout 2012). The movement of financial markets that had previously been largely irrelevant for managerial decisions now played an important role. Many argue that the orientation of managerial decisions on the price of stocks has led to short determinism and less investment into research and development (Stockhammer 2005; Rappaport and Bogle 2011). This trend undermines the long-term competitiveness of industrial companies and further amplifies the already existing trend towards the financialization of businesses. Even Jack Welch after the crisis commented that 'shareholder value is the dumbest idea in the world' (*Financial Times*, 12 March 2009).

Industrial companies are not just increasingly influenced by financial markets, but they increasingly become financial companies themselves (Krippner 2005). Companies such as General Electric, Sears, or General Motors became increasingly financialized, in that their financial subsidiaries overshadowed the activities of their traditional businesses. Originally these financial subsidiaries were founded to help consumers to finance their purchase of consumer goods and cars, but gradually they became an important source of revenue and allowed traditional companies from the 'real economy' with low profit rates to participate in the high-return financial businesses. During the financial crisis, this had the additional advantage that the world's largest industrial company, GE, could benefit from financial support from the Fed that was originally meant to support systemically relevant banks (*Washington Post*, 29 June 2009).

Shareholder capitalism and financialization have reinforced the market-based financial system. Unlike classic banking, share and bond markets are international, and investors can come from any part of the world. Companies have a strong interest to place bonds and stocks as broadly as possible and, more importantly, to be able to acquire companies abroad in order to expand into new global markets. This has major consequences for the relationship between businesses and the financial sector, as businesses align their own interests with those of financial companies. Because businesses become increasingly invested in the financial sector, they become proponents of globalized finance. Thus, financialization and shareholder capitalism have weakened business factions that have an interest in 'sound finance' and a strictly regulated financial market that would provide them with patient capital at low interest rates for long-term investments. In other words, by aligning their preferences with those of financial companies, manufacturing businesses undermined their ability to invest for the long term.

Finance and Globalized Outsourcing

Another factor accelerating the trend of financialization is global outsourcing of production. The globalization of businesses means that more and more industrial production has been moved offshore to countries with lower labour costs. As manufacturing is offshored, the share of manufacturing and the absolute number of industrial employment is declining. In the US, most of this offshoring was first done to Mexico (particularly the maquiladoras close to the US border), but since the 1990s in particular to China. This global expansion was made possible through globalized financial markets that allowed companies not just to raise enough money for their international investment but also to maintain and manage them. At the same time, the globalization of businesses triggered a new round of financial globalization, as banks rushed overseas to serve the needs of globalized businesses (Helleiner 1994). As production was offshored, the financial activities that were now seen as the core function of the company remained near the headquarter in the US (Krippner 2005: 193–8). Finance became the central element of the 'global control ability' (Sassen 2001: 11) that allows companies to manage complex global production chains through investments and/ or the extension of credits. The outsourcing strategy of the US again highlights the global orientation of US finance-led capitalism and broadens the camp of those businesses with a strong interest of maintaining a weak regulation of international financial flows. In addition, the interests of foreign investors strengthen policy preferences for active monetary policies that tend to weaken the value of the US dollar and thus increase the value of foreign investments.

The globalization of production allowed US companies to remain competitive and profitable despite intensified competition. The combination of outsourcing industries and the ability of the financial sector to facilitate foreign investment created a new economic dynamic in addition to attracting fee-generating activities, because long-term investments of the US in industries abroad proved to be much more profitable than foreign investment in the US (Schwartz 2009). At the same time, offshoring has contributed to a deindustrialization process and the massive current-account deficit. Finally, offshoring further reinforces financialization, as companies that offshore production tend to be more financialized, to focus more on shareholder value, and to be more active in share buybacks (Milberg 2008). This means that globalization is not just a result of financialization but further reinforces domestic transformation of financialization and deindustrialization.

Market-Oriented Finance and the Financialization Curse

Ever since the 1980s there had been the fear that finance and the rise of 'paper capitalism' would erode the competitiveness of US industries and crowd out manufacturing (Cohen and Zysman 1987: 66). Such a 'financialization curse' (Kalinowski 2011, 2013b) is similar to the Dutch disease or the 'resource curse' (Sachs and Warner 2001) in resource rich (particularly oil-exporting countries) in the sense that one extremely profitable sector of the economy crowds out other economic activities and particularly manufacturing. In the case of finance-led economies, the financial sector has higher profit rates and pays higher salaries, which lead to an allocation of capital and talented employees in the sector. The preference for free capital accounts leads to an inflow of capital, and the negligence of the external value of the currency leads to an overvaluation of the national currency, which further undermines export competitiveness. In such an environment, only the most competitive sectors—such as resource extraction ("fracking"), aircraft manufacturing of Boeing planes, iconic products such as Apple's iPhones, or software companies such as Microsoft and Google—can thrive. Other less sophisticated or less radically innovative sectors, such as car manufacturing and agriculture, can survive only if they are subsidized or protected by the government. For example, domestic car production in the US declined from a peak of thirteen million cars at the end of the 1970s to less than eleven million in 2011. From a dominant position in the 1960s, the share of the big three US-produced vehicles in the US market declined and dropped below 50 per cent for the first time in 2008 (Katz et al.

2014: 52–3). In 2009, GM and Chrysler had to file for chapter 11 bankruptcy and received bail-out funds from the federal government, and in 2014 Chrysler was bought by Fiat.

The financialization of the US economy since the 1980s is associated with the decline of the manufacturing industry, often also described as a process of deindustrialization (Cohen and Zysman 1987). Deindustrialization was a direct result of financialization, as the increasing power of shareholders shifted the focus of firms in the direction of short-term profits, which impeded investment in long-term productivity and the economic sustainability of firms. Manufacturing became less important and less attractive for college graduates as salaries and bonuses in the financial sector grew much faster than those in other sectors.[4] Suddenly, working in the financial sector, which until the 1970s had been considered a dull job for the less ambitious, became attractive, and more and more of the top college graduates went into banking. Consequently, traditional industrial heartlands, such as the rustbelt in the US and the north of England, suffered as talents moved to the financial centres.

In the 1980s, the process of deindustrialization was largely lamented and seen as a disadvantage compared to Europe and particularly Japan, which, it was feared, was emerging as 'No.1' (Vogel 1979, 1986). For most observers, it was obvious that the US would be unable to maintain global leadership if it lost the productive industries and focused only on service and the controlling ability of finance. Cohen and Zysman (1987: p. xiv) summarized this verdict in the simple formula that 'over time, you can't control what you can't produce'. In the 1990s the notion changed completely. After the collapse of the real-estate bubble in Japan, weak growth in Europe, and the new US self-confidence at the end of the cold war, this weakness was reinterpreted as a strength and heralded as the long-anticipated transformation into a 'post-industrial society' (Bell 1973)—an economy that could grow without the limits of physical production. The US dominance in financial industry and particularly its well-developed financial markets were now seen as the US reaching a new stage of economic development. Financial markets were considered the 'brain of the economy' (Stiglitz and Chang 2001; Mishkin 2006). The victory of neoliberalism meant that finance was the new commander in chief on the 'commanding heights' (Yergin and Stanislaw 1998) of the world economy.

---

[4] Jobs in the financial sector paid a premium of about 50% over non-financial jobs in 2005. In 1980, the premium was just 10% percent (Lahart 2008).

One of the most important insights of the Varieties of Capitalism (VoC) debate was the recognition of the institutional complementarities between a dynamic economy driven by the financial market and 'radical innovation'—for example, in the IT sector (Hall and Soskice 2001). As we have seen, capital in finance-led economies tends to be short-term oriented and can be moved easily from one sector of the economy to the other. There is a willingness to move capital into riskier investments such as venture capital, in a search for higher returns. This gives start-up companies access to capital that they would not get through regular bank credits. When their business fails, innovators are not burdened with debt, but share the loss with the investors. Finance-led capitalism thus provides a facilitating environment for risky start-up companies and radical innovations.

In general, one should not confuse the financialization curse with a complete deindustrialization. Schwartz has shown that US productivity remains high because US multinational companies have been most active in global offshoring of production (Schwartz 2009: ch. 5). This enables them to take advantage of low labour costs in Mexico, China, and South-East Asia to a much higher degree then their European competitors. In reality, the deindustrialization in the US is not a decline of industry but a crisis of domestic industrial employment and particularly a decline of the traditional stable and high-wage industrial employment with high levels of unionization and welfare provided through corporate schemes. For example, from 2003 to 2009 the number of auto workers in the US declined by 42 per cent from 970,000 to 562,000 (Katz et al. 2014: 65).Within the car industry there was a dramatic shift from the traditional 'big three' producers (GM, Ford, Chrysler) in the north to Japanese and German car makers producing in the south, where labour costs and unionization are lower, as we shall see.

Financialization is not a symptom of deindustrialization per se, but is rather one indicator of the emergence of a finance-led model of capitalism that is characterized by the hegemony of financial motives, the globalization of production, and the decline of the industrial workforce. Financialization does not lead to a complete deindustrialization, but it shapes a certain form of industry that can survive amid financialization and the 'predatory formation' (Sassen 2014: 13) connected to it. In turn, this kind of industry shares many of the preferences of the financial sector for capital-account liberalization and the need for active macroeconomic policies and the maintenance of the US dollar as the most important global currency.

3.3.3. The Decline of Industrial Labour and the Domestic Sources of Global Imbalances

This combination of financialization and the globalization of production has resulted in the decline of the industrial workforce, labour unionization, and, more broadly, regular wage-earners, on the one hand, being compared to 'bonus receivers' in management and finance as well as rentiers living from the return of their financial assets, on the other hand. As an example, Figure 3.3 shows that employees' compensation in the industrial sector is declining in all countries, although it remains higher in Germany, Korea, and Japan, while it is lowest in the US and the UK. The decline in the industrial workforce in combination with a declining share of wages in the GDP has led to an increase in social inequality between wage-earners and capital owners. This trend of increasing inequality of wealth and income has been described and criticized extensively (Stiglitz 2013; Geoghegan 2014; Piketty 2014). What is particularly relevant here is that this increasing inequality has given rise to a specific form of labour market and consumerism that complements and reinforces the dominant role of finance in the economy. Most importantly, social inequality has increased the amount of financial wealth in the higher-income strata of society, while at the same time increasing

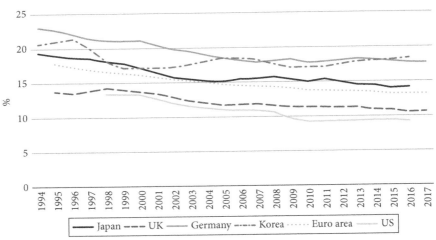

Figure 3.3. Share of employee compensation in the industrial sector of total value added (%)

Source: OECD (2019), Employee compensation by activity (indicator). doi: 10.1787/7af78603-en (Accessed on 05 January 2019)

the need for credit for consumption and subprime mortgages in the lower-income strata of society.

Deindustrialization and financialization are closely linked to a consumer-oriented economy in which economic growth depends not primarily on domestic investment and production but on consumption and the connected services and financial products. Indeed, the decline of the US as a producer economy is connected to its rise as the global financial centre and its role as the global consumer of last resort. While finance became the engine of the economy, consumption served as the fuel that kept the engine running. Financialization shapes a specific form of consumer culture, in which people are characterized by their consumption patterns, and what products they purchase are important for the way a person is characterized (Garon and Maclachlan 2006; Garon 2011). Unlike in the past, people are defined primarily not by their profession or their social status but through their ability to consume and the product choices they make. Conspicuous consumption has created an increasing market for high-priced iconic domestic products, such as Tesla's electric car or the iPhone, as well as imported brands and luxurious products from Europe. At the same time, lower-income consumers have benefited, as offshoring allows production costs to be reduced, and prices are kept down through reimports of offshore production. The offshoring strategy allows even low-income families to participate in the consumer society. This 'Wal-mart effect' (Fishman 2006) had the additional effect of keeping overall inflation down, thus allowing for lower interest rates and higher credit growth. Consequently, in international comparison, the US has a high level of domestic consumption and thus a low level of domestic savings (see Figure 3.4).

Finance-led capitalism thrives, not just because of the increasing financial wealth at the top that needs to be recycled, but also by allowing the losers of deindustrialization to consume through credit cards and consumer credits. Consumers can increase spending, despite the process of deindustrialization and the associated loss of employment and depressed wages, because of their ability to access credit and particularly home mortgages and credit-card financing. These financial innovations allowed many to consume beyond their means and constituted a lucrative business for the financial industry. The US became a 'credit card nation' (Manning 2000), where consumers used credit cards and consumer loans to buy products that otherwise they would not have been able to afford. Low interest rates with zero down payments allowed access to more expensive cars, and tax-deductible mortgage credits allowed access to the housing market. Through subprime mortgages, owning a house was available, even to those with very low or

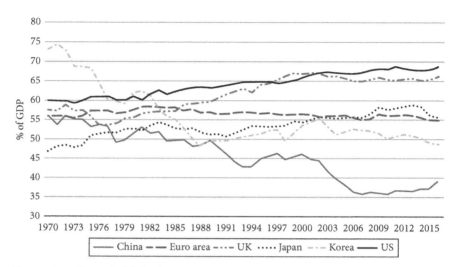

Figure 3.4. Household final consumption expenditure (% of GDP)

Source: World Bank, WDI Database, https://databank.worldbank.org/source/world-development-indicators.

even no income (Shiller 2008). Rising house prices went hand in hand with increasing consumer and mortgage debt, allowing Americans to use their houses as a piggy bank to finance consumption, which further fuelled the real-estate bubble. Consumer credits and subprime mortgages were the finance-led answer to the problem of social inequality. As long as the system of financialization worked, it successfully masked the weaknesses of the US style of capitalism, but it was a house of cards waiting to collapse. As long as the global financial markets had appetite for debt made in the US, the system worked quite well, but every asset bubble has to deflate or pop at some time, and this one collapsed in 2008.

3.3.4. The US as the Financial Centre of the World

While the US has lost its dominant role as a global producer in manufacturing, it maintains the global financial centre of gravity, towards which international financial flows are pulled. Despite the relative decline of US industries, the US financial market remains attractive and indispensable to store and recycle global funds. As already stated, this attractiveness has first of all to do with 'the willingness of other private and public actors to buy and hold US assets.' (Schwartz 2009: 227) The US remains the ultimate safe haven, owing to its global leadership position, and status of the dollar as the most important global currency, as well as the size and liquidity of the US market. In this sense, there is a strong path dependency, as the US is the global leader owing to the size and liquidity of financial markets, and its financial markets are large and liquid because of their global leadership position. Most importantly, the role of the dollar as the global currency forces all internationally active entities to hold US dollars. As in the long run financial markets always depend on the credibility of the state, global investors ask themselves which state would ultimately be the last one standing, even in the event of the most catastrophic global economic and/or political crisis imaginable. Despite the relative economic decline, the answer as to which is the safest vault for international capital is still the US. But the US is much more than just the banker of the world offering a safe haven and borrowing short term while investing long term around the world. As we have seen, the rise of the US financial market was connected with global outsourcing and foreign investment. Gourinchas and Rey (2007) have thus proposed to call the US not the banker of the world but the 'venture capitalist of the world' borrowing short and globally investing long term (Gourinchas and Rey 2007). However, the US is much more than just a venture capitalist or a banker. It is much more broadly the financial centre of the world, recycling global excess capital into all kinds of financial products.

It is not just the size and liquidity of the US financial market that create its attractiveness but more importantly the amount, variety, and sophistication of financial services and products on offer. This unique set and variety of services for a global customer base can only be found in the US and to a lesser degree in the City of London. Other financial centres might offer comparable services in some niches, but the breadth of services available in the global financial centres in New York and London is matched by none. Only the US market offers the variety of products satisfying every possible need for saving, borrowing, or investment. It is not a surprise that European MNCs, East Asian governments, and banks from all over the world rely and depend on the services of Wall Street and the City of London.

Even though the separation of banks and investment houses has been revoked, brokering of financial products and not the classic credit business of deposit-taking banks is dominating. This does not mean that the classic credit business is obsolete, as credit remain the most important source of external funding for investment. However, the expectation is that the classic credit business will lose relevance and be replaced by market-based or peer-to-peer based brokerages. Meanwhile US companies are leading in financial technology (or fintech) in diverse areas from crowdfunding to mobile payments.

Some argue that it is not the US that is finance-led but just New York, which is the financial centre and which is more connected to other 'global cities' (Sassen 2001) such as London, Tokyo, and Frankfurt than to the rest of its own country. While the global-city argument does have its merits, I want to highlight that the US role as the global financial centre depends on much more than just the cosmopolitan elite of New York. Financialization has created a distinct model of capitalism that can be felt in the political centre of Washington DC as much as in the venture capitalists of Silicon Valley and the consumer finance and mortgage industry operating everywhere in the country. Wall Street is the core, but it would not function without the rest of the country playing along and adjusting to the needs of the financial sector. Many of the global services provided by Wall Street would not be available without the political backing of the most powerful state in the world and a specific domestic political economy that complements the global role of the US financial sector. The dominant sector needs fitting into the complementary institutions in other sectors as well. Most importantly, the financialization of a wide range of industries creates a certain congruence of interests without which the ideological hegemony of Wall Street could not be understood.

The global position and the institutional affinities of the finance-led growth model shape the preferences of the US in the G20 and in global economic governance. Not surprisingly, the dominance of the financial sector implies that the US is imposed to limiting the free movement of capital because it would reduce the number of fee generating transactions. Instead, the US prefers to increase reserve requirements for financial institutes that hurt its developed financial markets less than the competitors.

3.3.5. The US Position in the Global Division of Labour

The US finance-led growth model essentially consists of three connected aspects. First, the global control ability necessary to manage a globalized system of offshoring that is far more developed in the US than elsewhere. Financialization does not mean deindustrialization per se but rather the globalization of value-added chains, which results in a decline of the domestic industrial workforce. Unlike in Europe or East Asia (as we shall see in Chapters 4 and 5), these production chains controlled by US companies are not primarily regional but truly global. The focus of the growth model thus changes from facilitating production to ensuring a global control ability. Second, the US financial market remains indispensable to store and recycle global funds. It is unique in its deepness and the variety of services, which are limited only by government regulation. Third, the finance-led growth model is complementary to a much broader sets of domestic institutions. It corresponds better with a market-based than with a bank-based financial system. Global investments require large amounts of capital, which can be raised more easily through financial markets than through banks. A lot of this capital is not raised domestically but originates in the global recycling of fund in US stock and bond markets, including the most important market of US treasuries.

The complementarities reach far beyond the financial sector and include a supportive state with a huge appetite for debt financing, fiscal expansion, as well as stagnant wages, which increase the need for consumer and mortgage finance. These economic structures are complemented by a specific kind of neoliberal ideology, as we shall see in the next section. A finance-led growth model is thus much more than 'buying time' (Streeck 2013) or a 'spatio-temporal fix' (Harvey 1989) but rather a relatively stable pathway from the decline of economic growth since the 1970s. Even economic crises such as the savings and loans debacle of the 1980s, the LTCM crisis of 1989, or the crisis since 2008 have not seriously threatened the position of the US as the financial centre of the world. Of course, the system can remain intact only as long as the global division of labour produces countries and regions in need of the services that the US financial centre offers. Given the need to recycle massive amounts of global capital owing to the sustained global imbalances, as well as the intensifying global production networks that need to raise funds and to maintain the ability to control international production through financial flows, it is hard to imagine that demand for US-based financial services will drop. As long as euro capitalism and East Asian capitalism exist, US finance-led capitalism will play its role, too. However, before we turn to the complementarities of different models on the global level, we need to investigate the domestic political economic structure that maintains the US finance-led capitalism. As we shall see in the following section, US finance-led capitalism is supported and reinforced by complementarities in the labour market, welfare state, consumer behaviour, and even ideology that are relatively stable.

3.4. Neoliberalism and the Political Economy of Finance-Led Capitalism

The previous section has described the economics of the US finance-led model capitalism. In this section we look at the political pillar of this model, which consists of a specific class compromise that is rationalized by a distinct type of neoliberal ideology. On the surface the finance-led growth model appears to be the dominance of financial over industrial ('real') capital, although, as we have seen, it is much more complicated than that if we take into account the globalization of value-added chains and consumption patterns. Most importantly, it is not per se the decline of the real economy but rather the decline of domestic employment in industrial manufacturing. This trend is connected to the decline of the economic, political, and economic power of organized labour—economic in the sense of stagnating wages and consumer debt, political in the sense of deregulation and a weakened welfare state, and ideological in the sense of the dominance of a specific US style of neoliberal ideology. This section describes how these broader developments are not just an essential part of the finance-led model of capitalism but also contributed to its rise. Economic realities are the driving force behind neoliberalist politics and ideology, but political decisions steer this dynamic one way or the other. After investigating the reasons why the US is so interested in capital-account liberalization and market-based exchange rates, this section also offers explanations as to why sovereign macroeconomic policies remain a necessity for the US model of capitalism.

3.4.1. The Neoliberal State and the Ideology of Finance-Led Capitalism

In finance-led capitalism, the interests of financial firms and financial investors began to dominate the agenda of economic and financial reform as well as academic and political discussions. Finance became the point of reference for the economy, and, as we have seen, even non-financial companies started to behave like financial firms. Financial markets and the sum of the decisions of financial investors became simply 'the market', and 'gaining the confidence of the market' became the primary goal of business and politics alike. Losing 'market confidence' and the resulting outflow of capital became the capital punishments for businesses and whole countries. Neoliberalism is the ideology of this market orientation. While in Europe the mandate of the state includes welfare policies and tripartite neo-corporatism and in East Asia state guidance and industrial policies are seen as essential, US style neoliberalism limits welfare spending and industrial policies. That does not mean the state is not actively intervening, but rather that the interventions should be market oriented in the sense that they apply to all market actors and limit resource allocation.

Neoliberalism differs from the pre-Keynes dogmatic liberalism in that it acknowledges the role of a capable state in ensuring the functioning of the market. In this sense, the neoliberal ideology is not about fewer state interventions and economic liberalization per se but rather about a form of market fundamentalism. As the market is seen as efficient and containing all relevant information at any given time, the state should refrain from 'market-distorting' interventions and rather provide a legal framework for the market. In this view, the market is a 'catallaxy', a system of exchange in which anonymous actors are merely connected through the price mechanism and where no other forms of coordination or cooperation exist (with the conspicuous exemption of the family). Not surprisingly, the neoliberal ideology in the US connects to the collective memory of the supposedly golden age of the free market and the internal expansion to the 'Wild West' until the First World War. More recently, the memory of the Great Depression has been shaped by Milton Friedman's account that central bank failure, as well as protectionism leading to the collapse of world trade, were the main causes of the World Economic Crisis of the 1930s. These collective memories have created a certain ideological bias that made the US far less aware of the need carefully to watch the rise of the financial sector and in particular the shadow banking sector and of the systemic importance of investment banks such as Lehman Brothers (Eichengreen 2015).

Neoliberalism also differs from classic liberalism in the way crises should be managed. The ideology that the market is always right is at the core of classic liberalism, but in neoliberalism this applies only during 'normal times', and neoliberals would agree that the state has to intervene in a crisis situation, when the 'normal operation' of the market has failed. As the financial crisis since 2008 clearly constitutes a market failure, there was little doubt in the US that the government should intervene to stabilize banks and stimulate the economy. Still, as we have seen in Chapter 2, it could be seen as surprising that a regulatory state like the US intervened more forcefully than neo-corporatist states in Europe and was equally decisive as the developmental states in East Asia. Superficially, the massive macroeconomic intervention and fiscal stimuli can be explained by the fact that finance-led countries were initially hit most severely by the collapse of the global economic crisis that began in the US financial markets in 2008. However, the reason for the more active intervention can also be explained by the institutional complementarity of institutions dealing with macroeconomic policies. In fact, studies have shown that there is a strong affinity between finance-led capitalism and expansive macroeconomic policies (Carlin and Soskice 2006; Soskice 2007).

During the crisis, finance-led countries like the US were characterized by decisive macroeconomic interventions and particularly by expansive monetary policies and large fiscal stimulus packages. Monetarism is the specific American version of neoliberalism, in which monetary policies and thus the central banks play the central role in steering the economy, while the government remains largely passive. Monetarism basically claims that monetary policies are a way of guiding the economy, particularly in economic downturns, without distorting the market. Consequently, finance-led countries tend to have central banks like the Fed that are dominated by the interests of the financial sector, but at the same time have a dual mandate not limited to price stability but also including economic growth. On first sight, this seems counter-intuitive, because financial assets are those mostly affected by inflation, but, as we have already argued, it is the strength of the financial industry and not the power of finance as such that characterizes finance-led economies. Financial assets can be held in many different ways, such as savings, bonds, stocks, and other financial products. Owing to the more developed financial markets in finance-led countries, savings tend to be parked in more inflation-protected assets such as stocks. The low saving rate and the tendency for debt-financed investment and consumption also mean that debtors are a much bigger interest group than in countries dominated by saving and thrift.

When it comes to fiscal policies, the US is again more active than European countries, as we have seen in Chapter 2 (Figure 2.5). Most of these interventions have been in the form of tax reductions, which are generally seen as market friendly because they reduce the redistributive ability of the state. Another reason why finance-led countries tend to have larger fiscal stimuli is that they have the advantage of larger and more liquid financial markets, which make it easier for the government to finance deficits. In the case of the US, the attraction of the public bond market is further increased by the position of the dollar as an international reserve currency (see Chapter 5). US treasuries are not just a debt instrument but also a global asset to store international currency reserves. In addition, there is also a close affinity between structural fiscal deficits and a majority voting system, which makes it difficult to increase taxes and at the same time demand election sweeteners or pork barrel projects from office-holders. In the US, the ideology of tax reductions provides a powerful legitimization for fiscal deficits and at the same time limits the role of the government to make institutional changes that would reduce the need for macroeconomic activism such as strengthening the welfare state.

The self-image of the 'neoliberal state' (Plant 2010) is essentially that the state should provide a legal framework for the market and guarantee the rule of law but not have any intrinsic goals itself. Unlike in Europe and East Asia, rule of law means the common-law principle, which is particularly suitable for a liberal market economy like the US (Pistor 2005). Common-law principles are the adequate legal system for a liberal market economy, because they put the private contract at the centre of the legal system instead of enforcing universal laws, as under the civil-law system. The common-law system leaves much more room for private contracts, and the market is the arena in which private contracts are signed. The market is regulated not primarily by legal rules but by the interaction of market actors and the occasional clarification of contracts by the courts in the case of diverging interpretations. Unlike the welfare or developmental state, which we shall see in Chapters 4 and 5, in theory the neoliberal state has the function of a 'night-watchman', without influence on what kind of decisions are made either in the economy or in society. The idea is that the sum of the individual decisions by the market are the optimal outcome and that no single institution can understand or improve this outcome. In practice, this utopian laissez-faire state has never existed, and, on the contrary, neoliberals have been very actively utilizing the state to implement their political agenda on the economy and the society as such. In fact, rather than being laissez-faire, the neoliberal agenda in practice was an active 'reengineering [of] the state' (Hilgers 2012: 81) to suit the interests of asset-owners and the financial sector as their service providers. This reengineering was not just a political project serving a certain economic interest but rather a more profound reform of existing models of capitalism. Neoliberalism did not become just one political philosophy among many but affected the whole ideological spectrum. Jessop (2013) distinguishes three phases of the neoliberal project since the 1970s: the first conservative one under Pinochet, Thatcher, and Reagan in the 1970s and 1980s, the second global one under the Washington consensus in the 1980s and early 1990s, and the third 'liberal' or 'third way' incarnation in finance-led capitalism under Clinton and Tony Blair, Gerhard Schroeder in Europe, and to some degree Koizumi in Japan in the 1990s and 2000s. It is important to note that neoliberalism differed quite substantially not just over time but also between the three major models of capitalism, as we see throughout the book. While in all models power was shifted from the state to market actors ('the market'), there are substantial differences on what kind of regulatory or framework setting power the neoliberal state should have. In the US, active monetary and fiscal policies are seen as compatible with a free market, while in Europe welfare policies are a natural part of the ordo-liberal framework of a 'social market economy'. In East Asia, few neoliberals would doubt that increasing national competitiveness needs state interventions in the form of industrial policies.

3.4.2. A Weak Welfare State and the 'Flexible' Labour Market

The choice of a weaker welfare state in particular reinforces the need of the neoliberal state for macroeconomic interventions. A weaker welfare state means that automatic stabilizers are smaller than in European welfare states and direct government intervention is thus more urgent and crucial. Indeed, the size of the welfare state is negatively correlated with the size of fiscal stimulus packages (Figure 2.5). A small welfare state also reinforces the trend for financialization, both directly and indirectly. It reinforces it directly by making it necessary for people to buy financial services for unemployment, healthcare, and retirement. In fact, the total social expenditure in the US is not much lower than in Europe, but it is the *public* social expenditure that is considerably smaller (Streissler, in Gustenau et al. 2006: 49). Instead, Americans have to purchase privately the protections that their European peers receive from public institutions. This has created a massive market in the financial and insurance industry. The indirect influence is because the failure of the welfare state in the US to reduce social inequalities has contributed to the massive growth in consumer credits, as we have seen.

At the same time, US manufacturing companies have a disadvantage in competing with European manufacturers in most sectors of manufacturing, because, directly or indirectly, they have to shoulder large parts of social spending. Because employees have huge private healthcare bills, they will either demand higher wages or ask their employer to contribute directly to their healthcare and pension savings. In particular, for old manufacturing companies, such private welfare spending is a large burden, as they have to provide for a large number of retirees. At the same time, newly started US companies in the high-tech sector remain very competitive, not just because they have a superior ability to raise capital but also because their employees are younger and so they have fewer retirees to care for.

In combination with a 'flexible' labour market, the weak welfare state also reinforces wage stagnation and the process of financialization in general. In the US, the liberal labour laws mean that employers can easily hire and fire workers. This type of labour-market flexibility allows US companies quickly to adjust to demand and to restructure their operations. US companies are thus able to reduce costs in a crisis situation much more quickly than European companies. This is particularly true for the service sector, where labour unions are too weak to negotiate job protection on the company level. For employers, this flexibility is a great benefit, but it also corresponds with the hollowing-out of traditional industries, as employers prefer to fire unproductive workers instead of using their experience to move into more specialized production. Amid a weak welfare state, laid-off workers have to rush to find a new job, even if wages and productivity are far below the previous employment. In the US, the flexible labour market is complemented by a weak 'workfare' welfare state, which is seen as a last resort, targeted at preventing absolute poverty but not as a way to reduce social inequality or to allow those laid off to take their time to find a new suitable job. This is the reason why those laid off in the US often have to accept lower-paid jobs when rehired, while their European colleagues can take their time to find a job that is comparable to the one they had before. This explains why US unemployment rates tend to be lower than in Europe but at the same time why there is a downward pressure on wages and a substantial loss in the job-related specific skills that would be needed for high-quality manufacturing.

As workers are easily replaceable, neither employers nor employees have an incentive to provide workers with extensive training. In consequence, US manufacturing companies focus on simplicity (Geoghegan 2014: loc. 418). They simplify work processes and focus less on training but instead invest a large amount of effort on improving management and quality control. This strategy differs substantially from European companies, which follow a strategy of quality-oriented specialization that requires extensive training and experience, as we shall see in Chapter 4. As pointed out by the VoC debate, the flexibility of the labour market also complements an education system that is focused on general skills. Employees with general skills can switch jobs more quickly. While this is a downside for manufacturing requiring specialized skills, it is an advantage for cutting-edge radical innovations that are based primarily not on experience but on creativity and the capability to combine existing technologies and skills in new ways. For example, the iPhone became a successful radical innovation not because it was technologically advanced but because it combined existing products (mobile phones, mobile organizers, and the iPod) with successful marketing. In this sense, the weakness of the US model in its deindustrialization and wage stagnation is just the other side of the coin from it strength in radical innovation and the growth of the service sector and in particular financial services.

3.4.3. The Declining Political Power of Organized Labour

The characteristics of US finance-led capitalism are not per se the decline of manufacturing and the real economy but more specifically the decline of domestic industrial production and workforce. While US industries remained competitive through financialization and globalization, the industrial workforce suffered and with it organized labour interests. Both union membership and the share of work contracts based on collective bargaining are much lower in the US than in Europe and East Asia (see Figures 4.1 and 4.2). For example, while car production in the US has declined by about 15 per cent since the 1970s, membership in the United Auto Worker (UAW) Union has declined by 75 per cent from 1.5 million members in 1979 to 381,000 in 2011 (Katz et al. 2014: 52). Geoghegan (2014: loc. 386) shows that, because of declining unionization, workers in car manufacturing in the US earn about half of what German car workers earn, and many earn even less. Originally, US laws from the 1930s and 1940s, like the Wagner Act of 1935, were very favourable to labour and even allowed unions to force non-members in a unionized factory to pay union fees. At the same time, the privilege to represent all workers within a factory has created a timid labour movement, which had few incentives to push for industry-wide collective bargaining. While labour unions might be strong in individual companies, they lack industry-wide wage-setting power that would affect the share of wages in the overall GDP. Consequently, when the political and legislative tide turned against them in the 1980s, organized labour was too weak to achieve neo-corporatist solutions with employers that would protect employees from hire-and-fire practices and wage depression. The threat to offshore production further undermined the power of unions. In addition, there was a domestic challenge as more and more industries moved from the traditional industrial centres of the north with a high unionization rate to the conservative and economically underdeveloped south. Most of the states in the south have 'right-to-work' legislation that makes it difficult for unions to represent all workers in a factory. Consequently, wages in the non-unionized plants are lower, which provides a competitive edge over those factories in the north.

Organized labour was an important political force enabling the rise of Keynesianism and social-democratic welfare reforms. With the decline of organized labour, business-friendly positions strengthened, not just on the conservative side of first- and second-generation neoliberals such as Reagan, but even within those parties that were closer to organized labour such as third-generation neoliberals like Clinton and Blair. Labour unions have lost substantial influence in the political sphere and particularly within the Democratic Party since the 1990s, when business interests started to dominate not just the Republican Party but also the Democrats. For example, while lobbying and campaign contributions from businesses were previously targeted at the Republicans, they became bipartisan and went almost equally to Republicans and Democrats (Reich 2007: 136). Labour unions are unable to compete with the massive business contributions, with the largest union organization, AFL-CIO, ranking seventy-fourth, far behind many individual business groups, with the US Chamber of Commerce coming in first (Reich 2007: 135). Labour-friendly candidates have consistently lost out against centrist candidates, as demonstrated by the defeat of Bernie Sanders by Hillary Clinton during the 2016 Democratic Party primaries. Centrist candidates do not only have the lead in direct donations; more importantly, they tend to have the overwhelming support from the party establishment, which is generally much weaker than in European parties but plays an important role in the selection of the presidential candidate.

While labour unions have substantially weakened, they still maintain an important role in advocacy work and influencing public opinions. Instead of long strikes to force employers to raise wages, as experienced in Europe and particularly East Asia, they employ 'guerrilla activities' such as short strikes and campaigns that create public support and lend credibility to their agendas (Geoghegan 2014). Most importantly, since the anti-WTO protest in Seattle in 1999, labour unions have been at the forefront of a critique of international trade agreements, which are criticized for facilitating the global offshoring of production. Unlike in Europe, where global challenges have let to more international cooperation within the European Union, there is a stronger general opposition to corporate globalization in the US. The remaining limited influence of labour unions also helps to explain why demand-side-oriented policies such as expansive fiscal policies are more acceptable in the US than in Europe. In short, in the US, labour unions are weak in setting wages and shaping the broad debate on welfare policies, but they remain politically relevant enough to demand government compensation for economic losses, particularly during economic crises.

3.4.4. The Neoliberal State: Market Fundamentalism and Macroeconomic Activism

Finance-led capitalism is much more complex and runs much more deeply than just the economic importance and power of the financial sector. It is facilitated by, complements, and strengthens institutions and power relations that have a long tradition in the US. The neoliberal state, and the weakness of organized labour and the welfare state, are the political foundation of the economic rise of finance and the decline of manufacturing. At the same time, these configurations correspond not just with financial liberalization but also with a strong regulatory state and active macroeconomic policies. Because the welfare state is weak, the state needs to be more active, particularly in a crisis situation, and because labour unions are weak, there is no need for a strong 'independent' central bank such as the ECB (and previously the German Bundesbank), which counters industry-wide wage increases with anti-inflationary measures. Consequently, the Fed is far less concerned with an 'inflation spiral' following a broad increase in wages then the ECB. This political foundation in the US is rationalized by a specific form of neoliberal ideology that has a global perspective, limits state interventions, but at the same time supports an active state in a crisis situation.

3.5. The Second Image of Finance-Led Capitalism

This institutional and political economic investigation of finance-led econo-mies has helped to clarify the position of the US (and to some degree the UK) in the trilemma triangle outlined in Chapter 2. We have found that the international position taken by the US complements the domestic, political, and economic institutions and power relations. The institutional regime con-sists of compatible institutions governing the relationship between finance and businesses, finance and consumers, and finance and state. This institutional regime is based on power relations with dominant financial institutions, weak labour unions, and a state focused on providing a regulatory framework, combined with substantial interventions in terms of fiscal and monetary policies.

First, the US finance-led capitalism has a clear global perspective as it establishes itself as the 'banker of the world'. Its goal is to recycle as many global funds as possible and create as many fee-generating transactions as possible. As industries are squeezed domestically by the dominance of the financial sector, they rush to offshore production in order to remain compe-titive. The 'financialization curse' thus speeds not only financial globalization but also the offshoring of production.

Second, and as a consequence, the main priority of the finance-led countries is capital-account liberalization in order to attract as much capital as possible.

As the financial sector has become the dominant capital faction, finance-led countries have opposed all attempts to curb international financial flows in the form of capital controls or financial transaction taxes, because they would reduce transactions and thus fee generation.

Third, finance-led countries like the US have been champions of global macroeconomic coordination. The US has been active in championing active monetary and fiscal policies to overcome economic crises. This state activism can be explained by the weakness of the welfare state in the US, which necessitates macroeconomic stimuli in economic crises to maintain social stability. At the same time, the US lacks corporatist coordination mechanisms that would help share the burden during economic downturns and distribute the gains during upswings.

Fourth, finance-led countries like the US prefer market-based exchange rates and are opposed to global monetary regimes that would limit either the flow of capital or their ability to undertake macroeconomic interventions. For large finance-led countries like the US, the lack of currency stability is not a problem, owing to the big domestic market and its position as an international debtor country that is indebted exclusively in its own currency.

4

Integration-Led Capitalism in the EU

The Rise of Euro Corporatism, and the Quest for Regional Stability

The global role of the European Union and its position in the trilemma triangle differ substantially from the global–hegemonic approach pursued by US finance-led capitalism. This chapter first explores the historical choices that countries in Europe made after the collapse of the BWS and the internal, regional dynamics of an emerging integration led euro capitalism. We show that the EU (and until 1992 the European Economic Community) developed a distinct regional solution for the challenges of globalization with the creation of the single market and the European Monetary Union. As we shall then see, this growth model is based economically on a specific European complementary specialization production system and politically on a distinct form of euro-corporatism. Complementary specialization production refers to a European division of labour that is strong in making specialized and niche products. Euro-corporatism refers to a system of conflict management that is based on the close coordination between the system of multilevel governance of the EU, business associations, and civil-society actors such as organized labour. As already explained in Chapter 1, this does not mean that national governments and national political economies have become irrelevant, but rather that there is a convergence towards a common EU position when it comes to global economic governance. In the past, UK finance-led capitalism, which is closer to that of the US, was an obvious exception, but, with the planned UK exit from the EU in 2019, it seems plausible that the convergence towards a euro-capitalist model will accelerate.

4.1. The European Position in the Trilemma Triangle

As we have seen in Chapters 1 and 2, Europe's global role in the international political economy and the trilemma triangle can be summarized as focused

Why International Cooperation Is Failing: How the Clash of Capitalisms Undermines the Regulation of Finance. Thomas Kalinowski, Oxford University Press (2019). © Thomas Kalinowski
DOI: 10.1093/oso/9780198714729.001.0001

on the stability of currencies, a conservative approach to macroeconomic coordination, a commitment to the free flow of capital, and an approach to financial regulation that is focused on rules preventing financial excesses and ensuring the embeddedness of finance into the real economy (see Figure 1.5). Unlike the outward-looking and global approach of the US, the most important priority of the EU is to ensure the deepening of the European single market and regional stability, in particularly the stability of currencies and since 1999 the euro. The goal of the single market is to create a larger market through enlargement of the EU as well as the harmonization of rules. Like the US, the EU promotes the free flow of capital, but at the same time the EU is more concerned than the US about the volatility of global financial markets and is thus more inclined to curb speculation and market excesses—for example, by taxing international financial transactions or limiting bankers' bonuses. Although EU-style harmonization and US-style liberalization have many similarities, the EU ideal is not to have 'free markets' but rather to develop unified rules that facilitate the exchange of goods and to a lesser extent services and people. At the same time, the EU is reluctant to follow the US lead for tougher bank rules, because its financial system is bank based.

In order to facilitate the single market, the EU puts the highest priority on internal regional stability and in particular the stability of the euro. So far, the EU has not been interested in jeopardizing domestic stability for a stronger international role of the euro, nor does the EU have any need to use its currency as a tool for competitiveness, like East Asian countries, because its businesses operate in niche markets for specialized products that are less price sensitive than East Asian mass-consumer products. In addition, the euro-corporatism described in this chapter helps businesses to moderate wage increases and to increase productivity by co-opting labour unions. Consequently, the EU and its member states have sacrificed national sovereignty and in particular macroeconomic management. Euro members have given up not just their monetary sovereignty by delegating power to the European Central Bank (ECB); they have also sacrificed substantial parts of their fiscal sovereignty with the Maastricht Treaty. It is thus no surprise that EU member countries are very reluctant when it comes to coordinating macroeconomic stimuli in the G20. As we have seen in Chapter 2, EU member states have implemented smaller fiscal stimulus packages (Figure 2.5) and the ECB has been much more conservative and reluctant than the Fed to cut interest rates and 'print money'. This global role of the EU has thus created zones of conflict with the US, and a reluctance of European countries to participate in US-led macroeconomic coordination (see Chapter 3). At the same time, the relatively strong welfare states that automatically stabilize economies in times of crisis mean that state activism is less urgent in the EU.

4.2. The Emergence of EU Integration-Led Capitalism and the Struggle for Regional Stability

Since the collapse of the BWS, Europe has focused on a regional solution to the challenges of financial globalization and currency volatility by establishing a regional monetary system. The EU has been the only region to uphold the goal of international monetary coordination, but the commitment to promote a comprehensive 'New Bretton Woods' has remained largely a general instinct without much concrete action. Indeed, the EU has been so occupied with maintaining regional currency stability (and since 1999 the stability of the euro) that there has been little room and appetite for attempting to provide leadership and resources behind a new global monetary system.

4.2.1. The Successful Recovery of Europe under the BWS

Although the US was the indisputable hegemon within the BWS, Europe was the region that benefited most from the post-Second World War order of the BWS from 1945 to 1971. While the US, as the global leader after 1945, would have been able to survive in any kind of global economic environment, European reconstruction after the devastating war was dependent greatly on international institutions such as the Marshall Plan and the International Bank for Reconstruction and Development (better known as the World Bank). The BWS facilitated the post-war period of trade liberalization and economic cooperation. Most importantly, the BWS provided Europe with a global framework of relatively stable global financial markets and stable exchange rates. Stable exchange rates did not only provide a predictable environment for the expansion of trade; owing to the much faster growth in Europe compared to the US, they also effectively meant undervalued European currencies (Eichengreen 2007: 38–9).[1] This made European products more competitive and provided windfall profits in local currencies for export businesses. And businesses did not only profit from exchanging the dollars they had earned from

---

[1] France and Belgium were notable exemptions.

exports at a favourable rate; they also benefited from low real interest rates, which were largely predetermined by the US Fed, the unquestioned monetary leader in the BWS. While France in particular resented the US hegemony in the BWS and the 'exorbitant privilege' (Eichengreen 2011) of the dollar as a global currency, in general European countries were the strongest supporters of the system. They not only accepted the US hegemony, but were willing to contribute substantially to the diverse attempts to stabilize the BWS in the 1960s, as described in Chapter 3. They contributed to the gold pool, the General Agreement to Borrow, and the Roosa Bonds, they agreed to purchase American military equipment to reduce trade imbalances between Europe and the US, and they supported the Smithsonian Agreement (Zimmermann 2001: 51–9).

Ultimately, all rescue attempts failed, and the Nixon Shock ended the BWS (see Chapter 3). This end of 'hegemonic stability' differed quite substantially from the catastrophic collapse of the hegemonic stability dominated by the UK in the 1920s and 1930s, when the UK was too weak to lead and the US was unwilling to take over the leadership role (Kindleberger 1986). In the 1970s the US as the hegemonic power was clearly not too weak, but rather the Nixon administration was no longer willing to pay the price of monetary leadership. On the other hand, the Europeans were too weak to underwrite a new global system. Europe instead started to look for regional solutions to the issues of the increasing instability of the BWS and the economic imbalance between the Europe and the US at the end of the 1960s.

As we have seen in Chapter 3, the period after the BWS was dominated by a lack of global cooperation paired with ad hoc interventions led by the US. At the same time, the European Community (EC), as the predecessor of the EU, switched to an almost exclusively regional strategy. Formally the commitment to a stable global monetary system still holds. Ever since the 1970s, the general commitment to the IMF statutes 'to promote exchange stability, to maintain orderly exchange arrangements among members, and to avoid competitive exchange depreciation' (IMF 19944: art. I) has remained intact, and section 4 of post-Bretton Woods IMF still envisions the 'introduction of a widespread system of exchange arrangements based on stable but adjustable par values'. Compared to the US and East Asia, the EU was clearly closest to the spirit of the new IMF. However, the EC/EU has done little beyond a very modest proposal to establish a 'New Bretton Woods' or at least a stable exchange-rate system beyond the European region. As we shall see, the EC/EU was preoccupied from the start with the stability of the European monetary integration, which stumbled forward from crisis to crisis.

4.2.2. European Regional Answers to the Collapse of the BWS

When the BWS became increasingly unstable at the end of the 1960s, the European integration process was already at an advanced stage. The Treaty of Rome went into force in 1958, the introduction of the Common Agricultural Policy (CAP) in 1962, and in 1967 the European Coal and Steel Community (ECSC), the European Economic Community (EEC), and the European Atomic Energy Community (EAEC or Euratom) merged to become the European Community (EC). In retrospective, it seems almost inevitable that the weakening of the US as a global hegemon and the challenges of a BWS breakdown would lead to a European regional solution. Indeed, particularly the intra-European payments within the CAP would have become impossible to manage in a system of market-determined exchange rates. However, at that time the emancipation from US dominance was at least initially reluctant and full of conflicts between European countries. More fundamentally, France with its 'monetarist' position wanted to use regional monetary cooperation further to advance economic integration, while Germany's 'economist' approach saw monetary integration as the last step of economic integration (for an overview, see Maes 2004).

The collapse of the BWS and the economic slowdown in the 1970s induced a transformation in the agenda of European integration. Until the 1960s, the EC was largely dominated by the French goal to control Germany and to prevent Germany from having a dominant role in Europe (Schäfer 2005: 66–74). From the late 1960s, the focus shifted away from this defensive attitude to a view that primarily saw the economic benefits of European integration. European integration was now reinterpreted as a source for economic growth and a protection against the volatility of global economic and particularly financial markets. Politically this change was symbolized by the generational transition from French President de Gaulle to Pompidou and German Chancellor Kiesinger to Willy Brandt. As national reconstruction after the war was completed, governments looked for new engines of economic growth. The liberalization of trade, capital, and the movement of people in Europe was a source for a new economic dynamic, while the idea of Europe as an engine of liberalization gained importance. Regional monetary cooperation, economic liberalization, and the harmonization of rules within the EC would increase the market for European companies and make it easier for them to sell their products in all countries within the EC. From being primarily concerned with security, the focus shifted to a process of European integration as a reaction to economic globalization and the construction of a

European growth model. This growth model was, to a large degree, based on the interlinked process of monetary integration and the creation of the single market.

4.2.3. The Werner Plan and Early Monetary Integration

When the problems of the BWS became more and more obvious at the end of the 1960s, the EC started working on increased regional monetary cooperation. At the European summit in The Hague in 1969, the Werner Commission was founded to develop a plan for a European Economic and Monetary Union (EMU). In its final report, the 'Werner Plan', the commission outlined a new ambitious stage of European integration. 'Economic and monetary union will make it possible to realize an area within which goods and services, people and capital will circulate freely and without competitive distortions, without thereby giving rise to structural, or regional disequilibrium' (Werner Plan 1970: 9). In the beginning of the 1970s, most observers and policymakers still believed that the BWS would survive in a reformed version, and, from the European perspective, European monetary cooperation was seen as a part of such a reformed global monetary system. Initially, the EMU was seen not as an alternative to the BWS but as a way to reduce global economic imbalances in order to save the BWS. According to the Werner Plan, 'the implementation of such a union will effect a lasting improvement in welfare in the Community and will reinforce the contribution of the Community to economic and monetary equilibrium in the world' (Werner Plan 1970: 9). The Werner Plan envisioned a new global role for the EC as a strong supporter of global monetary stability, but did not in any way claim a leadership role that would challenge the US and the hegemony of the dollar.

As mentioned in Chapter 2, the Smithsonian Agreement of 1971 was an attempt to save the BWS and to create a more flexible but stable exchange-rate system. The problem was that the dollar remained the reference point of the new global system. An exchange rate band of ±2.25 per cent to the dollar would mean that currencies between European countries could fluctuate up to ±4.5 per cent against each other. This fluctuation was seen as incompatible with the European customs union and the CAP, because it provoked protectionist measures to compensate for potential losses of competitiveness from currency volatility (Schäfer 2005: 96–7). Consequently, the EC introduced its own exchange rate band of ±2.25 per cent between EC currencies, which would behave like a 'snake in the tunnel' (Schäfer 2005: 99).

Unfortunately, the new European currency arrangement did not prove to be sustainable and in retrospect was only an intermediate step towards Europe's emancipation from the dollar peg. Already in March 1973 the EC countries decided to 'leave the tunnel' and abandon the Smithsonian Agreement amid the continuous policies of the Nixon administration to devalue the dollar in order to achieve domestic economic goals of stimulating growth and exports (see Chapter 3). After the US had started the dismantling of the BWS by abandoning the gold anchor in 1971, the EC delivered the final blow of what remained of the fixed exchange-rate system of the BWS by abandoning its interventions to stabilize the dollar. The European currency snake left the Smithsonian tunnel, and the role of the dollar as an anchor for European currencies was history. From that time, Europe's priority shifted entirely to the goal of achieving regional monetary stability.

The work to achieve regional monetary stability advanced through many stages and faced many problems and ups and downs from the beginning. The UK and Ireland left the European currency arrangement in 1972, Italy in 1973, France in 1974, and, after re-entering again in March 1976, Sweden finally left in 1977 and Norway in 1978 (EC 1979: 18). At the end of 1978, only Germany, Denmark, Belgium, the Netherlands, and Luxembourg remained part of the regional monetary arrangement, which had become 'virtually a Mark zone' (Marsh 2009: 77) led by the German Bundesbank, and European monetary cooperation was in crisis. It became clear that stable exchange rates in Europe would be sustainable only with more institutionalized monetary cooperation and improved coordination of economic policies. Just like the global economic imbalance between surplus and deficit countries that had undermined the BWS (see Chapter 3), regional imbalances between surplus countries that stuck to the regional currency arrangement and deficit countries that abandoned the European currency snake undermined monetary cooperation in Europe. Several fixes were implemented to save the European currency snake. Already in 1973 the European Monetary Cooperation Fund was founded (EMCF Statutes 1973). It would supplement funding from the IMF to support deficit countries, but failed to improve regional currency stability. In 1979 the currency snake was replaced by the European Monetary System (EMS).

4.2.4. The EMS as an Alternative to Global Currency Cooperation

The failure of the European currency snake led neither to a renationalization of monetary policies nor to a new global initiative, but rather to further institutionalization of regional currency cooperation in the EC. Originally, the Werner Plan had envisioned a European Monetary Union until the end of the 1970s, but by that time the goals for a new European monetary arrangement were much more modest. As a watered-down alternative to an EMU, the EC countries established the EMS, which saved the currency snake by deepening the level of institutionalization and cooperation in the form of the European Exchange Rate Mechanism (ERM). The EMCF was also upgraded and would issue the newly created European Currency Unit (ECU) as a unit of account for transactions between EC member countries (EC 1979). The funds available to support countries to stabilize their currencies and overcome balance-of-payment problems were increased threefold to 25 billion ECU (25 billion Euro) and 20 per cent of EC countries' currency reserves in gold and dollars were pooled in the EMCF (EC 1979: 31).

Starting to operate in 1979, the EMS was a clear sign that the EC countries were committed to stable exchange rates and had reacted to a crisis of currency cooperation with deepened integration and institutionalization. While originally the EU had been driven politically to preserve peace in Europe and economically to support economic reconstruction through Keynesian-inspired national development plans, the focus now shifted to regional monetary stability and the strengthening of the regional market in order to keep up with intensifying global economic competition. In the second half of the 1970s, the two most important leaders in the EC, German chancellor Schmidt and French President Giscard, had both previously been finance ministers and thus understood the problems of increasing financial globalization. They accepted the leadership of the Bundesbank in European monetary matters, which had emerged during the currency snake era, and reluctantly subordinated their domestic goals under the regional goal for stable currencies and further integration. In fact, with the EMS, monetary integration moved to the core of the European integration process and was now redefined as an important element to maintain economic stability and revitalize economic growth. At the same time, monetary cooperation in Europe departed more and more from the notion of contributing to a stable global exchange-rate system like a reformed BWS. At the end of the 1970s, the confidence in the reforms of the BWS had vanished and the EMS was now seen as an alternative to the global system. European monetary cooperation was reframed as a regional protection against the volatility of the global economy. 'It was acknowledged by the Heads of State or Government that the Community must itself develop the necessary monetary and economic policy structures to ensure that it will no longer be at the mercy of external developments over which its individual member countries have only a small degree of control' (EC 1979: 31). The global role of the EC was redefined, not as a contributor to globally coordinated currencies, but as an engine for world growth. 'The rest of the world expects the Community to play an active part in helping the world economy to climb out of recession' (EC 1979: 32).

The EMS initially worked well, and Europe benefited from further loosening its ties to the dollar, which ended the problem of imported inflation from the US. On the other hand, the EMS could not overcome the other flaw of the snake, which was its dependence on the German mark and the dominance of the German Bundesbank in monetary policies. On the contrary, the Bundesbank became even more dominant as the EMS suffered from the 'Tyranny of the Mark' (Marsh 2009: 81–92). In fact, countries that were part of the EMS had little leeway in their monetary policies, and small countries had almost none. For example, when the Bundesbank changed its interest rates, it would call the central bank of the Netherlands five minutes before the announcement, and the Dutch would usually just follow the lead of the Bundesbank (Marsh 2009: 126–7). For larger economies like France, the limits of monetary sovereignty were less obvious, but the failure of the attempt by President Mitterrand to revitalize national Keynesian policies from 1981 to 1983 showed that even France could not escape the structural limitations imposed by the EMS and the European integration process more generally. President Mitterrand tried to stimulate consumption by increasing government spending, lowering interest rates, and strengthening the role of organized labour, while at the same time the US and the UK switched to a radical supply-side-oriented approach (see Chapter 3). In France, nationalization of companies and thirty-six of the largest banks, public work programmes, and the reduction of weekly working hours were implemented to boost investment and achieve full employment (Green 1984; Marsh 2009: 96). The programme was successful in stimulating the economy, and in 1982 the French economy grew by 2.9 per cent, faster than any other OECD economy that year although at the same time inflation soared to more than 14 per cent (Green 1984: 26). The high inflation became a big problem for the EMS, because Germany, under its new conservative chancellor Kohl, who came to office in 1982, followed a policy of strict price stability. The diverging levels of inflation put an extraordinary stress on the EMS and forced a couple of devaluations of the franc and other currencies compared to the German mark (Schäfer, 2005: 102).

Ultimately, the Mitterrand experiment failed because the stimulus did not just affect the French economy but was dispersed throughout the European customs union. This pushed French current accounts into a deficit, and at the same time higher inflation created by the expansion of government spending added to the pressure on the French currency to devalue. At this point President Mitterrand had three options. First, he could leave the EMS and erect trade barriers and capital controls, which practically would mean abandoning the European customs union. Second, he could persuade his European partners to coordinate Keynesian policies on the European level. Third, he could abandon the national Keynesian experiment. Giving up on the European integration process as the centrepiece of peace and stability was not an option and persuading the new conservative German government under Helmut Kohl to implement Keynesian policies was futile. Consequently, Mitterrand abandoned his Keynesian experiment and joined Germany's focus on price stability and a strong currency ('franc fort') (Schäfer 2005: 103).

4.2.5. The Creation of the Single Market up to 1992

The failure of the Mitterrand experiment paved the way for a remarkable convergence of economic policies, as France and Germany adopted a 'neoliberal consensus' of economic liberalization and a business-friendly regulatory framework (Schäfer 2005). Unlike in the US and the UK, the neoliberal turn was achieved not through dramatic changes at the national level but through a particular way of European integration focused on the removal of barriers to economic integration (Scharpf 1999). The most important result of this neoliberal consensus was the creation of the single market, which became one of the centrepieces of the European integration process. The single market consists of the 'four freedoms', meaning that there should be no restrictions of the movement of goods, services, capital, and people within the single market. In addition, all national rules that would favour national over EU products would not be consistent with EU law. The single market was agreed upon in the Single European Act (SEA) of 1986, with the goal for it to be completed by 1992. With the SEA, 'harmonization' of institutions became one of the main driving forces of European integration and the European counterpart of neoliberal reforms in the US. With the SEA, the transformation of the European integration project from coordinating national Keynesian economic policies to the creation of a single market as the engine of economic development was completed. The SEA also brought important institutional changes that created a new dynamic by reducing the scope of decisions that needed the unanimity of EU member countries and by expanding decisions made by a qualified majority in many areas under the remit of the EU. In addition, the European Commission, as the proto-government of the EU, was given the jurisdiction to

go beyond the specifics of the treaties and to address all measures 'which
have as their object the establishment and functioning of the internal market', with the exception of fiscal provisions and decisions relating to the free
movement of persons and the rights and interests of employed persons
(Single European Act 1987: art. 18). The SEA symbolizes the European
integration process most clearly, and in Europe, when there is mention of
'the market', it is not 'financial markets' that come to mind first, as in the US,
but the European single market.

The launch of the single market on 1 January 1993 completed the transition
of the European integration process, from a politically driven project to
preserve peace to one that was much more concerned with economic issues.
The new integration-led growth model aimed to revitalize economic growth
by deepening markets, harmonizing rules, and creating a business-friendly
regulatory environment. This new growth model created a new unprecedented
dynamic of European integration. In particular, the free movement of capital
and services created a new dynamic, because it touched on many national
laws, including labour regulations, environmental standards, and migration
policies. In effect, all national regulations that would constitute any kind of
disadvantage for EU-based entities over national entities would be inconsistent with EU law. Consequently, the European Court of Justice (ECJ) extended
its famous Cassis de Dijon decision (ECJ Case 120-78), which outlawed the
discrimination of EU-made products in 1979, to the discrimination of investments and services. The principle of 'mutual recognition' was strongly established, meaning basically that whatever was legal in one EU country became
legal in all EU countries, although the ECJ made some exceptions—for
example, by ruling that the Dutch government could forbid Dutch coffee
shops to sell marijuana to non-Dutch EU citizens (ECJ Case C-137/09).

4.2.6. The Maastricht Treaty and the Introduction of the Euro in 1999

The completion of the single market in early 1993 was immediately followed
by the Maastricht Treaty, which established the European Union in November
1993 as the successor of the European Community. Most importantly, the
Maastricht Treaty envisioned the EMU and the introduction of the euro by
1999. To tackle the instability of the EMS, the EMU created a common
currency and thus an area of irrevocable fixed exchange rates. The dominance
of the Bundesbank was replaced by a newly created European Central Bank

(ECB), in which all euro-area central banks would have an equal say. In the old EMS, member countries effectively lost their monetary sovereignty but had no say in the decisions of the Bundesbank. The humiliation of being informed about interest-rate changes without consultation just minutes before they happened was difficult to swallow in an EC that had originally been set up to rein in Germany. The EMU was the logical consequence of the constant crisis of the EMS and the strong reliance of the EMS on the German mark and the Bundesbank. Naturally, Germany, and particularly the Bundesbank as the monetary hegemon in the EMS, had a different opinion. In the 'economist' tradition, they claimed that Europe was not ready for an EMU, because economic policies would have to converge before a monetary union would be sustainable. In the end, Germany accepted the EMU proposal initiated by France only because it needed the support of France for German reunification in 1990 (Marsh 2009: 137). President Mitterrand feared that a reunified Germany—by far the largest economy in the EU—would have further strengthened the 'tyranny of the Mark', and thus he demanded the pooling of monetary sovereignty, which would give the central banks of all member countries a say in the decisions on monetary policies.

The long ongoing conflict between the German 'economist position', which saw full economic and political integration as a prerequisite to a monetary union, and the French 'monetarist position', which saw monetary integration as a stepping stone, was finally decided in favour of the French. Monetary integration was going ahead without deeper cooperation in economic policies, and Germany surrendered its monetary hegemony to the new European Central Bank (ECB). As a concession, Germany was able to secure that the ECB would be institutionally even more independent than the German central bank and would have its headquarters in Frankfurt, not far away from that of the Bundesbank. While the German Bundesbank had only a de facto independence, the ECB was made de jure independent from the political decision-making process (EU 1992a: art. 7). The ECB is not formally part of the democratically legitimized political decision-making process but a seemingly technocratic institution that reacts to developments in the financial markets based on academic theories and empirical experiences. Like the Bundesbank but unlike the US Federal Reserve (see Chapter 3), the ECB has a narrow mandate, with the primary goal of maintaining price stability (EU 1992a: art. 2). Compared to the remit of the US Fed and East Asian central banks, the ECB's ability to manage the economy through monetary policies is limited. Central bank independence and the priority of price stability were included later in the Lisbon Treaty (art. 130), and some EU countries such as Germany have even changed their national constitutions to leave no doubt about their surrender of sovereign monetary policies to the ECB (art. 88 of the German Constitution (*Grundgesetz*) was changed on 21 December 1992). While a definition of what exactly is meant by 'price stability' is missing from the treaties; the ECB Governing Council later defined it as 'a year-on-year increase in the Harmonized Index of Consumer Prices (HICP) for the euro area of below 2%'. The governing council also clarifies that, 'in the pursuit of price stability, it aims to maintain inflation rates below, but close to, 2% over the medium term' (ECB 2015).

In another concession to Germany, the Maastricht convergence criteria limited government debt and fiscal sovereignty. The Maastricht Treaty specifies that 'Member States shall avoid excessive government deficits'. In the annex 'Protocol on the Excessive Deficit Procedure,' the treaty limits the fiscal deficit to 3 per cent of GDP and the total amount of public debt to 60 per cent of GDP (EU 1992b: art. 104c (1-2)). Effectively, EMU members sacrificed a large degree of their sovereign macroeconomic powers, and not just monetary policies, for the sake of monetary integration. Additional criteria as a precondition for entering the EMU were membership in the ERM for two years, as well as the convergence of interest and inflation rates.

4.2.7. The Stability and Growth Pact of 1997

The Maastricht Treaty determined the criteria under which countries would be able to join the EMU, but it left open the question as to what would happen if a country failed to achieve the criteria after it had been admitted. Unlike monetary policies, fiscal policies remained entirely the responsibility of national governments, and the Maastricht Treaty even explicitly ruled out that member countries would become liable for the debt of other countries ('no bailout clause'). Germany in particular wanted to have a strong stability pact that would automatically impose sanctions if an EMU member country exceeded the Maastricht deficit criteria. This time Germany did not get its way, and, in 1997, member countries passed the Stability and Growth Pact, which not only stressed fiscal prudence but also highlighted the ability of governments to stimulate growth. The pact put sanctions at the discretion of the Council of the European Union, which 'is invited always to impose sanctions if a participating Member State fails to take the necessary steps to bring the excessive deficit situation to an end as recommended by the Council'

(Stability and Growth Pact 1997). Because a qualified majority would be needed and the Council represents the member countries, punishment was far from being automatic but rather a political decision. This was particularly obvious when Germany, as the biggest proponent of austerity, violated the convergence criteria in 2002 and 2003. Not surprisingly, no fines were applied by the Council to punish Germany. In 2005, the rules were further relaxed, and in particular the ability to run deficits in times of economic difficulties were extended—an increase in flexibility that became important during the World Economic Crisis after 2008.

4.2.8. Financial Integration and Liberalization in the EU

With the creation of the European Monetary Union (EMU), the EU emerged as an important global player and even a rival to the US in the field of international monetary relations. At the same time, Europe clearly lagged behind the US in matters of financial integration and globalization. Europe was a latecomer when it came to financial liberalization, and the creation of a single European financial market remains a slow process. Until the 1990s, financial markets in Europe remained largely national, and discussion on common rules for finance was in deadlock because of the 'battle of systems', which would allow harmonization only at the level of the lowest common denominator (Mügge 2006: 991–2). Financial integration and liberalization in Europe took off only in the 1990s, as a result of the creation of the single market and particularly the introduction of the euro. The preparation for the euro broke the deadlock and facilitated financial liberalization and the harmonization and integration of institutions regulating finance. In 1999, the Commission proposed a Financial Service Action Plan (FSAP), with the goal of creating a single market for financial services in the EU. The corner-stone of the FSAP was the establishment of a 'single passport', which would enable financial service providers that were legally established in one member country to provide their services in all other member countries (IP/99/327). In 2000, the EU adopted the 'CRD [Capital Requirements Directives] 1 package', which created a first proto-European Banking Act in connection with the debate about Basel 2 guidelines. In the same year, the EU created an ad hoc committee of 'Wise Men' under the leadership of Alexandre Lamfalussy, which published its report in December 2000 (Quaglia 2007). Since then, the 'Lamfalussy process' gradually shifted power over financial regulation from the nation states to the EU Commission (Mügge 2006). In 2004, the Lamfalussy process cumulated in the Markets in Financial Instrument Directive (MiFID) (2004/39/EC). MiFID established the single passport and the 'home state' principle, meaning that financial service providers are regulated by the authorities of the state where they have their main office. Since the global crisis, this process of Europeanization of financial regulation has continued, albeit with less focus on liberalization and more focus on sound regulation and supervision, as reflected in the CRD 2 (Directive 2009/111/EC) and the CRD 3 (Directive 2010/76/EU) packages adopted in 2009 and 2010. Finally, in 2013, the EU adopted the 'CRD 4 package', which makes Basel III requirements legally binding. Most of the provisions entered into force in January 2014, while others were phased in over the following years until 2019 (EBA 2013). CRD 4 is a directive, which means it dictates only the goals, leaving some regulatory leeway to nation states on how to achieve these goals.

The slow pace of financial liberalization compared to that in the US does not mean the EU lacks commitment to financial globalization and capital-account liberalization. The role of finance in Europe is contradictory. On the one hand, the Lisbon Treaty clearly forbids (new) restrictions on movements of capital not just within the EU but also with third countries (TEU/TFEU, 2012: art. 63). On the other hand, it does not restrict limitations that existed before the Maastricht Treaty came into effect in 1993. It also makes clear that the EU does not limit the ability of member states to implement 'requisite measures to prevent infringements of national law and regulations, in particular in the field of taxation and the prudential supervision of financial institutions' (TEU/TFEU, 2012: art. 65). In general, the EU is moving in the same liberalizing direction as the US but at a far slower pace. Essentially, as we shall see, the single market has remained to a large degree a project for extending the market for manufactured goods as well as further deepening the regional division of labour, in which finance plays a supporting role but does not become the centre of gravity, as in the US. This is also reflected in the Lisbon and Europe 2020 strategy, which aims to make the EU 'the most competitive and dynamic knowledge-based economy in the world capable of sustainable economic growth with more and better jobs and greater social cohesion'. Both strategies focus on building on the traditional focus on stability and market expansion and supplementing it with a more proactive approach for investments in education, research, and job creation. The global financial crisis after 2008, less than ten years after the beginning of the FSAP, also prevented a more radical transition to a finance-led growth model.

4.2.9. The Global Financial Crisis of 2008–9 and the Euro Crisis

While the EU was far less financialized than the US, it was nevertheless affected severely by the crisis in the US, particularly after the collapse of Lehman Brothers in 2008. Having 'underdeveloped' financial institutions in Europe meant that they were unable to create new financial products, as their US peers did. At the same time, however, they were some of the biggest customers of the 'financial innovations' created by the US banks. In fact, the first bank that had to be bailed out was the IKB in Germany in July 2008, two months before the Lehman collapse. IKB, which had originally been intended to finance investments of German SMEs, had instead invested heavily in CDOs created from US subprime mortgage credits (see Chapter 3). In particular, North European countries like Germany had recycled their current-account surpluses, not just in Southern Europe but also on the global financial markets run by the big US banks. The 'dumb German money' (Wilhelm 2009) flooded international markets, owing to low growth and investment at home. The massive involvement of European banks in the crisis after 2008 thus does not contradict the idea of more reluctant financialization. Unlike US banks, European banks got into trouble not because they had created sophisticated debt products that hid risks but because they were unsophisticated and purchased these products that had been created by the US financial industry. In addition, with the introduction of the euro, the EU has triggered a massive flow of capital from Northern to Southern Europe, creating a massive financial and real-estate bubble in South European countries such as Spain, Portugal, and Greece, which are often referred to as the euro periphery.

The euro crisis after 2010 with the collapse of asset bubbles in Southern Europe revealed at least three severe flaws in the construction of the EMU. First, EU rules such as MiFID and CRD proved to be ineffective to prevent the crisis. Countries like Ireland were able to build up a largely unregulated financial market in which European banks could speculate with US-issued financial products. At the same time, South European banks could build up huge amounts of debt, which fuelled an unsustainable real-estate bubble. The EMU restricted only public debt, while private debt was not seen as problematic, because in theory creditors would take greater default risks into account. However, with the exchange-rate risk gone, financial markets dramatically misjudged the general risk involved in lending, for example, to South European countries. This misjudgement was reflected in the convergence of interest rates in Europe towards a lower German level. When banks in Ireland and Southern Europe collapsed, the governments were forced to step in, which transformed the euro crisis into a public debt crisis.

A second institutional flaw of the EMU connected to the financial crisis was that the Maastricht criteria (unsuccessfully) focused on stability by limiting fiscal deficit and public debts, but there was no mechanism to deal with a crisis once it was there. This created the absurd situation that national governments were left on their own during crisis time, and, when they intervened to rescue their banks by nationalizing their debt, they almost automatically violated the Maastricht criteria. Not only had the EMU failed to provide a regional crisis management mechanism, but it also threatened to penalize countries that took actions themselves to save the economy. Just when it was needed most, the Lisbon strategy of investing more in innovation and social cohesion took a back seat.

A third underlying structural problem of the EMU emerged in the different levels of economic development and the diverging levels of productivity between the mature low-growth economies of the north and the fast-growing emerging economies of the south. Since the introduction of the euro, Germany and most other Northern European countries had had low growth rates and had focused on maintaining economic stability and increasing productivity by implementing reforms to lower labour costs, loosen regulations on precarious work contracts, and generally make labour markets more flexible for employers. This had massively improved productivity without any accompanying wage increases and had pushed current accounts into surplus. These surpluses were then lent to Southern Europe. Countries such as Spain, Portugal, and Greece had high growth rates and were hungry for capital, which led to current-account deficits, high inflation, and thus lower productivity and high labour costs.

4.2.10. EU Crisis Management

Compared to the situation in the US, crisis management in the EU after 2008 was slow and timid. This was true both for macroeconomic reactions as well as for financial reforms. Fiscal stimulus packages were smaller than in the US and East Asia, and the ECB engaged in full-blown expansion only in 2015, when all other options had been exhausted (see Chapter 2). The initially much less decisive crisis management in the EU can be attributed to the introverted perspective that highlights stability. The EMU had no clear crisis-management mechanism and relied on the (wrong) premise that financial crises could be prevented by following strict fiscal rules and limiting government debt. When the euro crisis struck, it became obvious that the global economic and financial crisis was not just a problem of financial globalization and weak global rules for finance, but that the construction of the EMU itself had some serious deficits. Consequently, after 2010 the EU became more active in reforming EU institutions and establishing new ones. Essentially, the crisis management consists of four main elements: the creation of a European Stability Mechanism (ESM), new fiscal rules ('six pack'), a banking union, and the introduction of a financial transaction tax (FTT).

The need for a more institutionalized crisis-management mechanism became obvious when the Greek government requested a rescue credit in April 2010 and there was no EU institution that could handle such a request. EU member states had to create a new ad hoc institution, the European Financial Stability Facility (EFSF), equipped with up to 500 billion euros to facilitate the rescue package. As an ad hoc mechanism, the EFSF was created outside the EU treaties, and in September 2012 it was replaced with the permanent ESM, which operates like a European IMF. In 2011, the ECB also belatedly followed the lead of the US in implementing quantitative easing policies (see Chapter 3) and started to purchase government bonds of crisis countries in order to reduce spreads on interest rates. This step was massively criticized by the German members of the ECB governing council, and its two German members, Axel Weber and Jürgen Stark, quit over the dispute in 2011. In 2012, the ECB decided to institutionalize the bond-purchasing programme by introducing the Outright Monetary Transaction (OMT). OMTs are similar to the quantitative easing practised in the US (see Chapter 3) but with the important difference that initially all bond purchases of the ECB were 'sterilized'. This meant that OMTs initially only had the goal of bringing down interest rates, while the ECB took steps to prevent an increase of the monetary base—for example, by auctioning interest-bearing deposits at the ECB. Only in early 2015, the ECB finally abandoned sterilization, intensified its bond-purchasing operations and joined the US in full-fledged quantitative easing.

While monetary policies gradually diverged from the expected path of a sole focus on stability, the strengthening of fiscal rules is a clear example of path dependency. Despite the fact that the euro crisis was (with the partial exemption of Greece[2]) caused not by excessive government debt but by a financial

---

[2] Even in Greece, fiscal deficits were to a large degree the result of stagnating tax income and not excessive government spending.

and banking crisis, fiscal reforms were by far the most decisive reforms. Instead of a focus on the causes, the crisis was used to push through largely unrelated reforms that had been on the agenda for some time but had faced political opposition. Under the leadership of Germany, the euro crisis was used to push through the 'six-pack' reform of the Stability and Growth Pact with the long-envisioned goals of tougher fiscal rules. The six pack includes three EU regulations (1173/2011, 1175/2011, and 1177/2011) and one directive (2011/85), which strictly require countries to reduce their deficits below 3 per cent and their debt below 60 per cent of GDP with an Excessive Deficit Procedure (EDP) that is triggered automatically and can fine countries of up to 0.2 per cent of GDP per year if they do not comply. The measures can be stopped only if a majority in the Council of the European Union votes against them. Although at the time of writing no fines have been imposed, the EDP further limits the fiscal ability of EU countries to stimulate the economy and improve productivity through public investments. The two remaining regulations (1176/2011 and 1174/2011) address the problem of imbalances between Northern and Southern Europe. Again, Germany prevailed in pushing through regulations that would put deficit countries with an average deficit of more than 4 per cent over three years in the spotlight, while surplus countries like Germany would be allowed a 6 per cent surplus. Penalties of 0.1 per cent of GDP are possible for those that have excessive imbalances and fail to take actions against them.

The banking union was the measure that most directly tackled the origins of the euro crisis in the financial sector was finalized in May 2014. During the euro crisis, governments of relatively small countries such as Ireland (and later Cyprus) did not properly assess the risks that large banks posed for their economy and failed to shut down banks that often held assets exceeding the national GDP. This was a major flaw in both the Basel 1 and 2 regulations, because they took into account the stability of individual banks and not the stability of the banking system as such. The Single Supervisory Mechanism (Regulations 1022/2013 and 1024/2013) empowers the ECB to supervise 119 large and internationally connected banks holding about 82 per cent of banking assets in the euro area (ECB 2019). The ECB supervises these banks using the 'single rulebook', which includes the Capital Requirements Directive IV implementing the Basel 3 rules (see Chapter 2) but also includes European specialities like caps on bank bonuses paid to employees. The Single Resolution Mechanism (Regulation 806/2014) allows the orderly unwinding of failed banks with the support of the Single Resolution Fund.

The most original and most controversial European initiative was the introduction of a financial transaction tax (FTT). The FTT has long been championed by European civil-society groups like ATTAC and supported by the majority of the European public (*Eurobarometer 2011*), but has been fiercely resisted by the financial sector. Since the crisis of 2008, the plan to introduce the tax has entered the political mainstream, drawing support from all political directions in the EU, with the UK being the only major opponent. The FTT levies a small tax on financial transactions in order to reduce the number of transactions seeking to take advantage of small short-term fluctuations. As financial institutes earn fees for every transaction, they are opposed to an FTT. Long-term investors, on the other hand, usually support an FTT, because it aims to make the financial market more stable and prevent a redistribution of profits from long-term investors to short-term investors ('speculators'). The crisis created a window of opportunity for the FTT, and, in 2012, eleven of the eighteen euro area members (representing 90 per cent of its GDP) agreed on the introduction of an FTT levying a tax of 0.1 per cent on financial transactions and 0.01 per cent on transactions involving derivatives (see table 2.2). The remaining non-euro EU member countries—most notably the UK and most East European countries—opposed a regional FTT, although they agreed on the desirability of a global FTT (which is unrealistic, owing to the opposition by the US).

4.3. The Integration-Led Growth Model and the Emergence of Euro Capitalism

Throughout the history of the European integration process, challenges and crisis have been met with deeper regional cooperation. This process of an 'ever closer union' has created an integration-led growth model based on an economic structure and institutional framework that together form a distinct form of integration-led 'euro capitalism'.

4.3.1. Escaping the Financialization Curse and the Path Dependency of Euro Capitalism

Historically, the European strategy of manoeuvring in the trilemma triangle of economic globalization was regional integration and particularly monetary integration, compared to the global hegemonic approach of the US (Chapter 3) and the nationalist approach in East Asia (Chapter 5). This integration-led growth model was facilitated by a distinctive institutional regime and the convergence of national institutions to a specific form of 'euro capitalism' (Beckmann et al. 2003). In this growth model, regional monetary integration was closely and inseparably interwoven with the creation of a European single market. While monetary integration provided the stability needed to survive in financial globalization, the creation of a de facto single European economy expanded the market for European businesses.

Under the leadership of Germany and France, which represent different variants of non-liberal capitalism, Europe has taken a very distinct path away from liberal market economies like the US. Instead of reviving growth through financialization and becoming 'bankers of the world', European countries have reacted to the challenges of globalization through regional integration. European integration is driven by two major developments. First, the enlargement process, which increases the size of the market by including more and more countries. Second, the creation of the single market, which deepens markets by facilitating economic exchange through the harmonizing of institutions and policies in more and more areas and the delegation of an increasing number of competences to the level of the European Union. Regional trade and investment, and an intensifying regional division of labour, created new growth potential, particularly in the formerly underdeveloped regions of Southern Europe, and since the 1990s in Eastern Europe. At the same time, export-oriented countries of Central and Western Europe, most notably Germany, the Netherlands, Belgium, and Austria, were able to secure (export) markets and outsource production within the European economy. Unlike American and East Asian companies that outsourced production to China and South-East Asia, European countries had the advantage of a low wage region within the single market and increasingly within the euro area that is growing in membership in Eastern Europe.

In the literature, European integration is often explained through functionalist spillovers (Haas 1968) in which deeper integration in one area, such as trade or agriculture, creates the need for integration in other areas, like monetary integration. From a comparative capitalism perspective, this means that the integration-led growth model increasingly led to a convergence of policies and institutions within the EU and that this convergence spread from one sector to the next. In other words, the convergence of European national political economies has created a new model of capitalism with its own path dependency. This is even more significant within the euro area, where a distinct form of euro capitalism emerged. Even EU countries outside the euro area are forced to follow the leadership of the ECB, either because they are member of the ERM, such as Denmark, or because they cannot escape the gravitational forces of the euro. Just as the EMS was a German mark zone, the European Union is now dominated by the euro, with little monetary independence, even for non-euro member states. The British pound was the only currency in the EU that has maintained some independence from the euro, owing to the large size of the UK economy and the pound's role as an international currency.

The distinct form of euro capitalism has not been created by a plan but has evolved as the result of structural and institutional changes in Europe. As we shall see, this euro capitalist system is a hybrid between a German corporatist style system and French state activism. It is also substantially influenced by the much more liberal approach of the UK and the necessarily more arm's length approach mandated by the size of the European economy. The intense coordination within the EU multilateral governance system follows the German example of coordinated capitalism. The distinct character of euro capitalism is particularly obvious, if we look beyond the institutional level and take into account the interdependent economic structure and Europe's role in the international division of labour. Unlike the US and the UK, core continental European EU members have avoided the financialization curse and maintained a strong manufacturing base.

4.3.2. Preserving Industrial Structure through Enlargement and the Deepening of the Single Market

Industrial structures were preserved in Europe because of the dynamic of the European integration process. The EU economy is still economically less integrated than that in the US, which creates a huge potential for new markets and productivity improvements through a regional division of labour. Consequently, there is less need to financialize and move towards a finance-led growth model in order to generate profits. From the original six member states and a population of 169 million in 1958, the EU expanded to twenty-eight countries and tripled its population to 507 million in 2014. The emerging regional division of labour can be seen in the share of new East European EU members' trade with the Western EU members, which increased from 48 per cent of exports and 46 per cent of imports in 1994 to 69 per cent and 62 per cent in 1999 (Eichengreen 2007: 331). In recent years, East European countries have depended even more on intra-EU trade than most Western countries: Slovakia (84 per cent),

Czech Republic (81 per cent), Hungary (76 per cent), Poland (76 per cent), Romania (70 per cent), Slovenia (69 per cent) and Estonia (66 per cent) all exported two-thirds or more of their total exports to EU countries in 2012. This is more than the EU average of intra-regional exports of 63 per cent (EUROSTAT 2014).

Economic integration not just increased the size of markets for businesses, but also broadened investment opportunities for companies. It is much easier for them to lower production costs through outsourcing and subcontracting production—for example, to Eastern Europe. Unlike the US, Japanese, and Korean companies that outsourced their production to China and South-East Asia, European companies had the advantage that their outsourced production remained within the European single market. Institutional convergence facilitates exchange, because business can count on the same rules being applied everywhere in the Union. In the preparation for EU admission, all new members have to adopt the *acquis communautaire* and subscribe to all existing EU rules and regulations. As of 2019, only a few smaller East European countries have joined the euro (Slovakia, Slovenia, Estonia, Latvia and Lithuania), but all others have committed themselves to introducing the euro in the future while only Denmark and the UK have opted out. This commitment means that national monetary policies are more or less aligned with ECB decisions, and exchange-rate volatility is supposed to decline. Thus, companies are less inclined to move offshore production to countries outside the EU, because the potential for cost savings within the Union are still substantial (Zysman and Schwartz 1998a). Common EU standards on copyright and the option of settling conflicts with business partners in European courts are other advantages of regional supply chains compared to global ones. At the same time, the lack of a European minimum wage and the lower level of unionization in Eastern Europe makes the region attractive for investors interested in outsourcing labour intensive production, as we shall see.

From an institutional perspective, more and more rules and regulations are decided upon at the European level or are at least influenced at the European level. Euro capitalism is much more than Vivien Schmidt's view (2002: 310) of very distinct European countries going 'in the same liberalizing direction'. European institutions have a real effect on national political economies, and the trend of convergence within the EU is obvious. EU regulations are applied in all member countries, and EU directives provide standards that national regulations have to follow, although national adaptations can vary. While the popular claim that 80 per cent of all laws in member countries are made in Brussels is exaggerated (Toeller 2012), the EU level of the European 'dynamic multilevel governance system' (Jachtenfuchs and Kohler-Koch 1996) has clearly become more and more influential over time. All new treaties and treaty changes, and particularly the Maastricht and Lisbon treaties, have always delegated more authority to the EU level—namely, to the European Commission, the ECB, and to a lesser degree the European Parliament. Functionalist spillover, where EU cooperation in one area tends to lead to more cooperation in related fields, is alive and well. The recent demonstration was the spillover from monetary integration to fiscal coordination during the euro crisis, as already described. In short, we can observe a convergence of institutional systems within the EU.

Convergence should not be confused with harmony or lack of conflicts. On the contrary, convergence often creates conflicts—for example, the emergence of euro capitalism to a large degree in effect means an extension of German-style conservative macroeconomic policies to the European level. One case in point already described was the creation of the ECB as a clone of the Bundesbank on the European level. A more important area of conflict is that common regional institutions have different positive and negative effects on different regions and interest groups. For example, the euro and the common monetary policies have facilitated economic imbalances between current-account surplus and deficit countries in the years leading to the euro crisis, because ECB interest rates were too high for Northern European countries and too low for the Southern periphery.

4.3.3. European Complementary Specialization and the 'Workshop of the World'

Unlike American businesses, European companies have the alternative of outsourcing production within the single market. This strategy has created a new European production system, which can be described as 'complementary specialization' (Faust et al. 2004). This production system takes advantage of the strength of different previously nationally limited production models in particularly by combining the German 'diversified quality production model' (Streeck 1995) with labour-intensive production in Eastern Europe. Instead of offering high-tech products like the US or mass-production consumer items like East Asia, Europe is strong in high-quality products in a broad variety of specialized niche markets. Instead of competing over prices, European manufactures have occupied these niche markets, where competition is limited and profit margins remain high. While East Asia became the 'factory of the world' (see Chapter 5), Europe remained the 'workshop of the world' in many crucial markets where price competition is less important. Classic examples are capital goods such as specialized machines or machine parts and expensive consumer goods such as cars and upmarket fashion items.

A good example is the automobile industry. West European manufacturers have boosted productivity by outsourcing to Eastern Europe, while carmakers from Japan and Korea have invested in Eastern Europe to profit from direct access to the EU market (Jürgens and Krzywdzinski 2009). Because of the proximity of Eastern Europe to the West European economic centres, out-sourcing is far more likely to preserve industrial production in the west compared to Japanese or US companies outsourcing production to China or South-East Asia (Zysman and Schwartz 1998b). In addition, European pro-ducers have not only outsourced low-skilled labour-intensive tasks but have taken advantage of a well-trained workforce by investing in high value-added productions such as car engines.

Another example of European specialization is the European textile industry. The production of textiles is labour intensive and usually considered to be among the first industries to move to low-wage countries. However, in 2012, with exports of US$109 billion, the EU remained the second largest exporter of textiles behind China, while US exports were a mere US$6 billion, and the Japanese exported a tiny US$557 million (WTO 2013).[3] Textile companies in Germany, Italy, and France benefit from the regional proximity to their con-sumers and have better control over the supply chain (Tattara 2006: 7). Unlike US or East Asian producers, which have largely offshored their textile industry, Europe has been able to keep a substantial part of the value added of textile production in Europe—for example, by specializing in expensive high-quality products or quickly changing fashion.

At the same time, the southern and particularly the eastern enlargement of the EU has extended the possibilities of outsourcing labour-intensive produc-tion within the EU. The well-educated workforce in Eastern Europe has facilitated the outsourcing of high value-added production such as car engines, electronics, or capital and skill-intensive parts of the apparel industry. This regional division of labour moved many industrial jobs from Western to Eastern Europe, but it did not lead to a complete deindustrialization, as in the complete disappearance of the textile industry from the US or Japan. While offshoring production to countries with low labour costs far away leads to

---

[3] Within the EU, Italy remains the largest exporter, with US$22 billion and Germany the second largest with US$18 billion.

higher transportation costs, exchange-rate risks, legal insecurity in the case of a conflict, and possible tariffs, outsourcing to other EU member countries leaves the whole production chain within the single market and the same EU jurisdiction. Within the euro area and ERM countries, even the exchange-rate risks are eliminated. The single market also allows manufacturers to take advantage of a large market in business services, such as logistics, insurance, finance services, and legal advice. In general, it is much more difficult for services to cross borders than manufacturing, because they touch on many regulations, including sensitive issues of migration and work permits. In the European single market, these regulations are largely Europeanized, which makes an investment in another EU country almost like investing in your home country. European enlargement thus not only extends the western workbench to the east, but also leads to 'complementary specialization' (Faust et al. 2004: 53). Enlargement therefore does not just preserve a German-style specialization by outsourcing labour-intensive production and opening new markets for specialized products; to some degree the German specialization model itself is Europeanized.

Even in the IT sector, which is dominated by US companies, some smaller European companies have successfully occupied niches. US companies such as Microsoft and Intel have created standardized software and hardware for consumers and businesses. The 'Wintel' alliance has been very successful and profitable in setting global standards from which it is hard to deviate, because that would reduce the ability to cooperate with others running the same technology (Kim and Hart, in Rosenau and Singh 2002). On the other hand, European companies like STMicroelectronics (the ninth largest maker of microchips) or Infineon (the eleventh largest) focus on specialized chips— for example, for cars or automation machinery. They produce specialized products with high value added at a much smaller volume than US high-tech companies mass producing microprocessors, not to mention East Asian makers of memory chips operating at a lower level of the IT value-added chain. In the software sector, US companies such as Microsoft or Apple produce the ubiquitous Windows and iOS operating systems, while European software companies like SAP (the third largest software company) or Amadeus (the tenth largest) create specialized software solutions for companies.

Owing to the integration process, European companies have been successful in their specialization strategy, and deindustrialization was far less severe in continental Europe compared to the US or the UK. Unlike in the US, finance could not take over as the new growth centre of the economy. European MNCs with their European production chains depend much less on access to global financial services then American MNCs with their global production chains. Unlike in East Asia (see Chapter 5), the European specialized producers occupy niche markets, which makes them less vulnerable to price competition imposed by economic globalization. Unlike the breakneck price competition in East Asia and the offshore production facilities of US MNCs, this European model allows a more neo-corporatist approach lo labour relations, as we shall see, and fits well with a more 'patient' bank-based financial system.

4.3.4. The European Bank-Based Financial System

The European complementary specialized production has specific needs when it comes to financial services. Unlike the per se globally oriented process of financialization in the US and the UK, the European financial system has remained primarily bank-based and focused on recycling European capital within the region. Traditionally, European bank-based financial systems were analytically distinguished from market-based systems (Zysman 1983; Deeg 1999). These bank-based systems are good at providing long-term 'patient capital' through loans to industries focused on long-term investments and the occupation of niche markets based on decades and sometimes hundreds of years of incremental innovation, experience, and reputation. Instead of providing services for global investors, banks in Europe mostly recycle excess funds from surplus countries in Northern Europe to deficit countries in Eastern and Southern Europe. The recycling of excess capital through credits rather than a transaction-based global service provision remained the driving force of the financial sector. In this sense, the European financial sector remains strongly focused on intermediation and the active recycling of money and is not merely a broker focused on facilitating transactions between market actors.

Financial service providers in European countries differ in form and power from their counterparts in the US and the UK. They are primarily universal banks that make money from lending businesses, trading, and brokerage. While the classic connection between banks and manufacturing capital is weakening, banks remain wholesale markets for primarily domestic customers as opposed to specialized financial firms offering financial innovations or unique trading strategies. While the latter are aggressive and profit from unstable markets that create a need for hedging and trading, European universal banks are stability oriented. Representing a smaller share of the national economies, the private financial sector in Europe has also failed to gain the political influence of its American counterparts. At the same time, the manufacturing sector and the powerful interests of the export industry often conflict with those of financial service providers. In the EU, finance did not become the new centre of gravity in the EU economy, but financialization was primarily a phenomenon in the UK and the (particularly Southern European) periphery, where the massive inflow of capital from North European surplus countries and the weak financial regulations led to inflated asset markets.

Decision-makers and the public still see the financial sector not primarily as a profit-oriented business sector but as a quasi-public institution providing an infrastructure for the economy, similarly to roads or the electricity grid. In Europe, public banks, saving banks, and cooperatives maintain a large share of the depositor base. In Germany 43 per cent of all deposits, and in Spain 41 per cent, are held in savings banks, while in France cooperative banks have a market share of 56 per cent (Martín and Sevillano 2011: 122). That finance should play a 'serving role for the real economy' is not just a position held by the political left, but a broad societal consensus—for example, in the coalition document between the Social Democratic Party and Conservative Christian Democratic Union (CDU) after the 2013 German parliamentary elections (Koalitionsvertrag 2013). The 'underdevelopment' of financial markets in Europe can, for example, be seen in the low market capitalization of European *bourses* (see Figure 3.2). With the exception of Denmark and the Czech Republic, stock ownership in Europea is comparably low. For example, only 18.5 per cent of Germans and 14.7 per cent of the French own stocks at all.[4] On the other hand, stock ownership is at 30.8 per cent in the US and 45.5 per cent in the UK (Grout et al. 2009: 43–4). Consequently, there is limited support from shareholders for market-oriented reforms and inflationary policies in the EU that would boost stock markets and counter the stability orientation of European politics. Instead, the preference of European savers is to hold secure low-yielding bonds and to put money in savings accounts that benefit from low inflation; they can even live with deflation as long as real interest rates remain positive. In other words, the need for patient capital and the reluctant process of financialization are complemented by the saving behaviour of Europeans.

Among critical scholars, it is often argued that European economic integration and financial reforms in Europe have led to an 'Americanization' (Bieling 2006: 421) or an 'emergence of European financial capitalism' (Bieling 2013: 286)

---

[4] Based on the proportion of country population investing in equity, mutual funds, or optional pension schemes investing in equity.

that is converging with US-style financialization (Sablowski 2008). While there is little doubt that the creation of the European single market and the numerous liberalization initiatives have led to bigger financial markets and more leeway for financial institutions, this trend should not be equated with a full-blown convergence with US-style finance-led capitalism. Most importantly, the financial sector has not become the new engine of economic growth. Financialization remains largely a trend on the edges of the European financial system—Irish bank subsidiaries benefiting from lax regulations, unsophisticated German *Landesbanken* that tried and failed to play with the big ones, and niche markets such as currency derivatives concentrated in Frankfurt. In short, the number of financial transactions in Europe is increasing, but (with the exemption of the UK) they have not become the centre of the economy towards which all economic activities and institutional reforms gravitate.

Owing to the focus on savings and wealth generation as opposed to fee generation, European financial regulation is more concerned with the stability of the market and the security of assets, whereas the US is focused on supporting the financial industry to attract global businesses and conduct as many fee-generating transactions as possible. While transaction-oriented financial capitalism profits from transaction fees in boom times and in bad times, the rent-oriented capitalism in Europe focuses on the security of savings. Of course, we do not know how long the path dependency will last. Sweden, the Netherlands, and France have seen financial markets and the financial sector in general reach a level close to financialized countries, and, while the UK is schedule to leave the EU in 2019, its ideological influence defining the EU primarily as a liberal single market remains powerful. It also remains to be seen how the global financial crisis and the ultra-low interest rates in the euro area will affect financial markets, because low interest rates tend to inflate asset prices and deflate savings. For now, however, it seems that the agenda is not Americanization but an inward looking, 'introverted' (Bieling 2006) European strategy focused on consolidating the integration-led growth model.

Some of the reforms that look like Americanization on the institutional level have had a very different impact in the European context. For example, European and national laws have made it easier for investment funds to buy European companies, and ties between banks and industry have weakened. This reform, however, did not induce a full-blown transition to US-style shareholder capitalism. The extension of shareholder rights means something very different in the European context of neo-corporatist labour relations.

In Germany, for example, owing to co-determination, up to half of board members come from the employees and labour unions, strictly limiting the influence of shareholder representatives. While banks have been reducing their shareholdings in non-financial companies, bank representatives remain a mainstay on company boards. The changes are even weaker in informal relationships. Even while networks of capital ownership were weakened, the personalized networks remained (Freye 2009: 11–12). While there have been cases of spectacular mergers and acquisitions (M&A) and even hostile take-overs, like the takeover of Mannesmann by Vodafone in 2000 or the aggressive acquisition of Hypo-Vereinsbank by Unicredit Bank in 2005, most of these deals were intra-European and not per se a sign of financial globalization. While they do reflect some degree of US-style shareholder capitalism, they can also be interpreted as a consolidation of the European market, particularly in the previously heavily regulated areas of telecom and banking. Other features of shareholder capitalism, like stock-market buybacks, were also legalized in the 1990s (for example, in Germany in 1998), but they remain far fewer in number than in the US. This is partly to with the fact that, unlike in the US, where buybacks can be decided by the board of directors, in most European countries they have to be approved by shareholders (Manconi et al. 2018: 2).

The strong industrial base and the vast potential of market deepening and enlargement in the EU slowed down the financialization process. Instead of becoming global service providers, European banks followed the MNCs and their suppliers to Southern and Eastern Europe. With the eastern enlarge-ment, it was European banks not British or American megabanks that snapped up large parts of the East European financial sector.[5] Of the non-European banks, only Citibank managed to acquire a substantial share of the East European market and became the seventh largest foreign bank in the region (Havrylchyk and Jurzyk 2006: 22). While financial markets are ben-eficial to start-up companies and radical innovators, European established MNCs, and particularly SMEs expanding into Eastern Europe, depend far less on access to venture capital, because of their own resources and the established connections with their main banks. This attachment is particu-larly strong for SMEs, which, unlike MNCs, cannot depend on their own funds for investment. Unlike US MNCs, which have stretched global production chains, European MNCs remain largely oriented on the expansion

---

[5] With the exemption of Slovenia, East European countries' financial sector is dominated by foreign banks. In Hungary, the Czech Republic, Lithuania, Slovakia' and Estonia the share is more than 80% (Havrylchyk and Jurzyk 2006).

within the European market. Thus, for them, the harmonization of European financial rules is more important than the global presence of the European financial sector and the availability of financial innovations hedging risks of stretched global value-added chains.

4.3.5. Europe's Position in the Global Division of Labour

In the international division of labour, Europe has a unique position as an exporter of high-quality capital and consumer goods. This role requires a certain form of coordination, which can be delivered neither by the market nor by the traditional nation state. The integration process has allowed Europe to thrive in the global economy along the established path of high-quality manufacturing, and it has weakened the trend towards financialization and radical innovation. EU integration has allowed Europe to maintain a privileged spot in the international division of labour supplying high-quality consumer goods to the winners of globalization and specialized high-tech and capital goods for those struggling to catch up. Europe thus depends less on price competition than East Asia, which enables the region to maintain its stability orientation and a strong euro. While the US continues to use quantitative easing to increase domestic growth at the expense of trust in the value of the dollar as a reserve currency, the ECB has been much more reluctant to implement such inflationary strategies. Only since 2015 and after hesitating for seven years since the beginning of the global financial crisis has the ECB embarked on fully-fledged quantitative easing. The inward orientation also explains why the ECB is hesitant to promote the euro as a global currency because it would mean that larger quantities of the European currency would circulate outside the control of the ECB. Erkki Liikanen, member of the Governing Council of the European Central Bank, stated that 'I think we, as European central bankers, should not promote the euro and that the euro's international role should rather reflect the economic development of the euro area' (Pisani-Ferry and Posen 2009: 186). Stability and consolidation are clearly the main priority of the ECB and European policymakers in general, while a global role for the euro plays only a secondary role.

As already mentioned, Europe is a large net investor and saver, and its banks specialize in managing international savings, but they are far less transaction oriented than banks in finance-led countries. European banks recycle profits made in Europe around the world, but they remain more traditional banks and not global service providers that see their main role in brokering deals rather than in managing money. In other words, Europe is primarily a global investor and not a marketplace for financial products. This has led to a specific preference for global economic governance. It reinforces the obsession with monetary stability, as only a stable currency can ensure the safety of the investment, while a strong currency allows for further expansion of external assets. Unlike in East Asia, Europe's foreign investments are not in short-term government bonds; instead they are in long-term direct investments that bring higher returns and stimulate exports by increasing demand for intermediate products. This is another reason why stability and not a competitive exchange rate (as in East Asia) is more important for Europe.

4.4. Euro Corporatism and the Political Economy of Integration-Led Capitalism

So far in this chapter we have covered the historical origin, institutional development, and economics of the European integration-led growth model. In this section, we turn to the political–economic foundation of the growth model. What kind of compromises between interest groups are the institutions built on? In the previous sections, we saw that euro capitalism is characterized by a strong dynamic towards monetary integration and stability, as well as the slowed-down process of financialization created by an integration-led growth model. We have seen that the EU has opted for (regional) stable exchange rates and an integration-led growth model with a limited degree of financialization, but a strong commitment to the free flow of capital. According to our trilemma triangle, this implies a limited sovereignty when it comes to macroeconomic policies. The EU has been avoiding the financialization curse, but this does not mean the region has avoided the pitfalls of globalization altogether. On the contrary, the integration-led model has produced its own problems, imbalances, and crises. Most importantly, the focus on the creation of a single market, and the obsession with stability and austerity, have undermined the sovereignty of member states but have failed in many areas to build capacity at the EU level. This 'negative integration' (Scharpf 2009), however, took very different forms in the EU compared to neoliberal reforms in the US. As in the US, neoliberal reforms could be implemented because of the weakening of organized labour, but, unlike in the US, industrial capital remains hegemonic while financial markets remain comparatively underdeveloped. More importantly, unlike in the US, in the EU neo-corporatist tripartite arrangements have led to a specific form of euro corporatism that has a strong pro-business bias but that is not oriented towards the 'free market', instead following a coordinated approach to 'harmonize rules' and deepen the single market. This coordinated strategy had led to changes that are more gradual and that have prevented a radical takeover of finance as the centre of the economy. Instead, it allowed traditional industries to take advantage of the growing European market and to negotiate strict wage constraints with labour unions to increase international competitiveness. Unlike in the US and East Asia, the welfare state has remained important in Europe to prevent social disruptions caused by the creation of the single market and has so far restrained political opposition against the EU and integration-led capitalism at least outside the UK.

4.4.1. An Ever-Closer Union through Negative Integration in the EU

The distinctiveness of euro capitalism and the lack of convergence with US-style neoliberalism should not be confused with a kinder, gentler form of capitalism. The EU has neither preserved Keynesian policies of the 'golden age' nor (so far) found a new paradigm to build a social and democratic Europe. On the contrary, far from becoming a global driving force for progress, the EU has become inward looking and stability oriented. Instead of a grand vision for what the EU is standing for, the main goal is integration and the 'ever-closer union' itself. This strategy is based on the economic interests of businesses that want an expanding single market with harmonized rules, but it also corresponds well with the stability orientation in Europe. After the experience of two world wars, the world economic crisis of the 1930s, and the threat of a nuclear holocaust during the cold war, the success of the European integration process became a life-and-death issue. This stability orientation is particularly strong in Germany, not just because of the political disaster of fascism but also because of the collective memory of hyperinflation of the 1920s. The almost mythical stories about hyperinflation have been repeated again and again and have become deeply ingrained in the collective memory (Feldman 1997). In Germany, hyperinflation is something like the original sin of economic policymaking, similar to the Smoot–Hawley tariffs in the US (see - Chapter 3) or the premature financial liberalization in East Asia that led to the Asian financial crisis of 1997–8 (see Chapter 5). The period of instability and hyperinflation in the early 1920s was even made responsible for the rise of fascism in Germany by conservatives, despite the fact that the rise of the Nazi

Party only started long after the hyperinflation and during the period of *deflation* following the World Economic Crisis after 1929.

With the EU, and in particular the introduction of the euro, the German obsession with stability and in particular with conservative macroeconomic policies and limitations on public debt, became part of the EU institutions. When the Maastricht Treaty to introduce the euro was signed in 1992, even France, which is known for its rebellious national culture, had lost interest in economic experiments. The failure of Mitterrand policies of macroeconomic expansion and the plan to establish Keynesianism as the foundation of the European Community in the 1980s created a convergence with German stability orientation (Schäfer 2005: 102). With the introduction of the euro in 1999, the EU broke the hegemony of the German mark and the Bundesbank, but at the same time the EU became 'more German', as the German institutions seemed to work best in the context of a common currency. In 2011, French President Sarkozy even stated the previously unimaginable that France should become 'more like Germany' (*Financial Times*, 28 October 2011).

Europe has developed a very stability- and inwards-oriented mindset, which is focused on slowly expanding and deepening the Union but not on shaping global affairs or challenging US global hegemony after 1945. The European integration process became a goal in itself, but it lacked a positive vision of how a 'unified Europe' should look. Thus integration meant that rules were harmonized and national sovereignty in economic policies were delegated to the European level, but the EU did not use its new powers to build a European institutional system that could take over the role of the nation states it integrated. The EU largely failed to take over important roles from the nation states, such as fiscal policies and welfare, which could have helped positively to shape the EU. This has to do with the deliberate institutional design to allow decisions on liberalization to be made by a qualified majority, while most policies that would actively shape the EU still require the unanimity of all member states. This defect has often been called the 'neoliberal bias' (Scharpf 2009) or the dominance of 'negative integration' (Scharpf 2009). Negative integration seems to be a better term to describe the reality of the EU, because neoliberal bias seems to indicate a convergence with the neoliberalism of the US. As we have seen, the EU remains very different and the implementation of neoliberal reforms took a quite different path. Continental Europe lacked revolutionaries such as Reagan and Thatcher who were willing to antagonize large parts of the society through radical national programmes of liberalization and deregulation. Instead, the reforms were incremental, technocratic, and almost insulated from the public debate. During the 1990s, the European

Court of Justice emerged as a potent force for interpreting European treaties in the most business-friendly way. For example, it ruled that subcontractors in the building sector could circumvent national rules and rather use their home-country rules and wages when providing services in another EU member state (Menz 2005). The freedom of exchanging services in the single market was ruled to be more important than national labour laws. The same was true of decisions favouring the creation of the single market over collective bargaining arrangements, even though they are guaranteed in the EU Charter of Fundamental Rights (art. 28). The ECJ has consistently placed the four freedoms of the single market over (national) constitutional rights like collective action that could prevent wage dumping by companies (Höpner and Schäfer 2008; Joerges and Rödl 2009: 23–8).

At the same time, the creation of the single market to some degree strengthened and spread the European model of neo-corporatist coordination. While, for example, outsourcing to Eastern Europe was used by companies to undermine labour standards in Western Europe, investment of West European companies in Eastern Europe are not simply based on hiring and firing. Companies maintain their focus on maintaining skilled workers and focus on gradually upgrading production in the region (Jürgens and Krzywdzinski 2009). In this sense, corporatist arrangements are at least partly exported to Eastern Europe. In the EU, business-friendly 'neoliberal reforms' were mediated and facilitated through national corporatist negotiations, and the social effects were cushioned by national welfare states. From the beginning, the EU was driven by the dual dynamics of economic liberalization and corporatist arrangements.

4.4.2. Euro Corporatism

The neo-corporatist system has allowed Europe to remain socially and politically stable, even under the conditions of low growth rates and deflation. Unlike what the Anglo-American-trained economic profession and particularly neo-Keynesian observers such as Paul Krugman believe, stability orientation and austerity policies are not just policy mistakes made by decision-makers and their inept advisors. On the contrary, the stability-first principle constitutes a specific political economic model, reflecting the interests of dominant capital groups and cushioned from opposition through strong welfare states and corporatist arrangements. Already the Werner Plan of 1970 reflected the dual strategy that combines negative integration with neo-corporatist coordination. At that time, economic liberalization and the deregulation of national rules were combined with the goal of preserving ailing national Keynesianism by regaining political sovereignty of fiscal and economic policies on the European level. Distinct from the Anglo-American liberal democracies, the Werner Plan stressed the importance of an embedded liberalism that achieves economic liberalization in 'concertation with the social partners'. In the Werner Plan, these Euro-Keynesian objectives were meant to complement the elements of economic liberalization, and the free movement of goods, capital, and (to a much lesser degree) people. With the failure of Keynesianism in France in the 1980s, neoliberalism took over as the dominant ideology institutionalized in the creation of the single market and the EMU, as we have seen. Instead of replacing neo-corporatism with arm's-length anonymous market transactions, neo-corporatism arrangements were modified in a more business-friendly way. In this 'embedded neoliberalism' (Rhodes and Apeldoorn 1998) the capital side exercises its increased leverage through the creation of 'social pacts' or tripartite agreements for jobs and growth, like the German *Buendnis fuer Arbeit*.

The German Agenda 2010 is a good example of supply-side-oriented reforms in Europe and is, although highly controversial in Germany itself, often presented as a 'model for Europe' (*The Economist*, 14 April 2012; *Financial Times*, 5 June 2013; critically Dörre 2014). The Agenda 2010 was the more radical successor of the *Buendnis fuer Arbeit* and the German expression of the Lisbon strategy. The *Buendnis fuer Arbeit* that started in 1998 was a tripartite forum with the goals of creating jobs and increasing competitiveness, which included the government, businesses, and labour unions. Amid the weakened political power of labour unions and their declining influence in the political discourses, most importantly within the Social Democratic Party under Chancellor Schroeder, the *Buendnis fuer Arbeit* had a pro-business bias from the beginning. Due to this political weakness of labour, neo-corporatist institutions were used to implement neoliberal policies and co-opt potential opponents. After being re-elected chancellor in 2002, Schroeder pushed through the more radical Agenda 2010, which liberalized the labour market and reduced benefits for those unemployed for more than one year. The Agenda 2010 reforms effectively reduced wage costs for employers and created a secondary job market with precarious working conditions and subsidized wages. While the Agenda 2010 brought substantial benefits for companies and a retrenchment of the welfare state, it still remained substantially different from the more radical neoliberal reform implemented under Thatcher and Reagan in the UK and US. The German government under Schroeder was careful not to touch the rights and benefits of core constituencies of regular and unionized workers. German reforms were inspired by neoliberal ideology, but they were carried out through a neo-corporatist strategy.

Grote and Schmitter (1999) even speak of a 'Renaissance of National Corporatism' as a consequence of the European integration process and particularly the EMU, because the adaptation of EU rules and convergence criteria created a pressure to adjust to the Maastricht convergence criteria. Owing to the fact that the pressure for coordination is coming largely from the EMU and the creation of the single market, I think it is justified to speak of the emergence of a new form of euro corporatism that is the result of the increasing influence of EU institutions on national political economies. Old-style national neo-corporatism goes back to a kind of class compromise between capital and labour in order to assure productivity and competitiveness of business in return for growth with equity. Unlike authoritarian or even fascist corporatism, which constituted of collusion between business and government and excluded labour, neo-corporatism took a tripartite form. Neo-corporatism was facilitated by a welfare state that would provide a cushion against volatilities of the global markets. Since the 1970s, this welfare state has become much more comprehensive. At the same time, Keynesian policies of direct macroeconomic state interventions have always been weak in Europe, and the state either pursued a more micro-intervention strategy, as in France, or remained a facilitator of tripartite coordination, as in the case of Germany. Nordic countries in the EU followed another strategy by combining a strong market orientation and open economy with a comprehensive welfare state.

The integration-oriented structure of the European economy is an important reason why stakeholders including business remain interested in corporatist coordination. As we have seen, the regional outsourcing strategy is complementary and does not put factories in Eastern Europe into direct competition with factories in the west but rather ensures their productivity. Companies producing highly specialized or artisan goods also depend on experienced long-term employees with specific skills that cannot easily be replaced. All these factors make business in the EU far more open to a neo-corporatist model in which labour relations are coordinated. It is thus not surprising that other countries have been trying to emulate German-style elements of coordination, owing to the pressure posed by the European integration process. Austria and the Netherlands, the country most closely aligned with the German economy, have taken the lead. In many ways

Austria—and its 'Austro corporatism' (Bischof and Pelinka 1996)—is a country that is even closer to the ideal type of a corporatist country than is Germany. In the Netherlands, neo-corporatist arrangements ('polder model') had already been implemented with the Wassenaar Accord between labour unions, employers' associations, and the government in 1982 to overcome the 'Dutch disease' of an overreliance on gas production and exports that squeezed out all but the most competitive sectors of the economy. Other countries followed and created 'social pacts' in preparation for the EMU strengthening coordination between employees, employers, and governments (Enderlein 2008). Most explicitly, Finland introduced a 'euro buffer' in 1998. The euro buffer is a fund to which employees and employers contribute during times of economic upswing and that can be used to adjust labour costs during economically difficult times without reducing household incomes (Enderlein 2008: 441). Spain and Portugal, which would face low or even negative real interest rates under the EMU, tried to introduce elements of German-style corporatism and fiscal restraint in order to prevent an overheating in the 1990s. Even Ireland, the most liberal of the euro countries, has moved in the direction of a more corporatist style since the preparations for the EMU began in the 1990s. According to some accounts, Ireland is in many ways as coordinated as Germany and has a higher level of centralized wage bargaining (Driffill 2006: 15). Even France has been implementing reforms making the traditional state-centred capitalism more similar to the decentralized German coordination model (Fioretos 2011: 99–135). The outcome was that France's economic system evolved as a hybrid system much like the EU in general (Fioretos 2011: 135).

In short, this evolving euro corporatism can be described as the coordination between government, business, and labour unions to adapt to the European integration process. So far, euro corporatism is far less institutionalized than the national variants, because European labour and employers' associations remain weak, and it is the European commissions and the national governments that take the initiative while labour unions react. In this sense euro corporatism is more an old-style collusion between European commissions, national governments, and business than real neo-corporatist tripartism, but, unlike old-style corporatism, it is not simply an alliance between state and business to supress labour. Labour unions do remain a partner on the EU level, although they have become a junior partner that is co-opted in order to facilitate a smooth implementation process of policies decided by national governments and the EU Commission, with strong input from business lobbyists. Organized labour can still modify, slow down, or even prevent agreements, but it has lost the ability for initiative and agenda setting.

4.4.3. The Weakness of European Organized Labour

The weakening of organized labour is one of the strong similarities between the three models of capitalism, but there are still differences in the degree and the way that organized labour is weakened. Labour union density has declined in the EU, as in other regions (see Figure 4.1) although it remains at a higher level. More importantly, collective bargaining coverage, which is a much better measure for the power of labour unions and their ability to play a coordinating role, remains high in Western Europe (see Figure 4.2). For example, 60 per cent of all employees in Germany and 98 per cent of all employees in Italy are covered by such agreements, while in the UK the comparable figure is only 36 per cent and in the US 13 per cent (ILO 2014). In the US, labour unions have lost the ability to make corporatist arrangements and to have an influence on political decision-making. In Europe, labour unions have also been considerably weakened in their ability to shape political decisions and discourses,

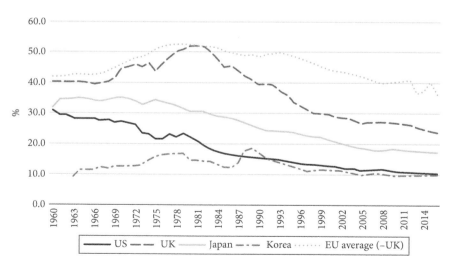

Figure 4.1. Trade-union density share of all employees (%)

Note: Administrative data except US 1973-2016, survey data
EU is unweighted average of Germany, France, Italy, Netherlands, Belgium, Sweden, Finland, Denmark, Austria, Ireland
EU countries data availability varies by year

Source: OECD, https://stats.oecd.org/Index.aspx?DataSetCode=TUD#

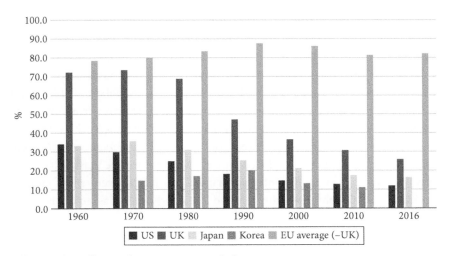

Figure 4.2. Collective bargaining ratio (%)

Note: unweighted average of Germany, France, Italy, Netherlands, Belgium, Sweden, Finland, Denmark, Austria
EU countries data availability varies by year

Source: OECD, https://stats.oecd.org/Index.aspx?DataSetCode=CBC#

and thus their ability to contribute to the macro-organization of the economy; at the same time, however, corporatist coordination has arguably intensified. Politically, labour unions remain influential, because of their close relationship with social democratic and socialist parties. While the times when socialist parties in Europe could be described as the 'political arm' of labour unions are long gone, labour unions have maintained substantial influence compared to their peers in the US and East Asia. In Hoepner's terms (2007), labour unions lost their ability to organize capitalism at the macro-level while at the same time remaining an important player in its coordination on the micro-level within companies. Instead of the traditional neo-corporatist arrangements, where state, business, and labour were equal partners, unions have been reduced to junior partners that are necessary largely to achieve wage moderation. Despite decreasing membership, labour unions remain a powerful actor. Of course, these arrangements could become more fragile given the declining unionization, but at the time of writing a collapse of a neo-corporatist style of wage coordination seems to be exaggerated.

The weakening of organized labour can partly be attributed to the European integration process itself. While businesses can take full advantage of the single market, labour unions are constrained by their national organization and by a lack of harmonization of European labour regulations that protect the rights of workers. For example, while a French company can easily invest in Poland or hire workers from the Czech Republic in order to reduce labour costs, labour regulations do not travel with the investments and labour unions cannot simply transplant their agreements at home to the new subsidiary. Within the single market, companies can play off employees and labour unions from different countries against each other by hiring subcontractors from other EU countries to do jobs at wages based on the home country of workers and not on the wages of their locally hired colleagues. While labour unions were successful in preventing an explicit country of origin principle in the Bolkestein directive on services in the internal market, the free movement of capital, services, and people gradually shifted neo-corporatist agreements in a business-friendly direction. At the same time, there is a counter-movement, and, although labour unions still face difficulties of cross-border organization there, EU-wide cooperation is improving. The European Trade Union Confederation (ETUC) brings together sixty million employees in its eighty-five National Trade Union Confederations and ten industrial unions (www.etuc.org/en). The acknowledgement of European Work Councils (EWC) in European MNCs by the EU in 1996 might be interpreted as a very modest first step to facilitate a corporatist method of coordination at the European level. While the EWCs have limited power, they have to be consulted by the management in important decisions, and they constitute a starting point for a European identity of employees. Because they apply only to large MNCs, they might also lead to a more East Asian style of coordination that focuses on a few large conglomerates (see Chapter 5) and does not depend on peak level associations.

4.4.4. The European Welfare State

The sustainability of corporatist arrangements despite the declining power of labour unions is connected to another distinctive figure of euro capitalism and that is the relatively strong welfare states (Figure 4.3). Average welfare spending in the EU is higher than in the US and East Asia, and it is still higher in the core EU6 countries (France, Germany, Italy, and BeNeLux). In addition, welfare states in the EU tend to be more comprehensive, in particular when it comes to unemployment benefits compared to the liberal welfare state in the US and the developmental welfare in East Asia (Esping-Andersen 1990; Holliday 2000). Welfare states cushion the negative effects of wage restraint and industrial rationalization that were often accompanied by the reduction of workforce and high unemployment levels. In the US, active macroeconomic

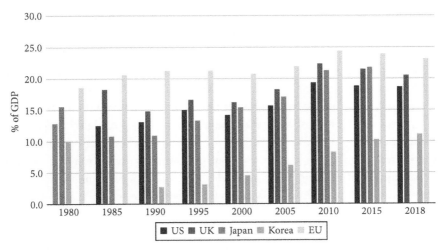

Figure 4.3. Public welfare spending in the US, the EU, Japan, and Korea (% of GDP)

Note: EU unweighted average, EU members the OECD is providing data: Austria, Belgium, Denmark, Estonia, Finland, France, Germany, Greece, Ireland, Italy, Latvia, Luxemburg, Netherlands, Poland, Portugal, Slovak Republic, Slovenia, Spain, Sweden

Source: OECD, Statistical Database, https://stats.oecd.org/Index.aspx?DataSetCode=SOCX_AGG#

policies stimulated the economy and reduced unemployment; in East Asia, active industrial had the same effect of creating jobs. In Europe, the welfare state allowed a weakening of labour unions and wage repression without a massive decline in economic demand and social cohesion. During economic crises, social safety nets act as automatic stabilizers that make macroeconomic activism less crucial. This explains the relatively small fiscal stimulus in EU member countries (see Figure 2.5). From the domestic perspective, these automatic stabilizers have the advantage, compared to macroeconomic measures, that welfare benefits will be used mostly for domestic consumption and less for imports, because people receiving welfare benefits will be more likely to spend them on daily necessities and not on important consumer goods. On the other hand, from a global perspective, automatic stabilizers contribute less to global growth than macroeconomic stimuli.

Strong welfare states play an important role in the European corporatist framework. The state effectively takes over large parts of the financial burden from stakeholders, who are negotiating, for example, the restructuring and downsizing of production in a company during crisis times. This makes it much easier for stakeholders to agree on measures to increase productivity and preserve competitiveness in the event of an economic crisis. For example, in

Germany, *Kurzarbeit* (shortened work hours) allows companies and labour unions to agree on reducing the work time (and thus the wages) of employees in a crisis situation for up to six months with the possibility of renewal (Crimmann et al. 2010). The Public Labour Agency will then compensate employees by paying 60 per cent of the amount they are losing from the wage reduction. Such schemes prevent unemployment, maintain the purchasing power of employees, and retain qualified workers for highly specialized companies. Corporatist arrangements are thus closely linked to the needs of specialized quality production. Similar programmes exist in most (West) European countries, and some countries like Spain have strengthened their short-time work programmes based on the German model as a reaction to the 2008–9 crisis (Walz et al. 2012).

A strong welfare state connects the European growth model and the ability to preserve industrial structures in many other ways. Strong public pension systems reduce the reliance of savers on financial markets and private pension funds. This slows down financialization because it weakens the role of financial markets and particularly bond and stock markets. In a crisis, this adds stability, because retirement benefits are not invested in the stock market but are underwritten by the state.

4.5. The Second Image of Euro Capitalism

The investigation of euro capitalism and its distinctive reaction to the challenges of globalization allow us to draw conclusions about the EU's global role and its position as regards international economic regulation. The EU's approach differs substantially from the global hegemonic way of the US investigated in Chapter 3 and the nationalist approach of East Asian countries that will be covered in Chapter 5. First, Europe follows a distinct regional strategy when reacting to global challenges. The European instinct is to solve problems by expanding regional cooperation, particularly by enlarging and deepening the European single market. This regional inward-looking strategy has created a Eurocentric approach focused on stability and the consolidation of the European integration process, while neglecting the global perspective. The European integration-led growth model is dominated by the creation of the European single market in combination with the consolidation of the euro and the EMU. Not surprisingly, the EU sees the G20 as a mere expansion of the EU stability orientation in macroeconomic coordination, currency cooperation, and financial market regulation to the global level.

Second, like the US, Europe has a strong interest in open capital accounts that allow its global engagement, but, unlike the US, the EU dislikes financial volatility. The commitment to the free flow of capital is supported by the EU's role as an international saver and investor and not by the goal to attract financial deal-making. Unlike the US, the EU has avoided a regulatory capture by the financial sector and the transformation to a finance-led growth model. The expansion and deepening of the EU single market have preserved the industrial base and created a European complementary specialized production model. This establishment of Europe as the specialized 'workshop of the world' has prevented full-blown financialization. Unlike in the US, the European financial sector is focused on recycling European savings in Europe and around the world, but plays little role in global financial deal-making, which explains the preference of European governments for a taxation of international financial flows. In Europe's bank-based system, financial institutes face structural limits to access capital, and financial markets remain underdeveloped, which explains the reluctance to adopt stronger capital requirements. The limited financialization does not, however, automatically mean more financial stability, because financial regulations also tend to be weaker in Europe. Indeed, European banks were among those most heavily buying (but not emitting) risky 'financial innovations'.

Third, for Europe, internal stable exchange rates and the stability of the euro are an important priority. For the EU, stable exchange rates were possible because of the expanding external market and because companies in the region tend to focus on specialized niche products that depend less on the price mechanism to be competitive. This integrated specialized production system slowed down financialization, while the expansion of the single market to Eastern Europe opened new opportunities for investment within the EU, which made offshoring to globalized facilities in China and elsewhere less urgent than for the US economy. At the same time, because of the broadening and deepening of the single market, the EU depends far less on the global market than does East Asia. Because of the priority of stable exchange rates, it is not surprising that the EU is the only major player in the G20 to support a new global monetary system, because that would support the internal stabilization of the euro.

Fourth, when it comes to international macroeconomic coordination, the EU is a global troublemaker. Because the stability of the monetary integration process is the prime focus, euro area countries implement ultra-conservative macroeconomic policies to stabilize the euro. These rules were first institutionalized in the Maastricht Treaty and later in the Stability and Growth Pact.

EU member states are able to follow a strict austerity regime because of their relatively strong welfare states and neo-corporatist institutions. This euro capitalism was facilitated by what we have imperfectly called euro corporatism. A comprehensive welfare state has further cushioned this form of European-style adjustment. In other words, euro corporatist arrangements have facilitated European integration and in particular they have allowed the surrender of sovereign macroeconomic policies. While the US and East Asia prefer to combat crises with expanding demand and stimulating inflation, the German and now the European model has been so far successful in managing deflationary adjustment while maintaining social stability.

5

State-Led Capitalism in East Asia

Export Orientation and the Quest for National Sovereignty

East Asia is the third world region that is crucial for an investigation of international economic conflicts and cooperation. Indeed the rise of East Asia as the 'factory of the world' since the 1970s is as important for the global political economy as US-led financial globalization and European integration. It would be impossible to reduce global imbalances in a cooperative and peaceful manner without cooperation from the region with the biggest trade surpluses. It would also be difficult to conceive of a new global monetary system without the involvement of the region that has by far the biggest currency reserves. East Asia has become a key region for creating a framework for the global economy in the sense that a successful global governance of finance will depend on its cooperation. As explained in Chapter 1, in this book by East Asia we mean the three most important countries for our purpose—Japan, Korea, and China. These three countries are not just the three (North-)East Asian G20 members; they can also be described as the core group of an East Asian model of capitalism (Kalinowski and Jang 2014). As we shall see, despite their differences, there are similarities between the three countries to justify subsuming them under the same term of East Asian state-led capitalism.

As in the previous two chapters, this chapter begins with an explanation of the region's role in the trilemma triangle, and then turns to an analysis of the historic genesis of the East Asian (developmental) state-led model of capitalism. We then investigate the economic origins of the East Asian success story and in particular the formation of large export-oriented business conglomerates. Finally, we look at the political foundation of the East Asian model, which can be described as an authoritarian corporatist model that is shaped by the alliance of state and business at the expense of labour.

Why International Cooperation Is Failing: How the Clash of Capitalisms Undermines the Regulation of Finance. Thomas Kalinowski, Oxford University Press (2019). © Thomas Kalinowski
DOI: 10.1093/oso/9780198714729.001.0001

5.1. The East Asian Position in the Trilemma Triangle

Since the collapse of the BWS, East Asian countries have positioned themselves between the 'Bretton Woods corner' and the 'activist state corner' of the trilemma triangle (see Figure 1.5). As export-oriented economies, East Asian countries are interested in stable and competitive exchange rates, so that they can give their exporters a competitive edge. They thus remain close to the Bretton Woods corner of the trilemma triangle. Unlike the countries within the EU, East Asian countries established neither a political integration process nor a regional currency system, but opted for unilateral currency pegs to the US dollar, as we shall see in more detail in the next section. Unlike in the EU, where stability and predictability have been the primary goals of macroeconomic and currency policies, the East Asian countries were much more concerned about improving national competitiveness and particularly about getting an edge over their rivals within the region.

Consequently, the second priority of East Asian countries has been to maintain sovereignty over national economic policies. Nationalist developmental states have been at the core of East Asian economic success. As we shall see throughout this chapter, it is the state and not the market or the coordination between stakeholders that plays the central role in the East Asian political economy. The most important aspects of this national sovereignty are active fiscal and industrial policies, guidance of the financial market, and a large degree of control over monetary policies. The legacy of active national economic and industrial policies makes countries in the region strong believers in active macroeconomic policies, and it is thus not surprising that they were among the most enthusiastic followers of the US call for fiscal stimulus packages in the initial stages of the crisis in 2008–9. While implementing the largest fiscal stimulus packages, they strictly followed their national development model by spending heavily on infrastructure projects and industrial policies that improved national competitiveness rather than introducing tax breaks or social security that would increase domestic consumption.

Subsequently, East Asian countries had to curb financial markets and the flow of capital. The close cooperation between state and large business conglomerates limited the influence of financial markets and a nationalist development strategy that kept out foreign investors. As we shall see throughout the chapter, this nationalist development strategy created a specific set of formal and informal institutions that limited the exposure of East Asian economies to the volatility of global financial markets. The international coordination of rules for financial markets is the least relevant issue for East Asian countries, because they have 'underdeveloped' financial markets and lack financial global players that would need or benefit from internationally coordinated regulation. The lack of interest in global standards for financial firms has furthermore to do with the fact that their banks remain mostly conservative in the business strategy, as a result of the Japanese financial crisis and the Asian financial crisis of the 1990s. More importantly, banks are kept under tight direct guidance by the government, because they are seen as quasi-public institutions subordinated to the national development strategy. East Asian countries do see stronger regulations in the established financial centres as a chance to increase the global role of their own financial centres, but governments fear the loss of control over sovereign economic policies and exchange rates even more than they desire to develop centres for global financial services. Consequently, instead of supporting international rules for financial actors, East Asian countries have maintained or reintroduced capital controls to insulate the domestic market from the volatility of financial globalization.

5.2. The East Asian Developmental State and the Export-Oriented Development Strategy

These policy preferences are deeply rooted in the East Asian model of export-oriented and state-led capitalism. To understand the East Asian position on the trilemma triangle, it is first necessary to investigate the differences between the East Asian path-dependent development since the 1970s and those in the US and Europe. In sum, unlike the global hegemonic strategy of the US and the regional solution pursued by the EU, East Asian countries followed national strategies to adapt to the changing global situation after the collapse of the BWS. When we look at the East Asian development path, three characteristics of this very successful East Asian solution to global challenges can be seen as central. First, East Asian countries have emerged as the factory of the world through a successful export-oriented growth strategy that rested on industrial policies, protectionism, export promotion, and a unilateral currency management. Second, East Asian countries have focused on state-led development strategies, carefully safeguarding the sovereignty of national economic policies. Thirdly, with their economic structure based on manufacturing and construction, East Asian countries have found ways to limit their vulnerability to financial globalization.

5.2.1. East Asia under the BWS

The BWS and the 'embedded liberalism' (Ruggie 1982) of the 1950s and 1960s were a very beneficial international environment for those East Asian countries that were part of the capitalist camp and allies of the US such as Japan and Korea. Stable exchange rates and declining tariffs under the GATT allowed East Asian newly industrializing countries to enter new export markets and grow quickly without concerns for wild currency fluctuations. The BWS invited East Asian countries to move beyond the traditional development focus on import substitution and focus on their international competitiveness. East Asian countries such as Japan and Korea as well as the coastal areas of China are resource poor and need to export in order to be able to import raw materials. Instead of withdrawing from the global market, they decided to mobilize all their national resources to compete in the market by pursuing a state-led neo-mercantilist strategy, as we shall see.[1] As industries in East Asia developed near the coast, they had easy access to ports and thus foreign markets. Initially exports were a structural dependence, and consequently East Asian countries had to start early to develop products that could be sold on the global markets. Over time, exports increasingly became the centre of gravity for East Asian economies, which is particularly obvious in crisis situations. The BWS provided an excellent stable international framework for this development strategy. As a credible system backed by the IMF, the BWS allowed stable and undervalued currencies, while currency speculators were deterred because they needed to bet against the deep pockets of the IMF. Japan's and Korea's important role as military allies of the US in the East Asian region also helped them to secure development aid and market access, in particular to the US. The IMF and the US tolerated the neo-mercantilist strategy, which included protectionist measures in East Asia, because it initially prioritized economic development and political stability in the region over market access for US companies. China, as the poorest of the three countries in East Asia, was obviously the exception in this initial phase of East Asian development. It stayed outside the BWS and the GATT and desperately tried to industrialize through classic import substitution, which culminated in the disastrous 'great leap forward' from 1958 to 1961.

---

[1] The separation of commercial centres and resource-rich regions in East Asia has often been cited as one of the reasons why Europe was able to soar ahead of East Asia in the nineteenth century; see Pomeranz (2000).

5.2.2. The East Asian Reaction to the Collapse of the BWS

When the BWS eventually collapsed in 1971, East Asia, with the exception of Japan, was still a very poor region, and China was suffering under the 'Cultural Revolution'. The collapse of the BWS was a massive external shock, because Japan and Korea had benefited greatly from the financial and currency stability the system had provided. Because both countries lacked the ability to stabilize the global system, and because of the absence of regional mechanisms of cooperation, they followed a national self-help strategy. They switched their currency policies to a currency management system that unilaterally pegged their currencies to the US dollar. This was done without international coordination, and the stability of the currency peg was based solely on the domestic currency reserves. China was a special case, in the sense that it remained outside the BWS with a non-convertible currency and an almost completely closed economy until the gradual opening to the world market that began in 1978. In 1980 China became a member of the IMF and a gradual convergence with the East Asian model of capitalism began.[2]

The US decision of switching to a free floating system was not an option for East Asian countries, because of the dependence on trade with the US and imports of raw materials that needed to be paid for in dollars. Thus they needed stable exchange rates to limit currency insecurities. At the same time, a regional approach was not possible, owing to the lack of multilateral cooperation and institutions in the region. Unilateral currency pegs meant that stability was maintained, so that the exchange rate now became part of the toolbox of macroeconomic policies to support national competitiveness and economic policies. This allowed the East Asian countries to have competitive exchange rates that supported their increasingly export-oriented development strategy. Unilateral currency pegs have two important advantages. First, they eliminate currency volatility as a source of economic insecurity for exporters, importers, and investors. Those involved in trade do not need to spend fees on hedging their trades for sudden changes in the exchange rate. Creditors borrowing in a foreign currency do not have to fear a sudden depreciation of the local currency and a resulting increase of debt payments. Second, unilateral currency pegs allow currencies to be used as a means to improve the national competitiveness. Unlike in the BWS, unilateral currency pegs have no cooperative adjustment mechanism. They are set unilaterally and can be adjusted to achieve a favourable exchange rate, favouring exports and

[2] From 1945 to 1980, China was represented in the IMF by the Republic of China on Taiwan.

penalizing imports. Consequently, the ability to manage exchange rates has become a crucial element of the toolbox of East Asian countries, while they have played little role in the US or Europe. As we shall see later, besides these major advantages, unilateral pegs have the disadvantage that the peg has to be defended solely with national currency reserves without support from the IMF, and that currency management in general raises suspicions about currency manipulation. Unlike the BWS, which was backed by US reserves and the IMF, unilateral currency pegs lack an intrinsic credibility that would signal a certain degree of reliability to exporters, importers, and investors. In order to have a credible unilateral peg, central banks need a substantial amount of currency reserves and a steady income of foreign currencies generated through competitive and stable exports.

Unilateral currency management not just facilitates export orientation; it makes it a necessity, because of the need to accumulate foreign reserves that are necessary to influence exchange rates. The first oil crisis and skyrocketing oil prices from 1973 added to the urgency to earn foreign currencies. As large oil importers, East Asian countries were particularly affected by the oil price shock. There was little choice but to expand their export industries, and in the case of Korea basically to build them from scratch. Korea since the 1970s and China since the 1980s have followed the Japanese model of a neo-mercantilist strategy that combined import substitution and protectionism with export orientation. This strategy relied on tariffs and non-tariff barriers for infant industry protection and at the same time promoted exports. The state made success in export markets a condition for access to cheap credits with government-controlled banks and gave almost unconditional support to companies that successfully conquered foreign markets. In this partnership between state and private companies (see Section 5.4), the state was the senior partner. The state also ensured a certain amount of domestic competition and later used trade liberalization to ensure companies would not abuse protection for rent seeking. Private companies were forced to invest the rents they earned through protectionism at home to upgrade the quality and price competitiveness to compete successfully in the world market. This strategy was very successful, and the economy of the East Asian countries became more dynamic, with Japan and the East Asian tigers Korea, Taiwan, Hong Kong, and Singapore achieving annual growth rates of 10 per cent and more. In the 1970s Korea followed Japan's path with a furious heavy and chemical industrialization, which was announced with the third five-year plan in 1972. By the end of the 1970s, and particularly in the 1980s, the East Asian development model began to draw the attention of academic observers, with publications such as

Japan as Number One (Vogel 1979) and studies on South Korea such as *Asia's Next Giant* (Amsden 1989).

Export-Oriented Development and the International Conflict about Currency Manipulation

In East Asia, currency adjustments have been a common, and often first choice, reaction to economic challenges. Instead of stimulating consumption like in the US, or providing support for industrial development through market enlargement and institutional harmonization like in the European integration process, East Asian governments tend to use export-oriented growth and recovery strategies. Indeed the East Asian share of world exports has increased from less than 5 per cent in 1960 to more than 17 per cent in 2016 (Figure 5.1). The preference for stable and undervalued currencies has facilitated export-oriented economies and has the tendency to produce current-account surpluses, but export orientation does not necessarily lead to current-account surpluses. In the initial stages of industrialization, the import of technology and capital goods often created deficits. In later stages of development, investment rates decline and export-oriented economies tend to produce surpluses. This was the case in Japan from the 1970s, in Korea from the 1990s and in China from the 2000s. To maintain stable currencies amid

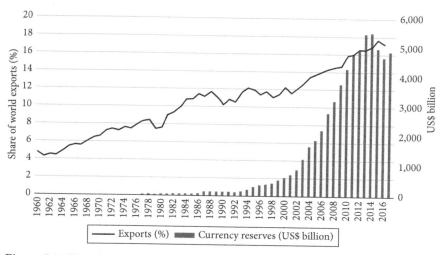

Figure 5.1. East Asian share of world exports in goods and services (%) and amount of currency reserves (US$ billion)

Note: Data for China, Japan, Korea, Reserve data for China from 1980 only

Source: World Bank WDI, https://databank.worldbank.org

current-account surpluses, central banks are forced to purchase excessive dollars and sell the local currency to prevent or limit an appreciation. This explains why East Asian countries accumulated a huge amount of currency reserves, which amounted to $4.8 trillion in China, Japan, and Korea alone (Figure 5.1).

As long as East Asia was not seen as a serious competitor and the US was determined to support East Asian capitalist development as an alternative to socialism in Asia, the 'manipulation' of exchange rates was not seen as a big problem. This changed in the 1980s with the emergence of Japan as a serious competitor in almost all industrial sectors. Chalmers Johnson's book (1982) on the Japanese developmental states, like many other publications in the 1980s, was an explicit warning that the Japanese nationalist development strategy would prove to be superior to the US market-oriented approach. In Chalmers Johnson's words (1999: 41), Japan was an 'economy mobilized for war but never demobilized during peacetime'. Consequently, the US government pushed back and pressured Japan to abandon currency interventions to undervalue its currency.

5.2.3. Retaliation against Currency 'Manipulation' and the Plaza Accord

With the Plaza Accord in 1985, Japan and European G5 members agreed to a massive depreciation of the US dollar and intervened into currency markets until the dollar depreciated by more than 50 per cent against the Japanese yen and other Asian currencies. The dollar depreciation largely failed to achieve its original purpose to reduce current-account imbalances between the US and Japan, but instead it had some severe effects on the Japanese domestic economy. First, Japanese banks and companies used the stronger currency to invest abroad, particularly in other East Asian countries but also in US assets and government bonds. To lower their production costs, Japanese companies offshored production to China and South-East Asian countries with lower labour costs. This strengthened Japan's global economic role and allowed current-account surpluses to be recycled, thus lowering the upward pressure on the Japanese currency. These intensified global economic activities were matched by some remarkable global political initiatives by the Japanese government, such as the 'Miyazawa Initiative' for debt rescheduling to manage the crisis of the developing world in the 1980s (Kojo, in Berger et al. 2007). While the initiative was never implemented, the US took over many aspects of the initiative for its own Brady Plan to reschedule debt.

Second, the most dramatic effect of the strengthening Japanese currency was on the domestic political economy. The strengthening yen lowered inflationary pressure, and the Bank of Japan used low interest rates to stimulate the economy and compensate for the rising yen. These loose monetary policies successfully preserved Japanese global competitiveness and fuelled an economic boom, but they also created a massive stock-market and real-estate bubble. These bubbles burst in the early 1990s and led to a long period of low inflation and low growth.[3] The Plaza Accord and its consequences are still an excellent case to study how a change of the international framework can have unintended consequences for domestic political economies. The Plaza Accord also signalled a revitalization of US hegemonic power and willingness to lead. With the collapse of the Soviet Union in 1991 and the end of the cold war, East Asia also lost some of its strategic importance for the US, which made the US even less tolerant of currency management and the protection of domestic financial markets. With its strengthened position as a hegemon and the only remaining superpower, the US also increasingly reinterpreted its current-account deficits, not as a weakness of its own economy but as the result of 'unfair' practices of currency manipulation and protectionism by others.

5.2.4. The East Asian Miracle and the Rise of China

The period from the Plaza Accord in 1985 until the Asian financial crisis of 1997–8 is characterized by the Japanese financial and economic crisis and the rise of the 'Asian tigers' (Kim 1998) Korea, Taiwan, Hong Kong, and Singapore as well as the 'high performing East Asian economies' (HPAE) (World Bank 1993). The HPAE included not just Japan, Taiwan, and Korea but also South-East Asian economies such as Thailand, Malaysia, and Indonesia, which were seen as following in the footsteps of North-East Asia. Although not included in the original 'East Asian Miracle' (World Bank 1993) literature, China later became part of the East Asian success story in the late 1990s and particularly with admission to the WTO in 2001. An illustration emerged of the East Asian model of development as a flying-geese pattern, with Japan at the front followed by the four tigers and the South-East Asian countries and China at the end (Kasahara 2004). To some degree, the rise of the East Asian region can be attributed to the rise of Japanese foreign investments, particularly in South-East Asia and China. With the rise of Korean and later Chinese

---

[3] For a very accessible account of Japanese financial markets from boom to bust, see, e.g., Tett (2003).

competitors with lower wage costs, offshoring production became a necessity for Japanese companies to reduce costs and remain competitive. More importantly, the rise of the East Asian region showed that Japan was not an outlier but indicated the existence of a distinct and successful East Asian model of development. This model has usually been seen as export oriented and state led, based on a long history of statehood, nationalism, and neo-mercantilist states. As we shall see, these 'developmental states' (Johnson 1982; Woo-Cumings 1999) shaped East Asian development, but the way they shaped this model was strongly influenced by the collapse of the BWS in 1973 and the economic and financial globalization that followed.

During the 1990s, the whole East Asian region experienced a massive inflow of international capital that was trying to benefit from the East Asian 'miracle'. This massive inflow of capital amid pegged exchange rates let to a massive asset bubble and an increase of particularly short-term international debt, which soon exceeded foreign-currency reserves. In 1994 China decided to unify its exchange-rate regime and gradually make the yuan convertible until 1996. At the same time, it dramatically devalued its official exchange rate by 33 per cent (Kanamori and Zhao 2006: 8).[4] Consequently, the Chinese yuan depreciated from the official fixed exchange rate of 5.77 RMB to the dollar to a pegged exchange rate of 8.28 RMB to the dollar (Morrison and Labonte 2013: 2). Owing to this massive devaluation, Chinese export competitiveness over its East Asian rivals increased, and it became an even more interesting destination for foreign direct investment (FDI) from companies in Japan, Korea, and Taiwan that were desperately looking for new investment opportunities. When the first signs of a cooling-down in East Asia emerged in early 1997, however, investors withdrew their money, and countries in the region were forced to abandon their exchange-rate pegs and ask the IMF for a bailout (Wade 1998; Haggard 2000; Blustein 2003).

5.2.5. The Asian Financial Crisis

The Asian financial crisis and the subsequent recovery were critical events in the rise of East Asia and became engrained in the regional collective memory. The crisis both showed the limits of the old development model and reinforced suspicion about financial globalization. The crisis revealed the limits of the

---

[4] The real effect of the devaluation was arguably lower, because the majority of transactions at that time were done on the swap market.

previous exchange-rate pegs amid increasing pressure for financial liberalization. Amid the hard-currency pegs that were in place until 1997, financial liberalization led to a massive increase of capital inflows, as investors wanted to have their share in the proclaimed East Asian miracle. In addition, domestic business groups favoured the opening of short-term capital flows but lobbied against the opening of long-term credit flows and investment because they feared that long-term foreign engagement would undermine their management control (Kalinowski and Cho 2009). The previous asset bubble and overinvestment reversed to a panic and massive withdrawal amid first signs of an economic downturn in 1997. Capital flew from the East Asian region to the safe havens in Europe and the US, and exchange-rate pegs came under pressure. Consequently, with the exception of China, currency pegs were replaced with a more flexible system of exchange-rate management. China, which remained closed to short-term capital, was largely able to avoid the crisis and maintained its exchange-rate peg until 2005, when pressure from the US forced it to take a more flexible stance.

The successful export-oriented recovery strategy and the remodelling of the East Asian growth model to be highly competitive in the global market shaped Asia in the decade from the Asian financial crisis to the global crisis in 2008. When the IMF moved in to bail out East Asian countries, many expected that IMF structural adjustment programmes would transform East Asian closed 'crony capitalism' into a 'modern' open US-style market economy. However, the Asian financial crisis also showed the limits of IMF measures, which in retrospect are often seen as misguided, and at least initially they worsened the situation for the region (IEO/IMF 2003). The Asian financial crisis constituted a critical juncture in East Asia, but, in contrast to what many expected at that time, the 'Wall Street–Treasury–IMF complex' (Veneroso and Wade 1998) did not 'tame' the East Asian tigers (Bullard et al. 1998). The crisis rather awakened the tigers, and they have been building on their strengths of high domestic saving and investment, export promotion, and incremental product innovations to improve competitiveness. Indeed, as we shall see, instead of abandoning their development model and initiating a convergence with a market-oriented model, East Asian countries 'remodelled' (Vogel 2006) their own system and created a reformed and more competitive state-led model of capitalism that is compatible with a Western-dominated international institutional system. East Asian countries abandoned the hard-peg currency system and replaced it with a managed floating system. In addition, massive national currency reserves were accumulated to protect the region from future crises. Ironically, the successful export-oriented recovery from the financial crisis in

East Asia confirmed the East Asian growth model when it comes to the neo-mercantilist export promotion strategy and the ability of states in the region to mobilize their resources for increasing competitiveness. Indeed, many of the biggest successes of East Asian businesses, such as Korean car company Hyundai and IT producer Samsung, became real global players only after 1998. In Japan and Korea, businesses also intensified offshoring to China and South-East Asia to decrease production costs and thereby become more competitive, which further fuelled the economic rise of China and its role as the factory of the world, particularly after its admission to the WTO in 2001. At the same time as the Asian financial crisis, China was going through a massive adjustment process to adapt for its accession to the WTO.

The Chiang Mai Initiative and the Failure of East Asian Regional Cooperation

The Asian financial crisis created a certain regional identity, in particular in reaction to the IMF intervention, and for a brief period it seemed possible that East Asia would overcome its nationalist development strategy and improve regional cooperation. The experience of the financial crisis showed leaders in the region that the global financial international organizations are primarily a tool of the US to export its own institutions and thus advance the interest of US companies and foreign financial investors. Until 1997, East Asian countries, with the exception of Japan, had little interest in shaping international institutions but rather tried to adjust and exploit them. The crisis showed that such a strategy was no longer viable and that a US-dominated IMF was a threat to the East Asian development model that was still generally seen as successful in the region. The initial reaction was to follow the European model to build regional institutions as alternatives for the Western-dominated global ones. Briefly, it seemed that Japan would be able to lead a regional alternative to global approaches by creating an Asian Monetary Fund (AMF) as a competitor of the IMF. However, the plan was opposed not just by the IMF and the US but also by China, which was even more cautious about a Japan-dominated East Asia than it was about Western-dominated international organizations. Because of the threat from North Korea and its dependence on the US military, South Korea also still found it difficult to balance its strong bilateral ties with the US with a stronger engagement in regional cooperation.

For the decade after the Asian financial crisis, it seemed that East Asian countries would at least move in the direction of a European model of regional cooperation within East Asia. In particular, the Chiang Mai Initiative (CMI) of the ASEAN+3 countries that was initiated in Chiang Mai, Thailand, in 2000 was a strong reaction to the humiliation felt in the region. The CMI was a watered-down version of the AMF and consisted of mostly bilateral currency-swap agreements of $90 billion, in which East Asian countries pledged to support countries in the region in case of a financial crisis (Park and Wang 2005). The CMI, however, lacked a dynamic that could create spillover effects towards deeper integration, because it was largely a system of promises and not an institutional system that would foster trust and cooperation in other areas as well. Indeed, national self-help remained dominant, and when the global financial crisis struck in 2008, the CMI proved to be ineffective, as we shall see.

Following the advice of the IMF and OECD, East Asia gradually adopted flexible but nationally managed exchange rates. Japan had been moving in that direction since the Plaza Accord in 1985, Korea since the Asian financial crisis in 1997, and China since 2005. However, East Asian countries never switched to a floating system, like in the US, nor did they adopt permanently fixed exchange rates, like in Europe. Despite much criticism of middle-of-the-road approaches by the IMF and a strong pressure to adopt one of the two 'corner solutions' (Mussa 2000)[5] East Asia opted for a balanced approach with flexible yet managed exchange rates (Grimes 2009: 65). This practice condemned as currency manipulation outside Asia is often euphemistically referred to in East Asia as 'smoothing operations' (*Financial Times*, 26 August 2010). The abolishment of a formal peg did not mean the end of state interventions into currency markets. In fact, China did not hesitate to reinstate a peg when it seemed appropriate in 2008 (Morrison and Labonte 2013: 3). Even in Korea and Japan, currency interventions remain frequent. The difference is that interventions became less predictable and technocratic, while becoming more political, as there is a constant debate on the 'right' value of the currency, and the use of the instrument is often dependent on the political background of the ruling party. This is reflected in the excessive attention that is paid to the external value of the currency by East Asian policymakers and the media alike.

5.2.6. East Asia and the Global Financial Crisis

When the crisis hit in 2008, the direct effects on East Asia seemed to be limited because, unlike European banks, East Asian financial institutions had bought

---

[5] 'With rising capital mobility and integration into world asset and goods markets, however, an increasing number of countries are moving, and are likely to continue to move, toward the ends of the spectrum that extends from purely floating exchange rates to very hard pegs' (Mussa 2000: 36).

few risky assets and most of East Asian wealth in the US was invested in safe treasuries. The 'decoupling' of East Asia was a popular hypothesis in the initial stages of the crisis (Park 2011). Large currency reserves would mean that short-term debts in East Asia could be easily covered, and China had the additional layer of protection from the limited openness of the capital account. Smaller economies like Korea (as well as South-East Asia), however, were still vulnerable, because domestic and foreign investors had fled the country, or rather the currency, into the safe havens of the yen, the euro, and most importantly the dollar, in order to be sheltered from (or even benefit from) an expected depreciation of the Korean currency. The depreciation of the Korean won by more than 40 per cent allowed currency speculators to earn a handsome rent but drained liquid currency reserves to an extent that the Korean government requested support from neighbouring countries under the CMI. Unfortunately, the CMI failed, and regional support did not materialize. Governments in the region had to revert to national and bilateral strategies. Particularly Japan and Korea took advantage of their special relationship to the US to secure bilateral central bank liquidity swaps. During the global financial crisis in 2008–9, severe weaknesses of the CMI were revealed, owing to its lack of any pooled resources or functional multilateral decision-making processes and the reliance on bilateral agreements and ultimately unilateral national decisions about the swaps. In 2010, leaders in the region agreed to multilateralize the CMI and strengthen the institution to avoid a repetition of the its failure in a subsequent crisis (Sussangkarn 2010).

While the immediate panic on the currency markets in East Asia could be stopped by currency swaps with the US, the situation became much more severe when the crisis spread from finance to trade. In 2009, world trade collapsed at an even steeper rate than during the world economic crisis of the 1930s (Eichengreen and O'Rourke 2009), and, as East Asian countries are extremely dependent on exports, they were hit particularly hard.

5.2.7. Currency Management since 2008

A distinct East Asian reaction to the crisis was the reactivation of more active currency management. Governments and central banks in China, Japan, and Korea used similar strategies to achieve competitive exchange rates and prevent currency appreciation amid current-account surpluses, but the degree of both their interventions and their success differed. China was most decisive by strengthening the currency peg and halting the gradual and controlled appreciation of the Chinese yuan in July 2008 after an appreciation of approximately 14 per cent since early 2007 (all fx data by Fed 2013). A controlled moderate appreciation resumed in September 2010, and by February 2013 the Chinese yuan had appreciated by approximately 25 per cent from its early 2007 value.

Korea was hit worst by the crisis, suffering a major currency crisis with a depreciation of the Korean currency by 40 per cent in late 2008 compared to its value in 2007. The main focus of currency policies was first to stabilize the depreciation of the currency, which was achieved in March 2009 with a bilateral swap agreement with the US Fed, and then to slow down the recovery of the country in order to take advantage of the competitive advantages of the depreciation. The controlled appreciation of the Korean currency was very smooth, and, in February 2013, the Korean won still remained approximately 15 per cent below its pre-crisis level. Under the rule of the Democratic Party, Japan initially refrained from stronger interventions and allowed a gradual appreciation of the Japanese yen until this strategy was reversed in September 2012 when the conservative LDP regained power under Prime Minister Abe. Although it is difficult to measure the real or 'fair' value of a currency, the IMF estimates that for 2013 the Chinese and Korean currencies remain under-valued by 5–10 per cent and 2–8 per cent, respectively. Because of the massive devaluation of the Japanese yen since the election of the new Abe government, estimates about its value fluctuate even more; these estimates, again for 2013, range from an overvaluation of 10 per cent to an undervaluation of 20 per cent (IMF 2013).

Increases in currency reserves are another indicator for the strategies used to keep currency values down. Since the beginning of the crisis in 2007, East Asian countries have dramatically increased their purchases of reserve assets (and thus sales of local currency) as we have seen in Figure 5.1. For China alone, its new reserve accumulation nearly doubled from $285 billion in 2006 to $461 billion in 2007. This accumulation amount remained above $400 billion a year until 2011. Beginning in 2007, Japan also accumulated reserves of between $27 billion and $44 billion each year of the crisis. Conversely, Korea was forced to prevent a further devaluation of its currency by selling a net $56 billion of its reserves in 2008. Since 2009, however, the Korean central bank has joined Japan and China in slowing down the appreciation of its currency by purchasing foreign reserves totalling $69 billion in 2009 and $27 billion in 2010 (IMF 2012).

Currency management remains an important element of the East Asian survival strategy in the global markets, but it is gradually becoming both less successful and more costly. This has been particularly since 2008 because of the US strategy to devalue the dollar not by directly intervening in the currency market but by reducing interest rates and increasing the amount of money in circulation through quantitative easing. This strategy has the advantage that it stimulates not just exports but the whole economy and it is less risky because it does not depend on the purchase of low yielding government bonds in a foreign currency. Quantitative easing has an additional advantage, because, following the G20 definition, it does not constitute currency manipulation, as it does not involve direct interventions in the currency market. The diminished effectiveness of currency management facilitated a revival of more direct government engagement and a stronger government engagement in areas such as infrastructure. The state also expanded into new areas of industrial policies supporting national competitiveness—for example, by supporting research and investments of private companies.

5.2.8. Fiscal Stimulus Packages

Beside currency management, the second distinct East Asian reaction to the crisis was the implementation of large supply-side-oriented fiscal stimulus packages (Kalinowski 2013a, 2015a). Implementing fiscal stimulus packages as a reaction to the crisis was initially very high on the G20 agenda (see Chapter 2). The East Asian governments, with their long tradition of state-led development, were naturally among the most enthusiastic implementers, and East Asian fiscal stimulus packages were among the largest in the G20 (see Figure 2.5). In fact, China and Korea had even larger fiscal stimulus packages as a percentage of GDP than the US, although their domestic economies were less directly affected by the global financial crisis than those of the US and Europe. At the same time, the global goal of fiscal stimuli was implemented in a very specific East Asian way. Unlike in Europe, which has relied on automatic stabilizers like strong social safety nets to cushion the effects of the crisis, government intervention in East Asian countries was much more direct, being administered through supplementary budgets. Unlike in the US, these large fiscal stimulus packages were not aimed at stimulating consumption, but were supply-side-oriented stimuli guided by the goal of improving national competitiveness. For example, instead of subsidizing the purchase of more energy efficient cars through 'cash for clunkers' programmes, as in Europe and the US, East Asian countries concentrated on infrastructure projects and industrial policies, for example, by supporting companies developing new 'green products' (Kalinowski 2015a). Other measures included large construction projects and investments in infrastructure, such as high-speed rail links, streets, and new airports. Rather than boosting consumption, these investments did little to reduce dependence on exports, but rather aimed at improving national competitiveness and securing bigger shares of the global market.

The East Asian self-help recovery strategy was very successful in the sense that it re-energized growth in East Asia through investments. While East Asian countries were frequently criticized in the G20 for their currency management, they were regarded as very cooperative when it came to fiscal expansion. At the same time, because of their supply-side-oriented nature, the stimuli did little to reduce global economic imbalances. To some degree, the increased demand for capital goods and machinery in East Asia helped exporters of capital goods, in particular in Europe. Economic imbalance, in particular with the US, however, narrowed only briefly, owing to the collapse of demand in the US. Since 2012, East Asian trade surpluses had increased again (see Figure 2.2), which is not surprising given that investments during the crisis improved productivity. Effectively, East Asia defended its position in the international division of labour by improving domestic infrastructure and advancing its competitiveness into new industries that benefited from government support for R&D or were more generally part of a 'green growth strategy'. These new industrial policies complemented measures in the West to improve energy efficiencies and reduce pollution and greenhouse gas emissions. While Europe and the US provided subsidies to install solar panels and for environmentally friendly products, East Asia concentrated on developing and producing these exact products. East Asian countries followed the path dependency of their development model and made sure to improve their international competitiveness, which over time would result in more exports. The conflict between China, on the one hand, and the EU and the US, on the other, about price dumping of Chinese solar panels is a telling example of the result of this strategy to support export industries (*Financial Times*, 27 July 2013).

5.2.9. Financial Reforms in East Asia

Improving financial regulations was the third major focus of the G20 and arguably the one that resonated the least with the political preferences in East Asia. East Asian countries are often criticized for their strategy of 'mock compliance' to international financial standards (Walter 2008: 5), but in the case of financial regulations after the global financial crisis East Asian countries had few problems in following new financial rules under the Basel 3 standards. This has to do first with the fact that East Asia had experienced a severe financial crisis exactly ten years before the collapse of Lehman Brothers, and thus asset bubbles had had much less time to build up. In East Asia, the crisis was primarily a problem of collapsing exports and not a financial crisis. In Korea, the crisis had the additional component of a currency crisis, because, as we have seen, the global crisis prompted a massive outflow of capital. Japan, China, and Korea are considered systemically important countries for global financial stability, and, once they were members of the G20, it became impossible for them to ignore the international standards set by the G20 and the BIS. In fact, East Asian countries not just agreed to the Basel 3 standards but were also among the first to implement them (BIS 2014). East Asia's rapid implementation might seem counter-intuitive, given the difficulties of East Asian banks to raise capital because of the underdevelopment of East Asian financial markets, but the new capital requirements of Basel 3 largely meant a reassessment of financial products that are little used in East Asia's conservative bank-based system. After the Asian financial crisis, national bank regulation also implemented much stricter capital requirements than were needed under Basel. In 2013, China implemented its own much stricter version of Basel 3 and raised its capital adequacy standards to 11.5 per cent for large banks until 2013 (Sekine 2011). This is a more ambitious goal than the 10.5 per cent until 2019 under Basel 3 (see Table 2.2).

In general, East Asian financial markets remain relatively 'underdeveloped', which means that they primarily still serve a domestic customer base of savers and businesses. Consequently, East Asian banks have fewer international connections and neither produced or even purchased the products created through 'financial innovation' that triggered a crisis in many of the Western financial institutes (Kawai et al. 2012: 9). This is not to say that East Asian banks are generally safer. In fact, East Asian banks tend to have a high exposure to traditional mortgage credits and feeble SMEs. Credits to SMEs are often conducted in the context of government initiatives to preserve or create jobs, which implies that the government underwrites these credits and would step in in the case of a crisis. In general, as we have seen, the connection between banks and the state is much closer in the East Asian model of capitalism than in Europe or the US, and even private banks are under a close guidance from the government, as we shall see. Consequently, Basel 3 hurts East Asian banks less than European ones, owing to their already high levels of capital adequacy and their traditional lending patterns. At the same time, Basel 3 standards do very little to mitigate risks stemming from an overexposure to domestic mortgage credits and the pressure from governments to channel credits into areas designated in their industrial policies.

5.2.10. Conclusions: National Solutions to Global Problems

Unlike the global approach of the US and the regional approach of Europe, East Asia reacted to the collapse of the BWS and the challenge of economic and financial globalization with national self-help solutions. Most importantly, measures to boost exports and improve national competitiveness were implemented. These consisted of intervening into currency markets to create competitive exchange rates, industrial policies and implementation of large fiscal stimulus packages concentrated on infrastructure, and investments in order to improve national competitiveness. Instead of trying to change the global system, East Asian countries accepted it and concentrated on using the system to their advantage as much as possible. While they have been unsuccessful in shaping global norms, they have been very successful in developing national strategies to operate within them. Since the 1970s, the international financial system and its institutions have been dominated by the US and to some degree Europe. In other words, the international system as it is to today is not something East Asians have had a substantial say in, and it is therefore perceived as something external and even hostile that is imposed on them. The strong representation of East Asia in the G20 might lead to a more active role in the future. So far, China and Korea have been focusing on using their stronger representation in the G20 to achieve more influence in other international institutions but without gaining or even attempting to shape their agenda.

5.3. The East Asian Neo-Mercantilist Growth Model and the Rise of Export-Oriented Business Conglomerates

The combination of national self-help strategy and export orientation just described represents the two core elements of the successful rise of East Asia in the world economy. So far, export orientation has been presented in a rather technocratic sense as a set of policies, a 'development strategy' or a 'solution' for managing economic challenges and crises. It is now time to look beneath the surface of such a policy-oriented view and discover the institutional underpinnings and economic structures that guide the hands of actors and decision-makers and lead to a certain path dependency of development in the case of East Asia. Export orientation is not just a policy choice; it corresponds with a specific economic structure that is supported by a web of institutions, interests, and ideologies. Export orientation is the visible characteristic of a distinct model of East Asian capitalism, which is introduced in this section. Economically, this East Asian capitalism is based on export-oriented business conglomerates that are closely interlinked with a specific East Asian form of mercantilism with a subordinated financial sector. Unlike past Western forms of mercantilism, this East Asian neo-mercantilism has shown a strong path dependency but has also proven to be very adaptive. So far, there are very few signs that this East Asian neo-mercantilism has been replaced by a liberal market model of capitalism, as in the US or a neo-corporatist strategy, as in Europe, which do not need to run current-account surpluses.

5.3.1. Exports as the Engine of the Economy

The first piece of the puzzle of East Asian capitalism is the region's structural dependence on exports in the sense that the dynamic of the economy depends on a strong export performance. This structure has created a strong path dependency that makes it difficult for any government to depart from policies favouring exports, such as intervening in the currency markets or international capital flows. The importance of exports for a country in general can be measured by the share of exports of GDP, indicating the importance or dependence of the economy on exports, and the share of the current-account balance of GDP, indicating the contribution of exports to economic growth. The share of export of goods and services to GDP (as measured by World Bank 2019) depends largely on the size of the overall economy, and thus China (19.7 per cent in 2016) and Japan (16.1 per cent) have a much lower dependency on exports than Korea (42.3 per cent). East Asian countries thus seem more export dependent than the US (11.9 per cent) but less so than the EU (43.2), although the latter figure is difficult to compare, because a large share of these exports represents trade within the EU (see Chapter 4). These figures, however, underestimate East Asia's dependence on export, because in some of the crucial industries export dependency is much higher. For example, 56 per cent of the cars produced by Toyota in Japan are exported (own calculations from Toyota 2013). While overseas production of Japanese cars is extensive, the offshore production depends on parts and technology from Japan, which further adds to its exports. The Korean car industry, which makes up 14 per cent of all Korean exports, exports an even a larger share of 70 per cent of the domestic production, while the share of imported cars in the domestic market is less than 9 per cent (own calculations for 2012, from Korea Automobile Manufacturers' Association 2013: 5–6). In some sectors of the Korean economy, such as semiconductors, export dependency is even bigger, at more than 100 per cent of the local production, which has to do with the re-exports of imported products (US Department of Commerce 2014). More importantly, when it comes to the contribution of exports to economic growth, the dependency becomes more obvious. The contribution of exports to economic growth can be measured by the share of the current-account surplus of GDP. All East Asian countries have strong surpluses, with an annual average of 5 per cent in China, 3.3 per cent in Japan, and 2.3 per cent in Korea in the 2000s (see Figure 2.3). Unlike the European Union, where current-account surpluses are largely a crisis resolution strategy (see Chapter 4), East Asian countries have had a much more structural dependence on exports since the mid-1980s.

Increasing exports became the first-choice strategy to react to economic challenges from the collapse of the BWS to the 2008 crisis. In the 1970s, the Japanese Ministry of International Trade and Industry (MITI) and the Korean Economic Planning Board (EPB) pushed private companies to export by giving them privileged access to credits through export loans (Woo-Cumings 1991). Korea followed an export-oriented recovery strategy after the Asian financial crisis of 1997–8 (Kalinowski 2005a), and China used the accession to the WTO to vitalize growth rates and weed out inefficiencies in the state-owned enterprise sector (Fewsmith 2001). It is important to note, however, that export orientation is not just a policy choice or strategy but a necessity deriving from the East Asian growth model. Exports have always been a necessary part of the development strategy, because the industrialized regions of Japan, South Korea, and coastal China are resource poor and thus depend on imports of natural resources and particularly imports for energy production. Later, export dependency became a logical consequence of high investment and low consumption rates, which were linked to the rise of large business conglomerates focusing on mass producing consumer goods for the world market. Even the emergence of global production chains did not alter the dependency. Unlike European and American companies that offshored production to low-wage countries and then re-imported products for the domestic market, Asian companies followed a 'home-market strategy'. Even companies with heavy foreign investments like Toyota Motors still organize their production around the core factories in Japan and produce cars sold in their domestic market in Japan. Korean companies such as Hyundai Motors and Samsung Electronics follow similar home-market strategies and maintain a strong presence in the home market in order to maintain their networks with the government and avoid protests from labour unions. Consequently, while outward FDI often has a negative impact on current accounts in the US, it further increases surpluses in East Asia, because products assembled abroad contain intermediate goods from the home market. In other words, the East Asian strategy of offshoring aggravates the export orientation and thus the challenge of how to recycle the inflow of foreign currencies, without risking an appreciation of the domestic currencies that would hurt not only exports but also the value of foreign investment.

5.3.2. Concentration on Price-Sensitive Mass-Consumer Products in the East Asian 'Factory of the World'

Equally important for East Asia's global role as the dependence on exports is the composition of these exports. The composition of exports determines East Asia's position in the international division of labour and has a strong influence on preferences for international regulation. The structure of East Asian exports means that competition is largely between companies in the East Asian region and is carried out mainly through the price mechanism. This means that competitive exchange rates are particularly important for the East Asian growth model. East Asian exports differ quite substantially from exports from the US or Europe. While finance-led countries dominate the export of financial services, European and East Asian countries both focus on the export of manufactured products. At the same time, they differ substantially in the type of manufacturing products they export as regards degree of specialization and quality. As was explained in Chapter 4, the European economy is shaped to a large degree by specialized high-quality products. These products cannot easily be replaced by competing products. In this sense, Europe was described as the workshop of the world for specialized production with a focus on quality, luxury goods, and customized solutions. East Asian countries, on the other hand, dominate in areas where products are more easily replaceable, price competition is intensive, and production volumes are large. Owing to the ubiquitous global presence of East Asian consumer products, the region has become the 'factory of the world'. This includes particularly mass consumer products and standardized intermediate goods ranging from textiles and plastic toys to electronic consumer products, cars, and standardized semi-conductors.

East Asian business conglomerates have been very successful in creating economies of scale and scope, but they have been far less successful in carving out niches that cannot easily be penetrated by competitors. Japan has to some degree evolved into that direction, as it competes with European specialized products and has even developed some unique consumer and cultural brands competing with the US service industry. On average, however, these products do not play a significant role in the overall exports, and they are usually able to compete only in the domestic and regional markets, while they have difficulties penetrating markets beyond the East Asian region. The focus on price-sensitive goods in highly competitive markets is indicated by the relative decline of terms of trade for East Asian countries that measure the price of exports as a percentage ratio of the price of imports (see Figure 5.2). A decline of terms of trade means that the prices of countries' exports decline compared to the prices for its imports. In East Asian countries that has been the case most of the time since the mid-1990s, with the notable exemption of 2008–9 and the period from 2014 to 2016. Both periods were very special, because they saw a massive decline in oil prices.

The competition over the price also undermines the building of customer loyalty, which further exacerbates the dependence on the price mechanism for competition. Even with very popular consumer products, like smartphones, for example, those produced by Korea's Samsung (for now) lack the loyalty enjoyed by European luxurious brands. East Asian consumer products have a high market share, but they ultimately remain replaceable, because customers

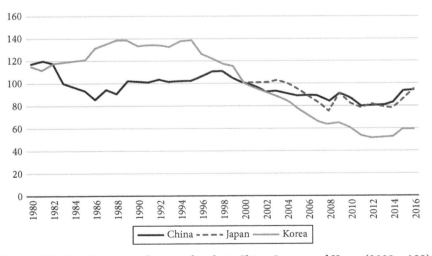

Figure 5.2. Development of terms of trade in China, Japan, and Korea (2000 = 100)

Source: World Bank, World Development Indicators, https://data.worldbank.org

of smartphones and other IT products are locked into the software 'ecosphere' of the operating system by US software giants Google, Apple, and Microsoft. The hardware is easier to replace than the software environment it is built for.

The type of products produced in East Asia is closely linked with the production process and the innovation regime. The character of the production process and the way productivity increases in East Asia are achieved remain strongly based on capital investment, long regular working hours, and routine overtime work. Krugman (1994) was clearly exaggerating when he called the East Asian economic miracle a 'myth', claiming that East Asian growth was dependent solely on increases in input of capital and labour and not on increases in productivity. On the contrary, productivity increases were substantial, and they were not just the result of capital investment but were also based on substantial process innovations. The 'just in time' production method that was developed by Toyota and that optimizes the supply chain is only the most prominent example of many incremental process innovations that helped East Asian countries to reduce costs and move products to the market much more quickly than their competitors. While these process innovations are less visible than radical product innovations such as the iPhone, they are no less important. The problem of the East Asian model is not lack of productivity and innovation, but the economic dominance of the hierarchically structured East Asian business conglomerate, which prevents a transition to a more balanced domestic consumption-driven growth model.

5.3.3. East Asian Export-Oriented Business Conglomerates as the Dominant Business Faction

The East Asian 'price export oriented' (Boyer and Freyssenet 2002) growth model is based on a specific form of corporate structure, regional cooperation, and financial markets. It was the rise of export-oriented business conglomerates that enabled East Asia to conquer the consumer markets of the world. Unlike European companies that thrive owing to their specialization on certain products or lines of related products, East Asian businesses are successful because of their economy of scale and scope as well as their ability for rapid adaptation. The emergence of the East Asian conglomerates was an almost inevitable consequence of the East Asian export-oriented development strategy. The high-volume export of standardized mass products corresponds with a business structure dominated by large vertically and horizontally integrated business conglomerates. These *zaibatsu* or since 1945 *keiretsu*

(Japanese) and *chaebol* (Korean) are written in the same Chinese characters. Since the 1990s, China has seen the Korean *chaebol* as a role model to reform its own SOEs (Baek 2005). To a large degree, the attempt to build national champions or 'big business with Chinese characteristics' (Nolan and Yeung 2001) copies the combination of hierarchical corporate governance under the control of the state (or the army) with a diversification of products.

The vertically and horizontally integrated business conglomerate is the corporate structure that enabled the East Asian consumer products to conquer world markets. The conglomerates systematically expand their businesses into related business sectors through linkages, synergy effects, and their ability to mobilize financial resources. Through this strategy, they create a large internal 'market' that guarantees stable sales and reliable business relationships. They also expand this conglomerate model to formally independent suppliers that are not part of the conglomerate but have exclusive contracts with companies within the conglomerate. The 'mothership' operates in a convoy of dependent SMEs and small suppliers, a structure that extends the conglomerate principle beyond the formal corporate structure. Moreover, East Asian conglomerates expand not just into related business fields to create synergy effects but also into unrelated business fields, because they are able to mobilize large sums of capital internally for investment. For example, the Korean *chaebol* Samsung builds mobile phones, semiconductors, as well as ships, and is active in construction, apparel, financial services, and amusement parks. The Japanese Mitsui group is active in banking, insurance, steel, chemicals, and logistics. In China, conglomerates are less diversified, because state control was much tighter, but since the 2010s state-owned companies such as Sinochem have increasingly been branching out from their core business (in the case of Sinochem, this is the chemical industry) particularly into finance and real estate.

Because of the integrated structure, East Asian conglomerates have the ability to adapt quickly to new products and achieve a competitive edge through process innovation. They developed the ability to imitate products quickly and to produce them more cheaply and at a quality that was competitive with the leaders in the field. This strategy of 'industrialization through learning' (Amsden 1989, 1991) was extremely successful and built the foundation for the region becoming the factory of the world. The weakness of the East Asian conglomerates is their hierarchical and bureaucratic structure, which prevents the sort of radical innovations seen in agile US companies. Their large size and diversification also prevent the sort of deeper specialization demonstrated by European niche players.

This specific business model needs a specific system of corporate governance that can hold the diversified conglomerates together and tolerate lower profit rates owing to cross-subsidizing of weaker companies within the conglomerate. The main goal of East Asian conglomerates is to achieve not profits but economic dominance by increasing market share (Dore 2000). In fact, profit rates in East Asia are generally far below those in the US and Europe. The appropriate governance structure is the dominance of majority shareholders and personal networks in management that thrives on the expansion of economic power and not profit or shareholder value. Personal networks are formed, usually through educational background, but often also through family ownership, with a founding father who is eager to expand businesses for the benefit of his children running different business within his empire. Indeed, the boundary between (extended) family and network is much more blurred in East Asia than in the West, while the gap between those inside and outside the network is much bigger. This is why the East Asian growth model has often been referred to as 'crony capitalism' (Fukuyama 1998). In East Asian companies, management backed by majority shareholders are relatively free from the pressure of shareholder value and can thus reinvest a much higher share of their profits. The conglomerates are also far less vulnerable to bank scrutiny than their European peers, as we shall see. The only institution that the conglomerates have to fear is the state with its power to pass and enforce laws. That is why, as we shall see, the conglomerates have extended their personal networks into the realms of politics and bureaucracy.

Admittedly, there are differences between the business conglomerates in East Asia. When it comes to corporate control, family links play a much greater role in Korea than in Japan and China. Chinese conglomerates are unique, because they are often partly or even completely state owned. Still they are similar, in the sense that they all have strong controlling shareholders and are vertically and horizontally integrated, combining businesses from very diverse sectors. In Whitley's (1992, 2007) academic terminology, East Asian business systems can be characterized by a high levels of ownership integration and a high level of coordination integration. Another difference of the Japanese-type conglomerate is related to the crucial link between the business sector and the financial market. In Japan, businesses within a conglomerate are usually grouped around a bank, while Korean *chaebol* are forbidden to own large shares in banks.

The structural power of conglomerates is immense, as they dominate not just one market but many different markets within the domestic economy.

This means that they are practically too big to fail by definition. Governments cannot let conglomerates go bankrupt, because they are either the only company in the sector or bankruptcy would create a monopoly. At the same time, the government is reluctant to break the conglomerates up, because that would undermine their export competitiveness and status as national champions. Consequently, export-oriented business conglomerates are the dominant business faction and form a formidable export lobby that has considerable influence on how policies and domestic institutions are shaped. This export lobby is not a unified actor in the sense of European peak-level business associations, but is dominated by a small number of competing business conglomerates. These conglomerates are run by families or highly connected groups of people who have extended their networks into the political parties, the government, and the whole bureaucracy. Unlike in the US, where lobbying is indirectly done via political donations, the influence in East Asia is very direct via personal networks within government and the bureaucracy. As we shall see, this close and personalized connection creates a very stable network between business and state that is able to exclude influence from competing interests such as small domestic market-oriented businesses, foreign investors, labour unions, and consumers.

5.3.4. How did East Asia Avoid Financialization? The Subordinated Role of Finance in East Asia

How could East Asian countries avoid the pressure of global financial markets and maintain a large degree of sovereignty in designing their national economic policies? One reason has to do with the above-described structure of businesses, which limits the exposure to international financial markets. The East Asian conglomerates have the ability to raise huge amounts of capital internally for new investments and thus rely less on banks and shareholder than their competitors in the US and the EU. Established profit-making businesses allow cross-subsidizing of new loss-making businesses and allow the conglomerate to grow into new business fields. Consequently, there is less need for external financing, particularly through stock and bond issues, which explains the relatively underdeveloped stock and bond markets in East Asia. The governance structure through personalized networks further limits the influence of minority shareholders, making East Asian conglomerates notoriously difficult to penetrate by foreign investors. Should external financing be needed, East Asian conglomerates prefer to borrow money from banks. In this sense, the East Asian financial system is similar to the European bank-based model, but with the twist that the state plays a strong guiding role in the banking sector.

State Guided Bank-Based Finance

In many ways, the role of finance in East Asia is the opposite of finance-led countries like the US. In East Asia, banks are seen as quasi-state institutions, even when they are formally in private hands. While in finance-led countries finance is the dominant business sector and the state frequently plays the role of serving the interest of the financial industry, in the East Asian development model finance has been and still is primarily a tool of the state to facilitate economic growth. The state used banks to finance its industrial sector and channel low-interest 'policy loans' into areas of the economy it wanted to develop (for the case of Korea, see Woo-Cumings 1991). Instead of using direct state funds and fiscal policies, the state facilitated private loans and occasionally bailed out companies that went bankrupt. When banks became insolvent, governments reacted with full nationalization, as was the case during the Asian financial crisis in Korea (Cho and Kalinowski 2010). By exercising control over the financial sector, the state helps to channel cheap credits from savers to businesses and forges a close relationship between banks and big business groups. This triangular partnership between state, banks, and business was very obvious in China as well as in Korea until the 1980s, when most banks were state owned.

In Korea, banks were formally privatized in the 1980s (and then again after nationalization during the Asian financial crisis), but the government maintains a tight leash on private banks. For example, the government has an important say in who becomes the CEO of private banks and has often exercised pressure in order to replace an unwanted CEO with a candidate closer to the administration (*Korea Times*, 23 April 2014). Industrial business groups are not allowed by law to exercise any ownership in banks, which prevents a close direct relationship between banks and business without the patronage of the state. In Japan, although many banks are formally part of business conglomerates, the state guides private banks in their lending and shelters them in case of crisis. In addition, state-owned banks and the postal banking system make sure that the state maintains its control over finance. Until today, the Japanese banking system remains one of the most 'centralized and controllable in the world', with an organization that is hierarchical, with the Bank of Japan at the top, which in turn is strongly tied to the Ministry of Finance (Pempel 1977: 736).

An independent financial market in the form of stock and bond markets where creditors and debtors directly interact remains weak. As we have seen in Figure 3.2, stock-market capitalization remains far below Western levels, with the exception of Japan in the post-Plaza Accord period 1985–91, during which the country witnessed massive asset bubbles. Bond markets also remain underdeveloped because of the low level of public debt that usually functions as a benchmark for private bonds (Eichengreen and Luengnaruemitchai 2004). Financial markets are dominated by the big business conglomerates, because they are the only actors that are seen as credible. For example, in Korea, the Samsung conglomerate represent almost one-quarter of the main Korean stock index KOSPI (*Yonhap News*, 24 December 2014). Because of the dominance of the founding families within the conglomerates, the expansion of businesses and the cross-financing of weaker companies in the same conglomerate have a clear priority over maximizing profit and shareholder value. This makes investments in stock markets highly risky and speculative. The speculative character is reflected by the much higher volatility of East Asian stock markets compared to markets in the West (Kittiakarasakun and Tse 2011). The specific corporate structure that allowed the successful economic rise of East Asian conglomerates is an obstacle to the development of financial markets in the region and prevented a financialization comparable to that in the US or other finance-led countries.

Domestic Savings and Investment-Driven Growth

The rapid development with high investment rates despite relatively closed and weakly developed financial markets was possible because East Asian countries have high savings rates. These high saving rates can be explained by a low consumption level and the weak welfare state forcing individuals to save for education, healthcare, and retirement. The flip side of the high savings rate is that the low level of domestic consumption perpetuates the dependence on exports. From a demand-side perspective, domestic savings are abstained consumption and thus an obvious reason for export orientation and current-account surpluses. The low levels of domestic consumption are relatively easy to understand in the case of China, which, despite its economic rise, remains a developing country with substantial poverty. With a per capita income of $8,100 in 2016, almost one-third of its population still lives below the poverty line, measured as a daily income of less than a purchasing power parity (PPP) of $2 (World Bank 2019). However, even in the East Asian OECD countries of Korea and Japan, at the end of the 2000s, poor households with incomes of less than 60 per cent of the mean (and thus limited ability to consume) accounted for 20.6 per cent and 21.7 per cent of the population, respectively, compared to the OECD average of 17.7 per cent. Not only is the number of low-income households far above the OECD average, but the depth of poverty, which is the gap between the mean income of poor households and the poverty threshold, exceeded the OECD average of 27.4 per cent in Korea (36.8 per cent) and in Japan (34.4 per cent). The large low-income sector is the logical consequence of the dualistic business system just described, which consists of export-oriented national champions as well as low productivity and low-wage domestic-oriented companies. It is also the result of the weakness of organized labour in East Asia, as we shall see.

Capital Controls and Limited Financial Flows

Initially, the large domestic savings exclusively fuelled domestic investment rates in the region that were much higher than in the EU and the US (Figure 5.3). These high rates can be explained only partially by the lower level of development and thus the higher need for investment in the region. Even Japan, one of the richest country with a very low economic growth rate, invests a larger share of its GDP than the EU and the US. Domestic investment rates were also higher, because East Asian countries kept their financial markets closed and strictly limited in and outflow of capital by outright capital controls and strict approval rules. In the initial phase of development, in Japan until the 1970s, Korea until the 1980s, and China until the 1990s, foreign

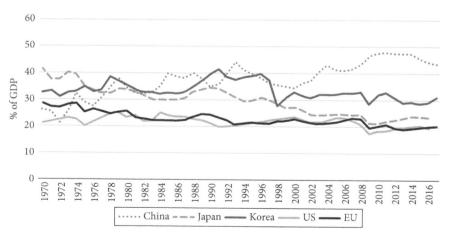

Figure 5.3. Gross capital formation in China, Korea, Japan, the EU, and the US (% of GDP)

Source: World Bank, World Development Indicators, https://databank.worldbank.org

investments played only a small role and foreign credits were channelled through state-controlled banks into the domestic market. Strict direct capital controls were liberalized gradually, but have been largely replaced by informal limits, such as the corporate structure and the oligopolistic structure of the market. East Asian countries still remain less liberalized, as the IMF financial reform index indicates (see Figure 2.3).

Four distinct characteristics stand out when it comes to limited financial liberalization in East Asia. First, capital outflow was liberalized faster than inflow. Originally, the outflow of capital was even more heavily restricted, and for some time Korea even punished illegal capital exports of more than 1 million US dollars with the death penalty (Amsden 1989: 17). This changed with increasing accumulation of capital and the need for companies in the region to penetrate new markets, offshore production, and the ability to acquire companies abroad. It might seem strange that East Asia has been liberalizing the outflow of capital more quickly, given that the literature on the 'competition state' (Hirsch 1995; Cerny 1997) suggests that in the era of globalization there is an increasing competition to attract global capital and thus capital inflows. East Asian countries, on the contrary, try to limit inflow of capital and support 'their' companies in investing abroad and thus exporting capital (for Japan, see Solis 2003; for Korea, see Kalinowski and Cho 2009). The contemporary developmental state is not limited to support industries at home but helps domestic companies to enter foreign markets—for example, by providing credit guarantees for foreign investments and using official development assistant projects as door openers (Kalinowski 2013a, 2015b). The preference for capital outflow can be explained structurally by the strong state–business alliance, together with sustained export surpluses that have to be recycled internationally.

Second, short-term inflow of capital was liberalized before long-term inflow of capital. As already mentioned in the context of the Asian financial crisis, East Asian countries liberalized short-term inflows of capital more quickly than long-term inflow. This sequencing made East Asia more vulnerable to short-term financial flows, but it protected the existing structure of corporate governance and control. Unlike long-term investors, short-term capital flows come without any managerial ambitions and were thus seen as less problematic from the perspective of the conglomerates.

Third, informal limits on capital inflow and outflow remain substantial, which is particularly true for Japan and more recently Korea, which have formally opened their capital accounts but remain difficult to penetrate by foreign capital. Both countries have relatively low levels of inward FDI at well below 1 per cent of GDP compared with an OECD average of 2 per cent (Alexander 2008: 3). Despite formally open markets, even in Japan 'foreign firms may find it difficult to gain access to the established networks and alliances that dominate such economies, at least initially' (Whitley 2007: 265). Cross-shareholding mechanisms and personal networks make it difficult for foreign investors to control an East Asian company, even if they are formally the largest shareholders. For example, the US hedge fund Cerberus failed in 2013 to increase the transparency of the management of the Japanese train company Seibu, despite being a major shareholder with a share of 35 per cent (*Frankfurter Allgemeine Zeitung*, 20 June 2013). In many ways, 'Japan Inc.', the strong connections between stakeholders, still trumps anonymous market transactions. The institutional regime of Japan itself creates a self-protection mechanism against foreign capital even without formal rules and laws. In Korea, many FDI projects have failed owing to legal and cultural barriers and the inability of foreign investors to adapt to the Korean market. Walmart, for example, was not able to adapt to Korean consumer habits. Idiosyncratic labour regulations and the feeling that foreigners are at a disadvantage when it comes to the enforcement of contracts have further limited foreign investment (Alexander 2008). While China has attracted a large amount of FDI due to its large market size, the OECD ranks China as the country with the most restrictions on FDI in its FDI Regulatory Restrictiveness Index (OECD 2013).

Fourth, the commitment to open capital accounts remains weak and tactical. Indeed, East Asian countries do not hesitate to consider or even implement new capital controls when they fear that their ability to develop sovereign economic and currency policies is undermined. After the Asian financial crisis, some Japanese policymakers started a debate in favour of implementing capital controls, but they failed to gain any international support (Grimes 2009: 66). With the global financial crisis, this changed, as they have gained some support from academics in the IMF, and, as we have seen in Chapter 2, especially Table 2.1, the recent G20 documents indicate a substantial softening of the position of the free capital account liberalization camp.

Owing to the concerns about global financial volatility and the lack of regulation and stability of domestic financial markets and banks, East Asian countries have little interest in completely open capital accounts and the free in- and outflow of money. Internally, these preferences can be interpreted as the legacy of a development model based on national industrial development that created an institutional regime that is compatible with limited capital flows. East Asian countries do not need massive amounts of capital flows, because they have high savings rates and current-account surpluses that are sufficient to finance domestic and foreign investment. This corresponds with business strategies that limit offshoring of production and particularly the reimport of foreign-produced products. Externally, the limited flow of capital complements the priority on stable exchange rates and East Asia's role as an international creditor.

5.3.5. International Creditors and the Dilemma of International Reserves

Sustained current-account surpluses have made East Asian countries substantial international investors and creditors. As we have seen, East Asian companies have been investing abroad, and particularly within the East Asian regions, to penetrate markets and take advantage of low labour costs. East Asian banks have also become major international creditors. For example, Japanese banks accounted for about 13.4 per cent of all external lending in 2013, more than UK banks with 13.1 per cent, US banks with 11.5 per cent, and German banks with 11 per cent (own calculations, based on BIS 2013: A60). Japanese banks have large net external assets, but, unlike their US and UK counterparts, they have remained largely domestic players with a weak international presence. Banks in East Asia are capital exporters, providing a service for domestic savers and companies, but they do not offer global services like their US and UK peers. East Asian banks export capital but not financial services like their Western counterparts.

The role of East Asia as an international creditor differs from the US and Europe because large parts of this foreign investment is held by central banks in the form of foreign-currency reserves. This corresponds with the experience of the Asian financial crisis and the need to insure volatile domestic financial markets against crisis as well as the preference for stable and managed exchange rates. East Asian countries are now the biggest holders of international reserves, as we have seen in Figure 5.1. Holding foreign-currency reserves is equivalent to purchasing insurance against financial crises and is the consequence of the interpretation of the Asian financial crisis as being caused by the external shocks of volatile global financial markets. Instead of aiming to achieve stability primarily by financial regulation, as in the US, or by taxing international financial transactions, governments in the region opted for a public insurance strategy by channelling excessive domestic savings into foreign-currency reserves. Those were invested mainly in US treasuries, which led to a massive flow of capital from East Asia to North America, fuelling asset bubbles there. Unfortunately for the East Asian region, these US government bonds earn very little interest, and further lock East Asian countries into a strategy of undervaluing their currencies, because an appreciation against the US dollar would mean a loss of value of foreign reserves. This also makes East Asian governments far less enthusiastic than Europeans to reform the global monetary system and reduce the dependence on the dollar. While Europe has at least partly freed itself from the dollar, East Asia remains completely locked into the dollar universe.

For East Asian countries, foreign reserves individually increase their protection against global financial instability, but globally these reserves add to the volatility of financial markets by interacting with the US-style finance-led growth model. As we have seen in Chapter 3, the financial merry-go-round administered in financial centres like the US have the knock-on effect that some of the Asian currency reserves are recycled globally as portfolio investment and credits in the region. Some of these funds eventually come back to the East Asian region. Given the difficulty that foreign investors have accessing East Asian markets, because of the dominance of main shareholders and personal networks, they prefer short-term investments over long-term FDI. These short-term investments not only come with much higher returns than currency reserves, but are also highly volatile, and can be withdrawn from the region at short notice. In effect, the East Asian unilateral self-help strategy is not just very costly, but indirectly also increases financial volatility in the region. We will return to these issues of international dependence in the concluding chapter.

5.3.6. Why No Regional Solution? East Asian Division of Labour and the Problems of Regional Cooperation

Why did East Asian countries not follow a European-style regional solution to the challenges of globalization or rather why have attempts in this direction failed so far? While strong nationalism and the legacy of war and colonialism are part of the explanation, the structure of the political economy in the region is the main reason why regional cooperation is lacking. The export-oriented model and the regional division of labour within East Asia is structured such that it is an obstacle to regional cooperation in three ways. Despite a large amount of regional trade in East Asia, there is a lack of a real regional market, as countries in the region compete to export to markets outside the region. The failure to create a single market and the general lack of regional cooperation also have to do with the preference for bilateral cooperation and the strong ties of many countries in the region with the US, but there are also deeper structural reasons, which are the result of the way economic exchange in the region is conducted. The lack of regional cooperation does not mean that trade and economic regionalization (as opposed to political regionalism) in East Asia is weak. Economically, East Asia is a relatively integrated region, with 37 per cent of the total trade in the ASEAN+3 being intra-regional, which is lower than within the EU and NAFTA, but higher than in any other world region (OECD 2016: graph 2.1). Trade between East Asian countries remains highly regulated and dominated by intermediate goods from regional production networks. Economic integration differs substantially from Europe, where economic integration is largely horizontal, while East Asia is vertically integrated (Ando 2006). Vertical integration means that the production networks in East Asia are created by offshoring labour-intensive production from companies in Japan, and since the 1990s also Korea, to China and Southeast Asia (Fukao et al. 2003; Ando and Kimura 2005). The goal is to reduce production costs in order to compete more successfully with other companies in the region for markets outside East Asia. East Asian companies are less likely to transfer their top-notch technology than their Western peers and have less interest in selling in the local market, although the latter trend is slowly changing, because of the massive growth of the Chinese market for consumer goods.

The difference between regional trade within Europe and East Asia is that in Europe exports from countries like Germany depend on markets within a European single market and are to a large degree accounted for in a single currency, while such regional patterns have not emerged in East Asia. East Asian countries see their neighbours, not primarily as a market for their products, but as competitors in markets outside the region, which corresponds with an ideology of nationalism and national competitiveness. One practical consequence is that governments use national economic policies, including exchange-rate management, to gain advantages over their regional competitors. Tariffs and particularly non-tariff barriers are employed to block competition, particularly from the region. This is the reason why it is possible to find many German cars in Japan, China, and Korea, but very few Japanese cars in Korea or Korean cars in Japan.

The focus on markets outside the region can also be seen by looking at the negotiation of bilateral trade agreements. All three East Asian countries have formed a substantial number of bilateral trade agreements with countries outside the region, but negotiations for a free trade area between them have stalled or they exclude large parts of bilateral trade that compete with each other. The lack of a free trade area, let alone a single market, further strengthens the focus on competition in East Asia for export markets outside the region and undermines regional cooperation. For example, regional monetary cooperation similar to the EMS in Europe would create few benefits for exporters who depend on markets outside the region. On the other hand, a competitive devaluation against an East Asian competitor would give domestic companies an edge over competitors in the region. This trend is reinforced by the focus of East Asia on price-sensitive mass products that compete against each other through the price mechanism, compared to the European focus on less-price-sensitive high-quality specialized goods and artisan products sheltered from competition because of their brand value (see Chapter 4). Much more than the stability of the currency, which is the main priority in Europe, the competiveness of currencies matters most for East Asian countries.

Consequently, East Asian regionalization is largely an extension of national development policies in which Japanese, Korean, and Chinese companies try to gain advantages in competition with their regional competitors without substantially reducing the reliance on export markets outside the region. In fact, Japan and Korea run current-account deficits with countries like China, which further increases the need for China to run surpluses with the US and Europe.

5.3.7. East Asia's Position in the International Division of Labour

The first essential element of the political economy of the export-led model of capitalism is the structural power of export-oriented big business conglomerates. In the international division of labour, East Asia is the factory of the world, focusing on the export of large quantities of consumer goods such as IT products and semiconductors as well as transport equipment from cars and trucks to giant container ships. Because of the large volume of non-specialized products, competition in export markets is done primarily by undercutting prices. This dominance creates a preference for stable and, more importantly, competitive exchange rates. This preference is not reduced by the increasing regional economic exchange, because, unlike in Europe, this regionalization is hierarchical in order to exploit lower labour costs in other countries, but it does not extend the regional market nor create a single market. Consequently, East Asian export-oriented businesses largely compete with each other for exports to markets outside the region and enlist their governments in supporting them in this competition.

This East Asian growth model is embedded in a distinct variety of capitalism with its own path dependence. As mentioned before, it is not an underdeveloped version of US style or European capitalism. It is a third distinct model, which is evolving but not converging with the other models of capitalism. In the following section, we will see that politically this system is characterized by a close alliance between export-oriented business conglomerates and the state. The financial sector offers little resistance to this policy, as it remains subordinated to the state. Organized labour and consumers are even more marginalized and have had little success in challenging the close business–state alliance that dominates capitalism in East Asia.

5.4. Authoritarian Corporatism and the Political Economy of State-Led Capitalism

As we have seen, export-orientation in East Asia is strongly interwoven with the state's active role in pursuing a nationalist neo-mercantilist growth model. State-led and export-oriented development has been the East Asian answer to the challenges of globalization since the 1970s. On the economic side, this strategy was achieved by the economic and corporate structure already described. This section looks at the political economic foundation that enabled and facilitated such a growth model. So far, it seems that the East Asian growth model is simply dominated by the almighty export-oriented business conglomerates. This would, however, underestimate the strong state autonomy that is characteristic of the East Asian model of capitalism. The business conglomerates in East Asia did not emerge spontaneously through a market process but were created and nurtured by a relatively autonomous developmental state 'governing the market' (Wade 2004). Unlike market-oriented or neo-corporatist models of capitalism, where the state plays a regulatory or facilitating role, the East Asian state is the driving force at the centre of a web of personalized societal relations. One relationship dominates above all others. The development partnership between big business and the state has been the dynamic at the centre of the East Asian model. Unlike the neoliberal regulatory state focusing on providing a framework for the market and on macroeconomic governance, it teamed up directly with businesses to achieve economic growth and international competiteness. Unlike in neo-corporatist states, it went about this, not with a tripartite deliberation but by excluding organized labour. This state–business alliance proved to be very stable and prevented the emergence of liberal or more social-democratic versions of governance in East Asia. The legacy of this authoritarian corporatism in East Asia has had strong repercussions for the preferences of East Asia in international economic relations, and most importantly the notion that international institutions constitute a limitation to national sovereignty and the preference for unilateral national self-help solutions. It is thus not surprising that East Asian countries have been carefully guarding the sovereignty of their national economic policies at the expense of capital-account liberalization.

5.4.1. Centralized State Structure and State Autonomy

As already described, in East Asia international institutions are seen not as an extension of the domestic institutional system but as imposed from the outside. This has to do, not just with the weak representation of East Asian countries in international organizations, but also with the internal structure of East Asian states. Unlike the federal state structure of the US and the multilevel governance in the EU, Japan, Korea, and China have a centralized political system with a central government that has a substantial amount of control over national economic policies. Decisions tend to be made in a top-down way from the president's (or prime minister's) office and the central planning agency or ministry down the line to the ministries and implementation agencies. The presidential system in Korea is the most centralized of the three, but Japan and China are also largely governed from the capital. While there is room for regional experiments in China, as we can see in the special economic zones from Hainan to Shanghai, the Communist Party (CP) provides a parallel and highly centralized quasi-state structure that prevents too much regional divergence. The centralized top-down state structure means that Asian governments have much more control over all aspects of economic policies compared to the US or the EU. For example, the lack of veto players has allowed East Asian countries rapidly to implement large fiscal stimulus packages and new financial regulations without a long political debate. On the other hand, this lack of deliberation often has the effect that the implementation process is hampered by mock compliance, corruption, and sabotage at lower government levels.

Industrial policies were initially planned by central agencies like the MITI in Japan (Johnson 1982), the EPB in Korea (Choi 1987), and the State Planning Commission in China. Since the beginning of liberalization in the 1970s in

Japan, the 1980s in Korea, and the 1990s in China, the power of central planning agencies has gradually been weakened and power moved to the president's or prime minister's offices as well as lead ministries like the finance ministry. Unlike the US Fed and the ECB, East Asian central banks are either not independent, as in China, or only formally independent, as in Korea and Japan. Their role has been generally to support the economic policies of the government, particularly by keeping interest rates low and exchange rates competitive. Unlike in the US and Europe, East Asian central banks are not primarily concerned with financial market stability and control of inflation; their primary objective is to support the economic policies of the government. This means that most state and state-controlled institutions are focused on the objective of development and economic growth. For example, the purpose of financial regulation in East Asia is not primarily to ensure the stability of the market or to limit the exposure of taxpayers to risks during a financial crisis, but to ensure that there is enough capital to support the growth objectives of the government.

State Autonomy and Stability

States in East Asia are not just highly centralized; they are also characterized by strong stability and autonomy. Political stability can take different forms, but here it refers to the almost unshaken dominance of a certain political elite that is organized by the CP in China and by the conservative parties in Japan and Korea. In China's one-party dictatorship the CP has ruled without interruption since 1949, and stability and gradual changes have become the doctrine since the traumatic experience of the Cultural Revolution in the 1970s. More surprisingly, even in Japan and Korea one party dominates the political landscape, despite the existence of free and fair elections. Japan in particular is effectively a one-party democracy, where the conservative Liberal Democratic Party has governed with only two small interruption in 1993–4 and 2009–12. In Korea, the dominance of the Conservative Party was recently weakened when its continuous rule in different incarnations since 1945 was interrupted by ten years of rule by the Democratic Party from 1998 to 2008. This interruption was possible due to the shock of the Asian financial crisis in 1997. Similar to the Japanese case, however, the more centrist Democratic Party in Korea has failed to establish itself as a serious alternative, and, when the Conservative Party regained power in 2008, it was quickly able to reconsolidate its dominance. It remains to be seen if the impeachment of conservative President Park in 2017 and the subsequent election of the candidate of the oppositional party candidate Moon Jae-in will be able to change the political power dynamics in Korea. So far, it seems that President Moon has had little success in challenging the established network between big business, conservative political elite, and bureaucracy

State autonomy refers to the insulation of the state from societal interest groups. It is one of the key feature of the East Asian developmental state that distinguishes East Asia from less successful 'predatory' states (Evans 1995). State autonomy has at least three elements: a competent bureaucracy, a top-down implementation of policies, and a relative independence of decision-making from societal interests—particularly organized labour but also to some degree the profit interests of businesses. First, East Asia has a long tradition of statehood going back about 4,000 years to the Chinese Xia dynasty in China. In fact, state structures emerged much earlier in East Asia compared to any other regions, because the cultivation of rice as the staple in East Asia requires an infrastructure of irrigation that is difficult to maintain by individual farmers. Wittfogel (1957) referred to this state tradition as 'hydraulic empires'. This has created a long state tradition that early on developed a sophisticated bureaucratic structure, including civil-servant entrance exams that ensured that the best-qualified students would enter public service.

Second, this long tradition of a strong state facilitated a centralized top-down state structure that was rationalized by a Confucian ideology. In this Confucian view, hierarchical structures are seen as the ideal form of organization of the state and society as a whole. It is not private initiative or civil-society engagement that is seen as the driving force of development, but rather the initiative of competent state leaders. The Confucian rationalization of the benign leader and his teaching of good government added to the attractiveness of civil services and the meritocratic selection of bureaucrats.

Third, state autonomy is possible because of a weakness of civil-society groups that could partly or completely capture the state. A strong state predated the emergence of strong societal and economic interest groups. While in Europe and the US the rising capitalist class gave birth to the modern state, in East Asia it was the other way round. It was the developmental state that created and nurtured a national capitalist class. While big business groups have an immense structural economic power, being too big to fail for the economy, they are not a united interest group. Unlike the European peak-level business associations formulating a coherent political pro-business agenda, businesses in East Asia are competing against each other to receive favours over their competitors from the government. Unlike in Europe, state auton-omy is thus primarily not the result of a compromise between business and labour but the result of the standoff between different business groups, which the government can play off against each other.

5.4.2. State–Business Relations and Embedded Autonomy in East Asia

Initially the study of East Asian developmental states highlighted their state autonomy. With the emergence of modern capitalism in East Asia, the government created a national capitalist class as a partner for development. Peter Evans (1995) highlighted that it was the combination of relative state autonomy and strong state–business links that distinguished Asian states from socialist planned economies and less successful cases of capitalist developmental states in Latin America and Africa. Unlike socialist countries or countries that were inspired by the initial economic success of socialist economic planning in the Soviet Union, Japan and Korea left most of the economy to private businesses. Unlike in the West, it was the state that created the capitalist class in East Asia. This meant that the state was the senior partner in the relationship with big businesses. Originally, this 'embedded autonomy' (Evans 1995) ensured that the state could maintain an active role without being captured by societal interests. While government and business worked closely together in developing and implementing economic plans, the government always remained in control. This allowed the government to achieve industrialization and a focus on macroeconomic growth, because it facilitated the needs of business in general without being influenced by the profit interests of specific businesses. The state supported the rise of the business conglomerates and at the same time ensured that they used their profits not to pay out dividends but to reinvest. This is the reason why profit rates in East Asia have always been much lower than in Western countries, as we have already seen.

Strong networks between state and business are central characteristics of East Asian capitalism. Unlike regulatory states that govern the economy through abstract regulations, and European corporatism that includes tripartite corporatist negotiations, East Asian state-led capitalism is based on strong direct personal networks. Most important is the link between state and industry, while the financial sector played only a supporting role to achieve industrial growth. For example, monetary and fiscal policies had the goal of supporting the industrialization strategy and, thus, had a generally expansionary tendency until the 1980s. This East Asian type of 'organized capitalism'

(Vogel 2003) or 'non-liberal capitalism' (Streeck and Yamamura 2001) is similar to its European counterpart in the sense that it is characterized not by the dominance of financial markets but by the close connection between industrial capital, state, and finance. The difference is that the state in East Asia took a leading role and acted not just as a facilitator of societal relations but as the initiator.

The embeddedness of state autonomy is important to understand, because it hints at the concept of the state as a dynamic political economic equilibrium that changes with the relative strength of actors. In Europe and the US, state autonomy is embedded in the balance between different factions of capital, finance, and labour; in East Asia the alliance between state and big business clearly dominates.

The state–business networks have been very stable, and they have existed under different governments, including governments from the non-dominant opposition parties. Even in Korea, with an extended period of ten years of non-conservative governments (1998–2008), the links between bureaucracy and business remain strong. This has to some degree to do with the weakness of SMEs in East Asia, as we have seen, which have failed to build powerful employers' associations like the ones in Germany. More importantly, however, the state is in danger of being captured by big business because labour unions as natural rivals are weak and fail to balance the power of the big business conglomerates.

5.4.3. Authoritarian Rule in East Asia and the Exclusion of Labour

In many ways, the East Asian developmental states are much more similar to the authoritarian European states in the nineteenth and early twentieth centuries and particularly to Germany than to late developers outside East Asia. This 'European lineage' (Menzel 1985) goes back to the fascination of the Japanese ruling class with German nation building and the authoritarian capitalism under the King of Prussia and later the Kaiser in the second half of the nineteenth century. Since the end of the nineteenth century, Japanese colonialism has also contributed to the establishment of modern bureaucracies with dictatorial political power in the East Asia region. Unlike many other dictatorships in the developing world, East Asian authoritarian developmental state had a competent bureaucracy that allied with business interests. The result was what Kohli (2004: 122) calls a 'cohesive–capitalist' state with 'overtones of fascism'. In South Korea, the developmental state was built largely during the brutal Japanese colonial occupation, and even after independence—particularly during the reign of General Park Chung Hee, who had served as an officer in the Japanese colonial army—Japan clearly remained the model for Korean development (Kohli 1994).

As we have seen in Chapter 4, in Europe the end of the Second World War brought fundamental structural changes that cumulated in the cultural revolution of 1968 and the 'fundamental liberalization' (Habermas, in *Frankfurter Rundschau*, 11 March 1988) since then. In Germany after the Second World War, state control was replaced or at least supplemented with a coordinated market approach based on cooperation between societal groups and the state, because of a strong labour movement and the terrifying experience of the totalitarian Nazi state. In East Asia, on the other hand, state control over the economy was maintained, and nationalist mobilization continued after the Second World War and the Korean War, which ended in 1953. Governments in East Asia used the nationalist mobilization that had been achieved during the war for economic purposes when it was over. They also used mechanisms of wartime economic planning to implement development plans.

This authoritarian developmental state was able to evolve only because organized labour in East Asia is weak and failed to demand the same kind of participation seen in the neo-corporatist coordinated or social-democratic varieties of capitalism in Europe. Unlike in Europe, where a neo-corporatist balance between capital and labour creates some democratic autonomy for the state (albeit with a business-friendly bias), there is no such balancing power in East Asia. China does not even have (legal) independent labour unions, and in Korea and Japan labour unions are organized at the company level and are strong only within certain big companies, where they have been very successful in forcing employers to increase wages. In general, the share of employees covered by collective bargaining arrangements remains very low (see Figure 4.2). The situation is worse when it comes to a broader political power; there was very little success in creating an employee-friendly political alternative that would challenge the dominant state–business alliance. Consequently, classic labour parties that function as a political arm of labour unions do not play an important role in the political sphere.

The East Asian 'corporatism without labor' (Pempel and Tsunekawa 1979), or, in its Chinese variant, socialism without labour, reflects the societal balance of power. The East Asian form of corporatism differs from European forms in its authoritarian suppression of the interests of employees and the exclusion of organized labour from any meaningful participation in political decisions.

This exclusion of labour allowed a specific supply-side-oriented growth regime that focuses on investments and exports while neglecting domestic consumption and welfare policies. As we have seen in Section 5.2.8, the supply-side bias of fiscal stimulus packages in East Asia has been a very recent example of this path dependency still dominating policy decisions. The weakness of labour in the societal relationship is the structural foundation of export surpluses and the focus of government policies on the international competiveness of businesses. Essentially the export orientation and the East Asian contribution to global imbalances have their root causes in the weakness of labour, which is unable to ensure that wages and so consumption keep pace with productivity increases. The tendency to react to external shock with state activism and export orientation is thus partly a result of the weakness of labour. A related aspect is the weakness of the welfare state.

5.4.4. The Weak Welfare State and the Compensating 'Neo-Developmental' State

The weakness of labour has also had an important impact on the transformation of the state under pressure from economic globalization. Since the 1980s in Japan and since the 1990s in the rest of East Asia, neoliberals and progressives alike have criticized the authoritarian developmental state as an obstacle to further economic development and democratization. Consequently, East Asian governments started a slow process of market-oriented reforms and particularly financial liberalization, which was accelerated by external pressure, particularly from the IMF, during the Asian financial crisis. From the 1990s, the model for East Asian governments has been US-style market capitalism, but, instead of a convergence of capitalisms, the reforms have led to a 'hybridization' of both systems (Yamamura and Streeck 2003) that is primarily shaped by domestic institutions (Vogel 2006). While neoliberal reforms were implemented, they were implemented in a specific East Asian way that did not lead to a convergence with the US liberal-market model.

At the same time, East Asian countries did not converge with a more welfare-state-oriented European model as well. Traditionally, East Asian countries had very weak welfare states. Initially, they were able to maintain a high level of social equality owing to their high growth and employment rates as well as the ability of big business conglomerates to lure their highly skilled workers with attractive bonuses and social benefits. In the 1990s, the World Bank (1993) hailed the essence of the East Asian development model as 'growth with equity'. Following the path dependency of the East Asian developmental state, governments prefer to support companies directly instead of increasing welfare spending. This is particularly true during times of economic crisis. Instead of creating a social-security system, the state focused on making sure that businesses were growing and investing in order to create new jobs. The 'development bargain' of low taxes and a weak welfare state remains a hegemonic concept in many Asian societies (for Korea, see Kim 2013). Citizens identify the state not as being a provider of economic freedom, like in the US, or of welfare, like in Europe, but as being a provider of economic growth from which they can profit as employees or shopkeepers. Their identity is that of a 'developmental citizenship' (Chang 2012). This mindset creates an extraordinarily strong resistance against rising taxes, which is at least as strong as in the liberal US, which partly explains the massive increase of government debt in Japan and to a lesser degree in Korea and China.

There is a significant negative correlation between the size of the welfare system and fiscal stimulus packages implemented in 2008–10 (Kalinowski 2013a: 20). The aggressive increase of government spending in the case of the crisis in East Asia can—as in the US—be explained by a weak welfare state. Countries with weak welfare states lack automatic stabilizers in the event of an economic crisis and thus need to intervene more strongly. East Asian countries strongly support fiscal expansion and they have a strong capacity to mobilize government funds in the short run. Besides official government budgets, state-owned companies and banks play an important role in mobilizing funds to stimulate the economy. At the same time, their capacity to increase tax revenues is quite limited. The lack of an ability to establish a more comprehensive welfare state corresponds with and aggravates the need for high saving rates, which represses consumption and explains why East Asia has become a major exporter of capital. This East Asian 'savings glut' has often been cited as a major contributing factor to the global economic imbalances (Bernanke 2005).

5.4.5. The Ideology of Nationalism and National Competiveness

Unlike the visions of a liberal global world order in the US or at least the construction of regional institutions within Europe, nationalism remains the dominant ideology in East Asia. In most Western discourses, global or regional markets are conceptualized as a neutral arena of exchange and a level playing field, while international institutions are shaped through cooperation. The East

Asian view on international markets is much more pessimistic and dominated by a 'realist' power-oriented perspective. From the East Asian perspective, the international arena is a place of ruthless competition in which the West has the advantage and international institutions are biased in its favour. As rising nations, East Asian countries see themselves as fighting an uphill battle in which they can rely only on their national strengths. Katzenstein (1996) has called this the 'Hobbesian' world view, in which each country is the other countries' wolf, as opposed to the Kantian vision of perpetual peace. This has created a combination of nationalism and focus on competiveness that can be found in many different aspects of East Asia, from international cooperation and economic competitiveness to the obsession with elite schools and international rankings in all areas.

This nation state-centred worldview affects how East Asian countries deal with global challenges and how they approach international cooperation. East Asian countries interpret crises as outside shocks to be countered by rallying all national stakeholders and resources to 'save and revitalize the nation'. In all East Asian countries, nationalism is a very strong force, originating first in the anti-colonial struggle against Western imperialist powers; in China and Korea, it is also associated with the national struggle for independence from Japanese colonial rule. Since 1945, this nationalism has primarily taken the form of economic nationalism, focused on national competitiveness, which is an obsession in all three countries. In China, the CP is a powerful instrument of social mobilization, and, unlike in European socialist parties, nationalism has been the most important element of the ideological toolbox of the CP from the beginning (North Korea is an even more extreme example of the combination of nationalism and elements of socialism).

In Japan and Korea, economic nationalism has taken more subtle forms. Government-initiated national mobilization campaigns are a distinct feature of East Asian capitalism. They are not just popular in China but have also been successfully used by the Korean government—for example, during the 'gold collection campaign' to refill currency reserves during the Asian financial crisis (Cho 2008) or by mobilizing helpers during the oil spill on the Korean east coast in 2007 (Park 2008). Nationalism was also used to support domestic savings that could be mobilized for the investments-oriented growth strategy. The high-investment and export-oriented model was complemented by campaigns that nurtured a culture of thrift and saving, and praises savers as patriotic and consumption as a waste of national resources (Garon and Maclachlan 2006). While conspicuous consumption has become substantial more recently, as witnessed by the large volume of luxurious goods imported from Europe, in general the increase in consumption has not kept pace with the increase of production and exports. Luxurious consumption is primarily a sign of increasing social inequalities in the region and does not signal a broader transformation to a consumer society.

Gradually, the East Asian developmental state is transforming into a form of authoritarian corporatism that reacts to challenges externally with nationalist solutions and internally by forming an ever-closer alliance between state and big business. This is why East Asia is clinging to the concept of economic sovereignty, which is primarily used to encourage national companies to improve their global competiveness and market share. The close coalition between state and business means that the government sees international negotiations to a large degree from the perspective of national competitiveness. On the other hand, we have seen that the state is not simply captured by business interests. As in Europe and the US, state autonomy is increasingly undermined, but with the specific East Asian twist where export-oriented business conglomerates are the dominant capital faction. Owing to the persistent weakness of organized labour in the region, possibilities for a more balanced approach highlighting domestic consumption and welfare are so far unlikely.

5.5. The Second Image of East Asian Capitalism

In the light of the discussion of internal political economic dynamics in East Asia in this chapter, it is now possible to understand the initial assessments about the global political role of East Asia and its position on the trilemma triangle presented in the introductory chapters. The second image of the East Asian region can be summarized by four major elements.

First, from the historical investigation we have seen that East Asian countries followed a national self-help strategy optimizing their position in the international institutional system but without much contribution to changing it. This East Asian development strategy has been extremely successful in the past and has shaped the political economy in a way that it constitutes a strong path dependency of interwoven institutions and interests. The East Asian mercantilist development model, led by a relatively autonomous developmental state, puts the main focus on the sovereignty of national economic policies, which are valued much more than a greater global political role. This is why countries in the region have so far showed relatively little interest in translating their increasing economic power into international political influence. The focus on national sover-eignty and the centralized state structure in East Asia mean that countries in the region will be reluctant to agree to any limits on their ability to shape national economic policies. This position is aggravated by a pessimistic world view and a catch-up mentality of constant uphill battles against established competitors. The general view that the international system is imposed by the West and that East Asian countries are impotent on the global stage has further reinforced the preference for national self-help strategies. Experiences such as the role of the IMF during the Asian financial crisis have reinforced views that the international system is rigged to their disadvantage. Finally, for all three East Asian countries and for most coun-tries in the East Asian region, the bilateral relations with the US are more important than any international institutions (or regional relationships). Global initiatives started from East Asia mostly aim at increasing the influ-ence in the global system but (so far) not challenging Western leadership or setting up regional East Asian alternatives to global or regional institutions. As Putnam (1988: 449) suggested, countries with a strong state autonomy have a weak position in international negotiations, because their governments are less credible when they use domestic opposition against an international agreement as a bargaining chip to gain concessions.

Second, the export-oriented growth model has led to a preference for a focus on competitive exchange rates that are compatible neither with the market system preferred by the US nor with the global currency stability desired by European countries. The management of exchange rates requires a limit of financial flows that is achieved primarily through informal barriers but also includes outright capital controls. East Asian countries have been criticized for currency manipulation by the US, and in turn have criticized US-style quanti-tative easing, which led to the inflow of volatile capital into the region. At the same time, the East Asian obsession with international competitiveness and current-account surpluses contributes to the global economic imbalances that fuelled the massive inflow of capital into the US, further contributing to global economic imbalances. The focus on competitive exchange rates reflects the interest of export-oriented businesses, which are the dominant capital faction making East Asia the factory of the world. In addition, the tradition of authoritarian corporatism and the weakness of organized labour prevent a transition to a more balanced growth model. In theory, it would be easy to lower current-account imbalances by increasing wages in the region, but in reality this is difficult to achieve, given the weakness of labour and the close alliance between export-oriented businesses and the state. While East Asian countries could easily avoid currency competition in the region by cooperating closely in the field of monetary policies, this is difficult because they see each other as their biggest competitors. Consequently, even a modest regional emergency support in the form of the CMI failed.

Third, East Asian countries have been strong in their commitment for macroeconomic expansion, in particular through fiscal stimuli. This strong commitment to active fiscal policies is another element of the path-dependent transformation of the developmental state from a focus on proactive macro-economic planning to a more reactive interventionism. Amid a weak welfare state and limited automatic stabilizers, the states have little alternative but to intervene massively through fiscal expansion. Because of the strength of state–business networks and the weakness of organized labour, these interventions are 'supply-side oriented' focused investments, and they offer support for business in order to improve national competiveness. This is in contradiction to the G20 concept of macroeconomic coordination with the goal to stimulate global demand and reduce global imbalances. In the future, these investments will further increase East Asia's global competitiveness.

Fourth, governments in East Asia have little interests in global banking rules. In East Asia's bank-based financial system, banks are seen as an exten-sion of the developmental state, and they remain under the influence and tight supervision of the state. Instead of the Wall Street–Treasury–IMF complex, the East Asian export–manufacturing–state complex means that the power of the financial industry is weak, and it is seen as a tool of the state to govern the economy. This means that the East Asian countries are less exposed to inter-national volatility and risks (although not necessarily domestic risks). Thus, international rules do not have much effect on the stability of the domestic financial system, but they might limit the ability of the state to use banks for domestic industrial policies. At the same time, East Asian governments see the strengthening of regulations in the West as a chance to attract financial services to their newly established financial centres.

6

Conclusions

Second-Image IPE and the International Regulation of Finance

International economic conflicts such as 'trade wars', 'currency wars', and the repayment of debt are often seen as clashes of nations and national interests. Such a problematic realist and even 'populist' view of international relations relies on a seemingly conventional wisdom about the anarchic 'nature' of international system or the conflict of national leaders and their exchange of statements and tweets. This book has offered an alternative interpretation that international conflicts are the result of a clash of capitalisms. The main aim was to show a way of looking beneath the surface of international statements and the shadow play of events such as G20 summits. Instead, this book has referred to historical developments, structural investigation, and the uncovering of power dynamics to investigate international cooperation and conflicts.

6.1. The Argument in the Light of the Empirical Investigations

In this book, we have looked at problems of international cooperation in regulating finance and traced the origins of conflicts to the competition of different models of capitalism. More specifically, we have found in the empirical investigation that the problems of regulating international finance can be explained by competing preferences for international regulation by distinct models of capitalism. Disagreements on the international level are thus not just political conflicts or the result of short-term thinking and national egoisms, but the outcome of the way global capitalism is structured as a competition of capitalisms. Thus international conflicts cannot simply be resolved by long-term thinking, goodwill, and good international institutions; they also require an altering of the domestic dynamic of different models of capitalism.

Why International Cooperation Is Failing: How the Clash of Capitalisms Undermines the Regulation of Finance. Thomas Kalinowski, Oxford University Press (2019). © Thomas Kalinowski
DOI: 10.1093/oso/9780198714729.001.0001

In addition, as we have seen, the competition of capitalisms is not just simply a defect of global capitalism, but is also its driving force and engine. International conflicts are neither the 'natural result' of competing national egoisms nor simple collective action problems that can be overcome by visionary leaders, good institutions, and trust building. Revisiting the six theses presented in Chapter 1 in the light of the empirical evidence, we can summarize the findings in the following way.

6.1.1. Hypothesis 1: IPE as an Interdependence of Different Models of Capitalism

In this book, we have shown that different models of capitalism have reacted in distinct ways to the challenges of the collapse of the BWS, economic globalization, and unstable global financial markets. Unlike what convergence or 'Americanization' hypotheses suggest, there is no clear convergence towards one superior 'best-practice' model of capitalism. As we saw in Chapter 3, the US overcame economic stagnation through a process of financialization. Following a different path described in Chapter 4, the EU focused on regional integration by expanding and deepening the EU single market. On a third distinct path investigated in Chapter 5, East Asian capitalist countries were shown to follow a state-led model of capitalism that focused on developing competitive national industries and exports.

These three distinct pathways placed the distinct models on different sides of our 'trilemma triangle', which we have developed from a modified version of the 'impossible trinity' originally introduced by Mundell and Fleming (Mundell 1963). As we have seen from the historical accounts, all countries face trade-offs between the three macroeconomic goals of achieving currency stability, allowing free movement of capital, and accommodating macroeconomic policies. The trilemma is thus not an impossible trinity, but a triangle in which different countries decide about different trade-offs and position themselves closer to or further away from the three corners symbolizing the three goals. We have named the corners according to their priority as the 'Bretton Woods corner' (stable currencies), the neoliberal corner (free movement of capital), and the 'activist state corner' (sovereign macroeconomic policies). We showed that different models of capitalism prioritized their goals differently. For the US, the first priority is the free flow of capital and the second priority sovereign macroeconomic polies, while currency stability played little role. The US was the first country to liberalize financial markets and establish

Wall Street as the global centre for recycling capital. The EU focused on currency stability within Europe, with the free movement of capital as the second priority, while sovereign macroeconomic policies were sacrificed in the Maastricht Treaty in order to ensure the stability of the euro. Europe maintained its industrial base and revitalized growth by enlarging and deepening the European single market. Finally, in East Asia countries combined sovereign economic (development) policies with fixed exchange rates while protecting domestic financial markets from the volatility of global markets. This allowed the East Asian region to strengthen its own industrial basis and become an export powerhouse. In other words, the US stayed closest to the 'neoliberal corner' of the triangle, the EU remained attached to the 'Bretton Woods corner', while East Asia stayed near the 'activist state corner' (see Figure 1.5).

As was stated in the beginning of Chapter 1, this competition of capitalisms constitutes the dynamic and crisis of global capitalism and not a neo-imperialist convergence towards one model. The US finance-led system cannot thrive without the inflow of capital from Europe and East Asia and without the services provided in recycling global capital as the financial centre of the world. East Asian export-oriented capitalism cannot thrive without the availability of the US as the consumer of last resort and its financial services, which allow East Asian countries to reinvest surpluses without risking currency appreciations. From the macroeconomic point of view, Europe seems to be a sustainable model without major current account imbalances, and indeed the focus of the EU is much more stability oriented and inward looking. At the same time, the European complementary specialized production system is highly dependent on the export of high-tech and artisan niche products to the US and East Asia.

6.1.2. Hypothesis 2: Competing Preferences for International Regulation

We have established that this divergence of capitalisms has led to different preferences and priorities when it comes to international economic regulation. For example, the US tries to push for opening financial markets and promotes capital-account liberalization through international organization and the 'Wall Street–Treasury–IMF Complex'. The free flow of capital is essential for the US to maintain its position as a 'banker of the world' and the home base for financial transactions involving investors and creditors around the world. As we have seen since 2008, the US did favour stronger regulation of financial institutions, with a focus on capital requirements that put US banks at an advantage. East Asia, on the other hand, is trying to limit exposure to global financial markets and maintains strong formal and particularly informal rules limiting the influence of foreign capital—for example, through strong personal networks between shareholders and management as well as between state and banks. East Asian countries were thus the biggest supporters of sanctioning unilateral capital controls within the G20. The EU is, like the US, a strong supporter of the free flow of finance, but because its bank-based financial sector finds it more difficult to raise new capital on financial markets it is hesitant to further raising requirements for capital reserves. On the other hand, EU banks are far less transaction oriented than those in the US, and the EU thus has been more open to measures such as an international FTT and limits on bankers' bonuses, which reduce financial volatility by reducing speculative or risky investments that can undermine systemic stability. In short, while the US prefers to provide a framework for self-regulation of financial institutions, the EU prefers curbing financial markets as such in order to improve stability.

When it comes to currency policies, we found that the EU is inclined towards the international stability of currencies and expanding the experience of regional monetary cooperation to the global level—for example, by implementing an international tax on financial transactions that would curb financial and currency volatility. In essence, the EU sees a new global monetary system as a logical extension of the EMU with the hope of helping to stabilize the euro. East Asia agrees with the EU on managing currencies, but, as the largest holder of currency reserves in US dollars, East Asian countries are also reluctant to devalue the US dollar as the global currency. In addition, countries in the region prefer unilateral management, which allows them to use currencies as a tool to boost exports and become more competitive than their partners in the region. While East Asia is trying to expand export markets, the US is trying to limit its current-account deficit, which explains why the US is eager to push for global standards that would limit currency management ('manipulation').

Concerning macroeconomic coordination, the US and East Asia have a strong preference for active macroeconomic policies, although the US prefers to stimulate the demand side during crisis times while East Asian countries would increase investments. For example, the US implemented a 'cash for clunkers' programme, subsidizing the purchase of new cars, while East Asian countries used fiscal stimulus packages to build new infrastructure and support companies in their R&D. The EU, on the other hand, is much more conservative, particularly concerning fiscal policies, owing to the restraints of the Maastricht Treaty and the focus of the EU on internal stability and on preventing rather than managing crises.

6.1.3. Hypothesis 3: Competition of Path-Dependent Models of Capitalism

Preferences for foreign economic policies and the international governance of economic relations are embedded in the domestic political economies of these models of capitalism. The conflicts just described about international regulation can be persuasively explained by a clash of different models of capitalism. Models of capitalism in this book refer to growth regimes, which consist of a distinct economic structure, institutional system, and dominant capital faction, as well as a certain balance of power within the civil society. The evolving economic structure within their hegemonic capital factions have created unique sets of institutions—organizations, rules, regulations, and norms—that complement each other on the domestic level. Substantial effort in this book has gone into establishing the hypothesis that each model of capitalism depends on distinct regimes of complementary policies, institutions, and structures. We have seen how specific economic structures, corporate governance, financial markets, labour relations, and the role of the state create a complementary regime in which the different elements reinforce each other. Table 6.1 provides a summary of this argument based on Chapters 3–5.

In the US, the finance-led model of capitalism relies on the market as the main coordinating mechanism, with a regulatory state providing the framework for the market. Finance ('Wall Street') is the hegemonic capital faction with the most political influence and the power to frame debates. The term 'market' in the US is a synonym for financial markets. The dominance of finance in the economy makes the free movement of capital an almost untouchable privilege and the free-floating exchange rate benefits the financial sector because it is concerned less with the stability of assets and more with the number of fee-generating transactions. The financial sector even benefits from volatility, as it can sell hedging products that insure customers against losses from currency fluctuation. The finance-led growth model is characterized by a global orientation, a deep financial market, and a dominance of shareholders in corporate governance ('shareholder capitalism'). These deep financial markets allow radical innovators such as start-up companies easy access to capital, and a hire-and-fire approach to labour relations with weak labour unions makes it easier to start a new business. Employees are generally educated with universal skills, which means they have a low loyalty to their employer. A weak social welfare system further stresses the necessity to be flexible, because unemployment benefits are low. This highly flexible system tends to create

Table 6.1. Stylized relevant characteristics of different forms of capitalism

	US	EU	East Asia
Growth model	Finance led	Integration led	Export led
Orientation	Global	Regional	National
Strategy	Hegemony	Regional cooperation	National self-help
Coordination	Market	Coordinated	State
Dominant capital faction	Finance	Specialized export	General export
Typical business structure	Financialized	Specialized SMEs	Integrated business conglomerates
Corporate governance	Shareholder capitalism	Stakeholder capitalism	Network ('crony') capitalism
Investment regime	Investment in radical innovations (venture capital)	Investment in incremental innovations (bank-based credit)	Capital intensive process innovation (bank-based credit)
Interpretation of crisis	Crisis of financial regulation	Macroeconomic regulation crisis	Export competitiveness crisis
Crisis strategy	Macro-management	Crisis prevention	Micro-management
Financial regulation	Facilitate private crisis management	Preventing bubbles	State-led crisis management
Dominant financial flows	Private and public inflow	Private outflow	Public outflow
Preferred fx rates	Market determined	Stable through multilateral system	Competitive through unilateral interventions
Meaning of market	Financial market	EU single market	Export market
Organized labour	Low collective bargaining but some political influence	High level of collective bargaining and political influence	Low collective bargaining and little political influence

high growth rates in good times but has few automatic stabilizers during bad times, which means the government has to step in with active macroeconomic policies. In the US, the interpretation of the crisis is largely one of failed financial regulation, and the reaction is thus a focus on stricter regulations of banks and financial product.

In Europe's integration-led growth model, the bank-based financial system plays a very different role. The financial sector is conceptualized as a service industry in which banks extend patient capital in the form of credits to established companies based on incremental innovation with strong vocational training focusing on conveying specific skills. A strong welfare system stabilizes household incomes and preserves specific skills even in times of crisis and unemployment, making discretionary macroeconomic interventions less necessary. The main system of coordination is based on tripartite negotiations between government, companies, and labour unions. Companies take advantage of the loyalty of employees, long experience, and brand value to export luxurious goods, artisan products, and specialized machinery to the winners of globalization. The gradual widening and deepening of the European single market allow European companies to produce and extend their market regionally within a converging institutional system. A European complementary production system emerges making 'the market' in Europe synonymous with the European single market. While the enlargement of the EU is driven by neoliberally inspired 'negative integration', we can at the same time observe an increase of neo-corporatist coordination in the implementation of reforms, as well as a necessity to remain competitive in the larger European single market. The establishment of the euro has permanently fixed currencies in Europe and reinforced the focus on stability, with moderate growth rates during upswings but fewer problems during times of lower economic growth.

In East Asia, finance is considered a quasi-public sector dominated by the state, even in those countries where banks have been privatized. In the state-led development model, finance was a tool of the state to facilitate industrialization. The legacy of this successful developmental state explains why sovereignty of macroeconomic policies remains a priority in East Asia, while the free flow of capital remains restricted in many formal and informal ways. The close connection between state and business is often referred to as network capitalism or 'crony capitalism'. The dominant capital faction consists of a small number of large export-oriented business conglomerates focusing on mass production of consumer goods. In East Asia, 'the market' is synonymous with export markets, and national competitiveness is an obsession in the region. Stable and competitive exchange rates are thus one of the main priorities in East Asia achieved by unilateral interventions. Organized labour is weak, not just in collective bargaining but in particular when it comes to political influence. This lack of power is a major obstacle towards a more balanced economic growth model and a transition to a welfare state that would not depend on high economic growth rates to curb social conflicts. The competition within the region for market shares outside the region has perpetuated a nationalist inward-looking strategy that leaves little room for regional cooperation.

These described complementarities within the three distinct models give the regime a path dependency that binds political actors and decision-makers. For example, when it comes to accommodating macroeconomic policies, conservative decision-makers in the US and East Asia are more progressive than most social-democratic decision-makers in Europe. On the other hand, even on the conservative side in Europe, there is support for taxes on international financial transactions and more broadly a general cooperation on international regulation of economic issues, while even within Democrats in the US and particularly in East Asia there is a strong sense of national sovereignty and a lot of scepticism about international cooperation. International monetary cooperation is, for example, equally popular among conservative EU leaders such as former French President Nikolas Sarkozy and leftist civil society activists such as ATTAC, while it is a non-starter for even progressive leaders in the US and East Asia.

6.1.4. Hypothesis 4: Complementarity of Capitalisms

Globally the three models of capitalism complement each other, creating a fragile equilibrium. The US provides financial services for the whole world as the bankers of the world. The US recycles large parts of the world's financial wealth, which enables it to consume much more than it produces. East Asia, the factory of the world, makes the products needed by consumers in the US, and in particular affordable products for those who have been losers or at least not the main beneficiaries of globalization. The EU acts as a workshop of the world by exporting artisan and luxurious goods to the winners of globalization in the US and East Asia, while at the same time providing the specialized machinery and intermediate goods for East Asian factories. This is a stylized and simplified view of the international division of labour. The US does have a vibrant high-tech and defence sector and small artisan producers able to survive, despite the trend towards financialization. Until BREXIT, the EU was home to one of the most important financial centres in the world, and the UK has been very influential in shaping EU legislation, which clearly had an impact in making the EU more neoliberal. At the same time, the BREXIT decision clearly fits into our hypothesis that the structural forces of the domestic political economy ultimately become relevant for political decisions and institutions. For some time, the UK has tried to combine a US-style model of capitalism with EU-style institutions, but, although political decisions and institutions can diverge from their political economic fundament for some time, ultimately the gravity of the political economic structure was stronger. Finally, East Asia also partly overlaps with Europe in advancing into specialized machinery and even entry-level luxurious goods such as Toyota Lexus or

Hyundai Genesis cars, although these products so far remain mostly regional in their reach. The reality is always more complex than any theory, but for the purpose of studying international economic conflicts the complementarities identified here have been crucial both for ensuring the dynamics of global capitalism but also for making it vulnerable to crisis.

6.1.5. Hypothesis 5: Path-Dependent Change

As we have seen throughout the book, path dependency and international complementarity do not mean that the different models of capitalism are not changing and that institutions cannot travel from one model to the other. On the contrary, path dependency and international complementarity are embedded in a dynamic domestic and international system. Following the perspective of a second-image IPE, we have traced international conflicts back to their origins in domestic social conflicts. In all studied models of capitalism, the power of business increased relatively, while interests of organized labour lost out, although the scale was different. It lost out most in the US, while it always has been weak in East Asia. Labour also lost out in Europe, but much slower and coming from a higher level. These structural changes were reflected in institutional changes such as labour-market liberalization. This business-friendly environment, however, took different forms in different models of capitalism. As we have seen, business-friendly re-regulations in the US has been described as neoliberalism, in the EU as negative integration, and in East Asia as authoritarian corporatism. Most importantly, in the three regions, different business factions dominate and have been able to shape policies and institutions in their favour. In other words, the different dominant factions of capital in different models of capitalism pit government against government at the global level to extend the domestic institutional system that is favourable to them to the international level. In short, the intensified competition emerged from a weakness of societal actors balancing the increasing influence of business interests particularly over those of organized labour.

6.1.6. Hypothesis 6: International Cooperation is Getting More Difficult and Easier at the Same Time

When it comes to the prospect of international cooperation, our analysis suggests that cooperation is much more difficult than liberal institutionalists think but at the same time more likely than realists believe. The global complementarity of capitalisms is far from being harmonious but rather creates many conflicts and problems. All institutional changes and improvements at the international level can work in a meaningful way only if they are accompanied by structural changes in the domestic models of capitalism (see Section 6.2). At the same time, this competition of capitalisms does not necessarily lead to an escalation of political conflicts or even military clashes, as realists fear. In fact, at the same time, changes have become easier in many ways. First, it is obvious in today's multipolar world that a global hegemon will no longer be able to provide stability for the international system. Thus, there is a strong incentive to cooperate. Second, and more importantly, all three models of capitalism are contested domestically. Policy preferences of different models of capitalism cannot be equated with the 'national interests'. Instead, these preferences are the result of domestic interest struggles and a specific balance of power. Most importantly, they are in the interest of the dominant capital faction and the institutions and discourses rationalizing and smoothing their dominance. Third, domestic changes are not a precondition for changes at the international level. Rather, as the domestic and international levels are interdependent, they can and have to go hand in hand. In fact, global changes can play a role in facilitating domestic changes as much as the other way round.

6.2. A Future Research Agenda and the Case for an Eclectic Approach to IPE

Before developing future scenarios and possible solutions, I want to revisit the methodological considerations of Chapter 1. Above all, the main contribution of academic research is not to solve problems but to improve the tools of understanding the problems we are facing in the world. I believe that the approach of this book offers practical tools to understand problems of international cooperation without relying too much on abstract theories, complex models, or elaborate thought experiments. Instead, the book shows a relatively straightforward path on how to investigate international conflicts by tracing their origins back to the domestic level. The book sees conflicts on the international arena as a result of domestic social conflicts and the distinct political economic structures, institutions, and policies they create. Unlike mainstream accounts of international conflicts that focus on the dealings of national governments at the international level, this book has investigated the origins of these conflicts in the domestic political economies. Bringing together Waltz's second-image approach to international relations and studies of critical international and comparative political economy, I call this the second-image IPE perspective. Such a second-image IPE account of international conflicts cannot replace classic international relations or IPE studies, but it can add value and depth to the investigation of the domestic sources of international conflict. Most importantly, unlike mainstream realist or liberal institutionalist studies, such a structuralist-inspired approach does not depend on theoretical assumptions of the 'natural' state of anarchy outside the 'wolf packs' of nation states nor assume a rational-choice functionalism that ignores the context of decisions made by (seemingly) rational actors. Neither conflict nor cooperation is rational per se; they are rational only in certain contexts. Unlike what realists tend to believe, the clash of national egoisms is not a 'natural' tendency to grab a larger share of the pie but the result of very concrete domestic political economic structures.

On the other hand, unlike what liberal institutionalists believe, functionalist institutions are not primarily the results of rational choices and institutional engineering, not to mention a quasi-automatic result of deeper economic interdependence. International conflicts are not just collective-action problems in which national egoisms or lack of leadership and trust prevent cooperation. In contrast, international conflicts can be traced to domestic political economies, social conflicts, and economic imbalances—or in Waltz's term domestic 'defects'. These defective domestic policy economies are solidified in distinct institutional arrangements within different models of capitalism. It is the clash of these models of capitalism that needs to be understood, if we want to understand international conflicts in global economic governance.

In this book, we have unpeeled the onion by looking below the layer of actors who conduct international negotiations and revealed that actors such as national governments are bound by internal domestic institutions. When we peeled off the institutional layer, we found that beneath these institutions there are political economic structures consisting of interest struggles between different factions of capital and between business and civil-society actors. Essentially, international conflicts are the result of these internal conflicts and the resulting balance of power. In this sense, this study could be described as neo-structuralist as opposed to a post-structuralist study, because I maintain the classic structuralist claim that economic structures and material interests are ultimately shaping discourses and not the other way round. Academics might want to believe that discourses, which are their bread and butter, play a superior role in shaping our world, but ultimately discourses are relevant, and can be understood, only in the material context (including the material context of academics who want to increase their own relevance by emphasizing discourses).

This kind of research strategy is applicable to all different kinds of international economic conflicts from trade wars to debt crises and restructuring. The regulation of finance just functioned as a case to demonstrate the usefulness of such a research strategy. It was not the purpose of this book to offer an all-encompassing analysis or a manual for future research. Rather the book aims to present a pathway for investigating 'big issues' within IPE and international relations without being too abstract and theoretical. A necessary and intended trade-off is that the book has not attempted to prove all its assumptions in detail nor to provide final answers. On the contrary, the goal was to stir curiosity and hopefully to inspire others to fill the pages that have been left empty. In order to do that I have tried to lay down the way I understand the problems to hand and how I came to these conclusions. There is no doubt that experts in the different fields touched on will find shortcomings and flaws in the details of my analysis. There are already much more detailed books on each of the areas touched upon, from financial globalization to East Asian capitalism and from European monetary integration to G20 negotiations. The purpose was to connect different approaches and traditions and highlight interactions and relationships that experts might not see, because of their narrow focus.

Throughout academic history, studies that dig deep in one specific aspect and those that connect different traditions have benefited from each other. Scholars conducting the former studies are often referred to as 'hedgehogs', while the latter are described as 'foxes'. The thinking of hedgehogs is of a 'single substance', while the thinking of foxes is 'compounded of heterogeneous elements' (Berlin 1966). Hedgehogs are specialists that focus on one approach and one theory, while foxes, on the other hand, pursue many pathways and connect different theories but without being specialized in any one of them. Foxes follow the classic Greek meaning of critique as discerning your own position from others, while hedgehogs interpret the role of criticism in a neo-positivist way of falsifying hypotheses. Both approaches complement each other. Theoretically (and practically when it comes to job hunting in academia), hedgehogs have an advantage. While foxes need the expertise of the specialists, hedgehogs can conduct their research without any references to seemingly unrelated fields outside their narrow focus. On the other hand, foxes have an upper hand in understanding the limits of such mono-theoretical approaches. Hedgehogs have a superior knowledge, but foxes have the advantages of understanding the context in which this knowledge is relevant. This is why I believe that foxes produce the more practically relevant knowledge.

Much more focused studies constantly adjusting the argument to the changing environment are needed. I hope students of Global Political Economy find the path I have taken plausible enough to investigate it further, and they will certainly come up with more precise and better works.

6.3. The Prospects of Cooperation in Regulating International Finance

Finally, what does our investigation tell us about the chances of a successful international cooperation in economic governance and more specifically in regulating out-of-control financial markets? This question is relevant for the prospects of international cooperation in general, because, if an international agreement in the central field of finance works out, it would indicate that cooperation is possible in other areas as well. I have sided neither with the pessimism of realists who are sceptical about the prospects of international cooperation nor with the optimism of liberal institutionalists who believe increasing economic interdependence will naturally lead to more international cooperation. If realists are correct and international conflicts are a natural result of an anarchic international system, there can indeed not be much hope for international cooperation, except in the unlikely case of the rise of a new hegemonic leader. In the realists' world view, international cooperation can work only temporarily, and nation states will find it easy to exit any agreement whenever this seems to suit their national interest. The assumptions on which realist thinking rests breathe a methodological paranoia that has misguided conservative thinking at least since Thomas Hobbes. Essentially the Hobbesian war of all against all is a self-fulfilling prophecy that becomes reality if leaders believe in it. Most importantly, the assumption that the world is a scary place plays an important role in the conservative ideology of creating national unity in order to quell domestic social conflicts. Indeed, this is exactly what US President Trump, Chinese President Xi, and a variety of realist-inspired nationalists are doing. They gradually make the world look more like their pessimistic theories about it. Unlike Hobbes, contemporary realists lack the imagination of a global Leviathan and view the wolf pack that is the nation state as the end of history. Realists fail to acknowledge the success of international institutions like the BWS or the ongoing process of European integration. In the tradition of critical theories, this book has tried to strip such views of their mythology in order to provide a more fertile ground for political solutions. 'Critical theory is concerned with the demystification of power and the development of alternative frameworks to expand human potentials and possibilities' (Gill 2012: 24). From the perspective of this book, our world is indeed a scary place, but international conflicts are not 'natural'; they can be traced back to very concrete imbalances (or 'defects') within the domestic political economy, without the need to refer to unproven and somewhat mystical assumptions such as the 'anarchic nature' of international relations, 'national interests', or the general evilness of human nature. This means that international conflicts can be overcome if we simultaneously address the domestic issues creating them.

At the same time, the view of liberal institutionalists that international cooperation is the logical and rational consequence of increasing interdependence hindered only by national egoisms and wrong political choices seems to be rather naive. The functionalist illusion is that the international system is a machinery that is running with suboptimal settings. In this view, there is an ideal solution, and the path in that direction is institutional engineering. The problem is the missing ability of political leaders to envision and implement the optimal solution. From this liberal institutionalist perspective, the solution could be easy. We would just extend the current national (or regional) best practice model to the global level, or invent new ones, where necessary, and elect visionary leaders who trust each other and can overcome international gridlock. Unfortunately, the problem is not the lack of leaders with visions— from President Trump's vision of the reindustrialization of the US to Xi Jinping's visions of balanced growth and the peaceful rise of China, and Chancellor Merkel's utopia of a world run by frugal Swabian housewives. The problem is not a lack of visions but their incompatibility with the domestic and global political economy. In particular, they neglect the connection between the global imbalances and conflicts that they want to solve and the domestic imbalances and conflicts over which they have little influence and about which they know little. In other words, these visions are either a reflection of lost paths or a projection of the domestic institutions to the global level, but they are not developed out of a sound understanding of the interdependence in the global political economy. The competition of different models of capitalisms over framing international institutions is real, and it will continue to limit and slow down agreements on international institutions.

The main practical conclusion of this book is that increased cooperation on the international level will have to go hand in hand with changes within the domestic political economies. These simultaneous changes seem to be difficult, if we apply a rigid interpretation of path dependency, as often employed in studies of historical institutionalism and comparative capitalism. The good news is that such studies tend to overestimate the path dependency of capitalist models. Globalization, financialization, European integration, and East Asian export orientation are neither just rational choices by actors that can be altered easily nor the automatic outcome of a static institutional regime that makes changes almost impossible. In the context of capitalism as a dynamic economic system, institutional regimes are dynamic and driven by real structural changes that undermine established institutions. These structural dynamics have created real changes in the political balance—for example, by undermining the fragile balance between capital and labour that existed after the Second World War until the 1980s in the US and Europe. While the pressure of globalization on institutional convergence has been exaggerated by many scholars and interested parties alike, the structural changes of the international division of labour are real. The interdependence of different models of capitalism could be unravelled only at the cost of major reductions in the standard of living within the capitalist centres. It would be possible to produce and sell the iPhone only in the US, and Chinese companies would still be operational without European machinery, just as Americans could live without cheap Chinese imports. However, all these changes would substantially reduce productivity and standards of living. More importantly, these changes would need a drastic adaptation of the domestic systems. For example, to maintain their standard of living without cheap Chinese imports, US workers would need wage increases that would be difficult to achieve without strong labour unions. East Asian companies would need to explore new markets, either through regional cooperation in the region or through more domestic demand. Both seem unlikely amid the strong nationalism and the weakness of labour unions in the region. US President Trump is trying to rebalance the US economy with a short cut of protectionism and so by increasing prices on East Asian products. If the argument of this book is correct, then mere changes in tariffs will fail unless they are linked to deeper structural changes. Leaders, governments, and their policies matter, but only if their actions correspond with deeper structural changes. Thus, it is unlikely that President Trump will be able to overcome the finance-led system in the US and reindustrialize the country. In fact, everything seems to indicate that Trump is further unleashing financial wealth, while bringing back coal and steel industries is merely a populist front to appeal to voters in underprivileged regions. While the EU seems to be least vulnerable to external economic shocks because it is more balanced as an economy, the European integration project has its own defects of an institutional system with a strong austerity and deflationary bias. In addition, the core idea of the EU as a multinational institutional system itself comes under pressure in a world that is increasingly pessimistic about international cooperation.

In Chapter 2, we briefly described a utopian global system that would ensure stable financial markets, support for development, and a balanced global economy: a system where a global (accounting) currency eliminates exchange-rate risks while national or regional currencies (at least for the mid-term) allow the coordinated re-evaluation of currencies based on economic fundamentals; a regime where macroeconomic policies are internationally coordinated and financial markets are regulated in a way that they support the real economy and not just syphon off rents; a system in which erratic capital flows are eradicated and trade imbalances are adjusted through international cooperative mechanisms. In many ways, these seemingly unrealistic goals are not a utopia at all. The original Greek meaning of utopia is 'no place'—a place that does not (yet) exist. In this sense, all of the elements just described of a new world order are strictly speaking not utopias but closer to what Ernst Bloch called 'concrete utopias', elements of a future world that can already be observed in the present, albeit in a very limited way. All elements of the utopian system just described already exist in some form today. In Chapter 1, we pointed out the puzzle that different models of capitalism have created ideological blind spots in which even sensible actors block policies or regulations that are almost common sense anywhere else. The US objection to even the mildest forms of regulation on financial flows, the EU's reluctance for accommodating macroeconomic policies, and the East Asian obsession with national economic sovereignty are examples of these ideologically based dysfunctionalities. On the other hand, each model of capitalism has already created some of the elements that would allow better international cooperation. For example, the US pursues an active macroeconomic management focused on supporting demand with a very pragmatic view on debt. East Asia has shown the world how finance can be subordinated to real economic development and sovereign economic policies. The EU has found a pragmatic position towards capital flows and has effectively abolished exchange-rate risks in the euro area. Putting these elements together, we would come close to an ideal system.

In the early twenty-first century, the utopian element left is that what is possible at the national or regional level in a specific area is not (yet) possible at the global level. But a unified nation state was a utopia in most of the world in the early nineteenth century and the EU was deemed impossible in the early twentieth century. Most importantly, the success of the BWS and the EU shows that international cooperation is possible, although any solution will always be imperfect. The global market economy is inherently unstable, and this instability can only be reduced but never abolished. The dynamic of the global economy will constantly demand a reform of international institutions that can be achieved only with an increasingly intensified global cooperation. As always, in theory the solution is easy. In order to curb the power of finance, the US would have to make sure that less wealth is redistributed from the real economy to the financial markets. A financial transaction tax and curbs on bankers' bonuses would make finance the 'boring' business it was until the 1970s. An improved social-security system would reduce the reliance on financial markets for savings. Wall Street would primarily focus on the domestic market instead of siphoning off global rents. These measures would reduce the influence of Wall Street and overcome the resistance against the global regulation of financial flows.

In East Asia, employees would strengthen labour unions and struggle for higher wages, which would increase their potential to consume and help rebalance the global economy. Governments would increase welfare protection, which would reduce the need to save and reduced working hours would lead to an improvement in productivity. These measures together would reduce dependence on current-account surpluses and reduce the need to manage exchange rates to remain competitive. Governments in the region would break up monopolies, reduce the influence of big business conglomerates, and fight cronyism between the public and private sectors. As a result, East Asian economies would become more balanced domestically, which would contribute to the reduction of global imbalances.

In order to overcome Europe's introverted attitude and obsession with stability and fiscal conservatism, the EU would abandon the focus on austerity and support Southern European countries in investing to increase productivity and help governments to increase tax revenues. In Northern Europe, countries such as Germany would increase investments, wages and consumption to reduce economic imbalances within the EU. Most importantly, the EU would supplement its successful 'negative integration' with positive integration, creating a real regional political economy beyond the coldness of the single market. By establishing a fiscal union, the redistribution between rich and poor regions would be strengthened and the EU would become much more like a federal state. Part of this 'ever closer union' would be an increased EU budget and an independent but pragmatic ECB, which would become a real central bank by moving beyond a sole focus on monetary stability, but it would also include other goals such as reducing unemployment. Consequently, the EU would become less reluctant to coordinate macroeconomic policies on the global level and increased employment and investment would contribute to global growth.

While these scenarios seem unlikely in their purest form, there have been some signs that there is movement in that direction. In the US, the Obama administration introduced stricter financial rules and strengthened the health-care system. Several of the Democratic presidential candidates for 2020 have announced policies along the line of a deeper rebalancing of the US economy, including previously unthinkable tax increases for the wealthy. In East Asia, governments have become aware of the necessity to rebalance growth and strengthen social-welfare systems and public investment. In Europe, Germany has introduced a minimum wage and lower unemployment has encouraged labour unions to demand high wages. French President Macron has proposed a fiscal union and the ECB has become far less orthodox in its monetary policies, while Southern European countries are seriously modernizing their institutions. Unfortunately, there are at least as many reasons to be cautious. The whole point of the book was to show that solutions are not the result of academic theories and technocratic designs but structural power changes and the political struggles about these changes. Often these political struggles are unpredictable and surprising, at least in the short run. The election of Donald Trump and his reversal of some of the financial regulation of the Obama administration show that progress can be reversed. The interests of the financial sector have ensured that the path dependency of US finance-led capitalism has been maintained. In Europe, Germany and other North European countries are determined to maintain the austerity focus of the EU, while right-wing populist leaders bet on a nationalist strategy and blame the multilateralism of the EU as such for economic and social problems. In East Asia, too, nationalism remains a persuasive narrative, and the region is a long way from kicking its addiction to exports. On the contrary, it has intensified industrial policies to improve its global competiveness for the future. Positive changes towards more international cooperation will surely not be easy. The point of this book was to help to understand the difficulties of theoretically plausible technocratic solutions and highlight the tension between technocratic decisions and political economic path dependencies.

From the perspective of this book, real changes are expected and sustainable only when the underlying political economy changes. Most important is the balance between labour and capital, as well as the balance between different factions of capital. Different factions of capital have gained the upper hand in different varieties of capitalism. This leads to a competition of capitalisms in which governments are pitted against each other in framing international arrangements. Key to the change would be either that in all world regions the same capitalist faction with the same institutional preferences would win, or that they would reach a compromise for the sake of a stable global system. The former option of hyper-globalization seems unlikely, given the global complementarity of the different models. As we have seen, a finance-oriented system needs an export-oriented one, and the other way round. The latter scenario is theoretically possible but unlikely given the different preferences of the different models of capitalism described in this book.

We do not know whether change will come, and in which direction it would go, but, following the logic of this book, all meaningful changes need to come from the bottom up. Chinese workers founding labour unions, American NGOs lobbying for financial regulation, and German civil society speaking out in solidarity with Greece—these are the factors that slowly bring about change by changing the awareness of economic interests and the discourses alike. Without such fundamental changes on the ground, any kind of technocratic fixes can be successful only in the short run. These are the changes we need to take into account, if we want to understand the International Political Economy beneath the noise (and tweets) produced by political leaders and the show of international events such as G20 summits.

A better understanding of the origins of international conflicts will help to manage international conflicts more effectively. We will never live in a world without conflict, but it is possible to understand that conflicts are neither inevitable, natural, based on a Darwinian law of the survival of the fittest, nor the result of a 'clash of civilizations' based on cultural values. On the contrary, conflicts can be traced to concrete political economic origins: a competition of different models of capitalism that themselves rest on distinct domestic balances of economic, social and political power. By understanding that international conflicts are the result of decisions and preferences shaped by sticky institutions that are ultimately the result of domestic conflicting interests, we can manage conflicts more effectively. It also means that struggles at the domestic level always need to be seen in a global context. What happens domestically in the political sphere and at the company level affects cooperation between states at the international level.

References

Acharya, V. V., Cooley, T. F., Richardson, M. P., and Walter, I. (2010). *Regulating Wall Street: The Dodd–Frank Act and the New Architecture of Global Finance*. Hoboken, NJ: Wiley.

Abiad, A., Detragiache, E. & Tressel, T. (2008). A new database of financial reforms. *IMF Working Papers*, 08.

Admati, A. R., and Hellwig, M. F. (2013). *The Bankers' New Clothes: What's Wrong with Banking and what to Do about it*. Princeton and Oxford: Princeton University Press.

Aizenman, J., Chinn, M. D., and Ito, H. (2008). 'Assessing the Emerging Global Financial Architecture: Measuring the Trilemma's Configurations over Time'. NBER Working Paper.

Albo, G., Gindin, S., and Panitch, L. (2010). *In and Out of Crisis: The Global Financial Meltdown and Left Alternatives*. Oakland, CA: PM Press.

Alexander, A. J. (2008). *Policy Implications of Korea's Low Level of Foreign Direct Investment*. Korean Economy Series. Washington: Korea Institute at SAIS (USKI).

Altvater, E. (1987). *Die Armut Der Nationen: Handbuch Zur Schuldenkrise von Argentinien bis Zaire*. Frankfurt am Main: Büchergilde Gutenberg.

Altvater, E. (1991). *The Poverty of Nations: A Guide to the Debt Crisis from Argentina to Zaire*. London and Atlantic Highlands, NJ: Zed Books.

Amable, B. (2003). *The Diversity of Modern Capitalism*. Oxford and New York: Oxford University Press.

Amsden, A. H. (1989). *Asia's Next Giant: South Korea and Late Industrialization*. New York: Oxford University Press.

Amsden, A. H. (1991). 'Diffusion of Development: The Late-Industrializing Model and Greater East Asia', *American Economic Review*, 81: 282–6.

Anderlini, J. (2011). 'G20 Struggles to Ease Monetary Reform Tension', *Financial Times*, 31 March 2011.

Ando, M. (2006). 'Fragmentation and Vertical Intra-Industry Trade in East Asia', *North American Journal of Economics and Finance*, 17: 257–81.

Ando, M., and Kimura, F. (2005). 'The Formation of International Production and Distribution Networks in East Asia', in *International Trade in East Asia, NBER–East Asia Seminar on Economics*. Chicago: University of Chicago Press, 177–216.

Andrews, D. M., Henning, C. R., and Pauly, L. W. (2002) (eds). *Governing the World's Money*, Ithaca, NY: Cornell University Press.

Angell, N. (1910). *The Great Illusion: A Study of the Relation of Military Power in Nations to their Economic and Social Advantage*. New York and London: G. P. Putnam's Sons.

Apeldoorn, B. (2002). *Transnational Capitalism and the Struggle over European Integration*. London and New York: Routledge.

Argy, V. (2013). *The Postwar International Money Crisis: An Analysis*. Abingdon: Taylor & Francis.

Arrighi, G. (1994). *The Long Twentieth Century: Money, Power, and the Origins of our Times*. London and New York: Verso.

Arrighi, G. (2005a). 'Hegemony Unraveling-I', *New Left Review*, 32: 23–80.

Arrighi, G. (2005b). 'Hegemony Unraveling-II', *New Left Review*, 33: 83116.

Arrighi, G. (2007). *Adam Smith in Beijing: Lineages Of The Twenty-First Century*. London and New York: Verso.

Baek, S. W. (2005). 'Does China Follow "The East Asian Development Model"?', *Journal of Contemporary Asia*, 35: 485–98.

Bakker, A., and Chapple, B. (2002). *Advanced Country Experiences with Capital Account Liberalization* (Epub). Washington: International Monetary Fund.

Barker, A. (2013). 'EU Ready to Set Tough Bank Pay Curbs', *Financial Times*, 17 February 2013.

Beattie, A. (2009). 'Team Ethos Fractures on Tough Route to Summit', *Financial Times*, 14 March 2009.

Beattie, A., and Jung, S. (2010). 'Doubts Grow on Prospects for G20', *Financial Times*, 19 October 2010.

Beckmann, M., Bieling, H.-J., and Deppe, F. (2003). *'Euro-Kapitalismus' und Globale Politische Ökonomie*. Hamburg: VSA-Verlag.

Beeson, M., and Broome, A. (2010). 'Hegemonic Instability and East Asia: Contradictions, Crises and US Power', *Globalizations*, 7: 507–23.

Bell, D. (1973). *The Coming of Post-Industrial Society; A Venture in Social Forecasting*, New York: Basic Books.

Berger, T. U., Mochizuki, M., and Tsuchiyama, J. (2007). *Japan in International Politics: The Foreign Policies of an Adaptive State*. Boulder, CO: Lynne Rienner Publishers; published in Association with the Japan Forum on International Relations.

Berlin, I. (1966). *The Hedgehog and the Fox: An Essay on Tolstoy's View of History*. New York: Simon & Schuster (1st edn 1953).

Bernanke, B. S. (2005). *The Global Saving Glut and the US Current Account Deficit: Remarks by Governor Ben S. Bernanke at the Sandridge Lecture, Virginia Association of Economists, Richmond, Virginia, 10 March*, online, <https://www.federalreserve.gov/boarddocs/speeches/2005/200503102/) (accessed April 2019).

Beyer, J. (2006). *Pfadabhägigkeit: Über Institutionelle Kontinuität, Anfällige Stabilität und Fundamentalen Wandel*. Frankfurt am Main: Campus-Verl.

Bhagwati, J. (1998). 'The Capital Myth: The Difference between Trade in Widgets and Dollars', *Foreign Affairs*, 77: P7(6).

Bieling, H.-J. (2006). 'EMU, Financial Integration and Global Economic Governance', *Review of International Political Economy*, 13: 420–48.

Bieling, H.-J. (2013). 'European Financial Capitalism and the Politics of (De-) Financialization', *Competition & Change*, 17: 283–98.

BIS (2010). *Group of Governors and Heads of Supervision Announces Higher Global Minimum Capital Standards*, online, <http://www.bis.org/press/p100912.pdf> (accessed 12 November 2010).

BIS (2010). *International regulatory framework for banks (Basel III)* [Online]. Available: http://www.bis.org/bcbs/basel3.htm?m=3%7C14%7C572 [Accessed].

BIS (2013). 'International Banking and Financial Market Developments', *BIS Quarterly Review*, September.

BIS (2014). *Seventh Progress Report on Adoption of the Basel Regulatory Framework*. Basle: BIS, October.

BIS (2016). *Triennial Central Bank Survey of foreign exchange and OTC derivatives markets in 2016* [Online]. Available: https://www.bis.org/publ/rpfx16.htm [Accessed].

Bischof, G., and Pelinka, A. (1996). *Austro-Corporatism: Past, Present, Future*. Piscataway, NJ: Transaction Publishers.

Bloch, E. (1986). *The Principle of Hope*. Cambridge, MA: MIT Press.

Blustein, P. (2003). *The Chastening: Inside the Crisis that Rocked the Global Financial System and Humbled the IMF*. New York: Public Affairs.

Bordo, M., Eichengreen, B., Klingebiel, D., Martinez-Peria, M. S., and Rose, A. K. (2001). 'Is the Crisis Problem Growing More Severe?', *Economic Policy*, 16: 53–82.

Boyer, R. (2000). 'Is a Finance-Led Growth Regime a Viable Alternative to Fordism? A Preliminary Analysis', *Economy and Society*, 29: 111–45.

Boyer, R. (2011). 'Are There Laws of Motion of Capitalism?', *Socio-Economic Review*, 9: 59–81.

Boyer, R., and Freyssenet, M. (2002). 'Globalization but Still a Large Diversity of Productive Models and Corporate Governance Styles', *Seoul Journal of Economics*, 15: 149–92.

Boyer, R., and Saillard, Y. (2002). *Regulation Theory: The State of the Art*. London and New York: Routledge.

BPB 2012. Das 19. Jahrhundert. Informationen Zur Politischen Bildung, 315.

Brenner, R. (2002). *The Boom and the Bubble: The US in the World Economy*. London and New York: Verso.

Brenner, R. (2006). *The Economics of Global Turbulence: The Advanced Capitalist Economies from Long Boom to Long Downturn, 1945–2005*. London and New York: Verso.

Bullard, N., Bello, W., and Kamal, M. (1998). 'Taming the Tigers: The IMF and the Asian Crisis', *Third World Quarterly*, 19: 505–56.

Carlin, W., and Soskice, D. W. (2006). *Macroeconomics: Imperfections, Institutions, and Policies*. Oxford and New York: Oxford University Press.

Carlin, W., and Soskice, D. (2009). 'German Economic Performance: Disentangling the Role of Supply-Side Reforms, Macroeconomic Policy and Coordinated Economy Institutions', *Socio-Economic Review*, 7: 67.

Cerny, P. G. (1997). 'Paradoxes of the Competition State: The Dynamics of Political Globalization', *Government and Opposition*, 32: 251–74.

Chancellor, E. (1999). *Devil Take the Hindmost: A History of Financial Speculation*. New York: Farrar, Straus, Giroux.

Chang, K.-S. (2012). 'Economic Development, Democracy and Citizenship Politics in South Korea: The Predicament of Developmental Citizenship', *Citizenship Studies*, 16: 29–47.

Chernow, R. (2001). *The House of Morgan: An American Banking Dynasty and the Rise of Modern Finance*. New York: Grove Press.

Cho, H., and Kalinowski, T. (2010). 'Bank Nationalization, Restructuring and Reprivatization: The Case of Korea since the Asian Financial Crisis', *Korea Observer*, 41: 1–30.

Cho, Y. (2008). 'The National Crisis and De/Reconstructing Nationalism in South Korea during the IMF Intervention', *Inter-Asia Cultural Studies*, 9: 82–96.

Choi, B.-S. (1987). The Structure of the Economic Policy-Making Institutions in Korea and the Strategic Role of the Economic Planning Board (EPB)', *Korean Journal of Policy Studies*, 2: 1–25.

Clark, C. (2013). *The Sleepwalkers: How Europe Went to War in 1914*. New York: HarperCollins.

Coates, D. (2005). *Varieties of Capitalism, Varieties of Approaches*. New York: Palgrave Macmillan.

Cohen, S. S., and Zysman, J. (1987). *Manufacturing Matters: The Myth of the Post-Industrial Economy*. New York: Basic Books.

Cooper, A. F. (2008). 'The Heiligendamm Process: Structural Reordering and Diplomatic Agency', in A. G. Cooper and A. Antkeiwicz (eds), *Emerging Powers and Global Governance*. Waterloo: Wilfried Laurier University Press.

Cova, P., Pisani, M, and Rebucci, A. (2010). 'Macroeconomic Effects of China s Fiscal Stimulus'. IDB Working Paper Series No. 211.

Crimmann, A., Wießner, F., and Bellmann, L. (2010). *The German Work-Sharing Scheme: An Instrument for the Crisis*. Geneva: ILO.

De Graaff, N., and van Apeldoorn, B. (2011). 'Varieties of US Post-Cold War Imperialism: Anatomy of a Failed Hegemonic Project and the Future of US Geopolitics', *Critical Sociology*, 37: 403–27.

Deeg, R. (1999). *Finance Capitalism Unveiled: Banks and the German Political Economy*. Ann Arbor: University of Michigan Press.

Diversity Office (2009). *IMF Diversity Annual Report 2008*. Washington: IMF.

Dore, R. P. (2000). *Stock Market Capitalism: Welfare Capitalism: Japan and Germany versus the Anglo-Saxons*. Oxford and New York: Oxford University Press.

Dörre, K. (2014). *The 'German Job Miracle': A Model for Europe?* Brussels: Rosa Luxemburg Foundation.

Driffill, J. (2006). 'The Centralization of Wage Bargaining Revisited: What have we Learnt?', *Journal of Common Market Studies*, 44: 731–56.

EBA (2013). *Implementing Basel III Europe: CRD IV Package*, online, <http://www.eba.europa.eu/regulation-and-policy/implementing-basel-iii-europe> (accessed 30 September 2013).

EC (1979). 'European Economic and Monetary Union.' European Documentation, 79.

ECB (2015). *The Definition of Price Stability*, online, <https://www.ecb.europa.eu/mopo/strategy/pricestab/html/index.en.html> (accessed April 2019).

ECB (2019). *Single Supervisory Mechanism*, https://www.bankingsupervision.europa.eu/about/thessm/html/index.en.html (accessed April 2019).

Eichengreen, B. J. (2007). *The European Economy since 1945: Coordinated Capitalism and Beyond*. Princeton: Princeton University Press.

Eichengreen, B. J. (2008). *Globalizing Capital: A History of the International Monetary System*. Princeton: Princeton University Press.

Eichengreen, B. J. (2011). *Exorbitant Privilege: The Rise and Fall of the Dollar and the Future of the International Monetary System*. Oxford and New York: Oxford University Press.

Eichengreen, B. J. (2015). *Hall of Mirrors: The Great Depression, the Great Recession, and the Uses—and Misuses—of History*. New York: Oxford University Press.

Eichengreen, B., and Bordo, M. D. (2002). 'Crises Now and Then: What Lessons from the Last Era of Financial Globalization.' NBER Working Paper, 8716, Cambridge, MA.

Eichengreen, B., and Luengnaruemitchai, P. (2004). 'Why Doesn't Asia Have Bigger Bond Markets?' National Bureau of Economic Research Working Paper Series, No. 10576.

Eichengreen, B., and O'Rourke, K. H. (2009). 'A Tale of Two Depressions', *VoxEU*, 1.

EMCF Statutes (1973). 'Regulation (EEC) No. 907/73 of the Council of 3 April 1973 Establishing a European Monetary Cooperation Fund', *Official Journal of the European Communities*, L 89, 5 April.

Enderlein, H. (2008). 'Wandel durch den Euro: Wie die Währungsunion die Nationale Fiskal- und Lohnpolitik Verändert', in M. Höpner, and A. Schäfer (eds), *Die Politische Ökonomie der Europäischen Integration*. Frankfurt am Main: Campus-Verl.

Epstein, G. A. (2005). *Financialization and the World Economy*, Cheltenham and Northampton, MA: Edward Elgar.

Epstein, G., and Power, D. (2003). 'Rentier Incomes and Financial Crises: An Empirical Examination of Trends and Cycles in Some OECD Countries.' Political Economy Research Institute Working Paper Series.

Esping-Andersen, G. (1990). *The Three Worlds of Welfare Capitalism*. Princeton: Princeton University Press.

EU (1992a). 'Statute of the European System of Central Banks and of the ECB', *Journal of the European Communities*, C 191, 29 July.

EU (1992b). 'Treaty on European Union (Maastricht Treaty)', *Official Journal of the European Communities*, C 191, 29 July.

Eurobarometer (2011). *Economic Governance in the European Union*. Brussels: Eurobarometer.

EUROSTAT (2014). EUROSTAT Database, online, <https://ec.europa.eu/eurostat/data/database> (accessed April 2019).

Evans, P. (1995). *Embedded Autonomy: States and Industrial Transformation*. Princeton: Princeton University Press.

Faust, M., Voskamp, U., and Wittke, V. (2004). 'Globalization and the Future of National Systems: Exploring Patterns of Industrial Reorganization and Relocation in an Enlarged Europe', in M. Faust, U. Voskamp, and V. Wittke (eds), *European Industrial Restructuring in a Global Economy: Fragmentation and Relocation of Value Chains*. Göttingen: SOFI Berichte.

Fed (2013). *Data Download Program*, online, <http://www.federalreserve.gov/datadownload/> (accessed April 2019).

Feldman, G. D. (1997). *The Great Disorder: Politics, Economics, and Society in the German Inflation, 1914–1924*. Oxford: Oxford University Press.

Ferguson, N. (2008). *The Ascent of Money: A Financial History of the World*. New York: Penguin Press.

Fewsmith, J. (2001). 'The Political and Social Implications of China's Accession to the WTO', *China Quarterly*, 167: 573–91.

Fioretos, K. O. (2011). *Creative Reconstructions: Multilateralism and European Varieties of Capitalism after 1950*. Ithaca, NY, and London: Cornell University Press.

Fisher, A. G. B. (1939). 'The German Trade Drive in Southeastern Europe', *International Affairs* (Royal Institute of International Affairs 1931–9), 18: 143–70.

Fishman, C. (2006). *The Wal-Mart Effect: How the World's Most Powerful Company Really Works–and how it's Transforming the American Economy*. New York: Penguin Press.

Freye, S. (2009). *Führungswechsel: Die Wirtschaftselite und das Ende der Deutschland AG*. Frankfurt am Main: Campus Verlag.

Frieden, J. A. (2007). *Global Capitalism: Its Fall and Rise in the Twentieth Century*. New York: W. W. Norton.

Friedman, M. (1970). *The Counter-Revolution in Monetary Theory: First Wincott Memorial Lecture, Delivered at the Senate House, University of London, 16 September, 1970*. Published for the Wincott Foundation by the Institute of Economic Affairs.

Friedman, M., and Friedman, R. D. (1982). *Capitalism and Freedom*. Chicago: University of Chicago Press.

Fukao, K., Ishido, H., and Ito, K. (2003). 'Vertical Intra-Industry Trade and Foreign Direct Investment in East Asia', *Journal of the Japanese and International Economies*, 17: 468–506.

Fukuyama, F. (1992). *The End of History and the Last Man*. New York: Free Press.

Fukuyama, F. (1998). 'Asian Values and the Asian Crisis', *Commentary Magazine*, 105/2, online, <https://www.commentarymagazine.com/articles/asian-values-and-the-asian-crisis/> (accessed April 2019).

G20 (2008a). *Communiqué Meeting of Ministers and Governors Sao Paulo 8–9 November 2008*, online, <http://www.g20.utoronto.ca/2008/2008communique1109.html> (accessed April 2019).

G20 (2008b). *Declaration. Summit on Financial Markets and the World Economy*, online, <http://www.g20.utoronto.ca/2008/2008declaration1115.html> (accessed April 2019).

G20 (2009). *Global Plan for Recovery and Reform, 2 April 2009*, online, <http://www.g20.utoronto.ca/2009/2009communique0402.html> (accessed April 2019).

G20 (2009c). *Leaders' Statement, the Pittsburgh Summit, September 24–25 2009*, online, <http://www.g20.utoronto.ca/2009/2009communique0925.html> (accessed 2010).

G20 (2010a). *The G20 Seoul Summit Leaders' Declaration, November 11–12, 2010*, online, <http://www.g20.utoronto.ca/2010/g20seoul.html (accessed April 2019).

G20 (2010b). *The G-20 Toronto Summit Declaration, June 26–27, 2010*, online, <http://www.g20.utoronto.ca/2010/to-communique.html> (accessed April 2019).

G20 (2011). *Communiqué G20 Leaders' Summit—Cannes—3–4 November 2011*, online, <http://www.g20.utoronto.ca/2011/2011-cannes-communique-111104-en.html> (accessed April 2019).

G20 (2012a). *G20 Leaders' Declaration, Los Cabos*, 19 June 2012, <http://www.g20.utoronto.ca/2012/2012-0619-loscabos.html> (accessed April 2019).

G20 (2012b). *The Los Cabos Growth and Jobs Action Plan*, 19 June 2012, online, <http://www.g20.utoronto.ca/2012/2012-0619-loscabos-actionplan.html> (accessed April 2019).

G20 (2013). *Communiqué of Meeting of G20 Finance Ministers and Central Bank Governors*, Moscow, 16 February 2013, online, <http://www.g20.utoronto.ca/2013/2013-0216-finance.html> (accessed April 2019).

Galbraith, J. K. (1967). *The New Industrial State*. London: H. Hamilton.

Galbraith, J. K. (1997). *The Great Crash, 1929*. Boston: Houghton Mifflin.

Gallagher, K. (2015). *Ruling Capital: Emerging Markets and the Reregulation of Cross-Border Finance*. Ithaca, NY: Cornell University Press.

Garon, S. (2011). *Beyond our Means: Why America Spends while the World Saves*. Princeton: Princeton University Press.

Garon, S. M., and Maclachlan, P. L. (2006). *The Ambivalent Consumer: Questioning Consumption in East Asia and the West*. Ithaca, NY: Cornell University Press.

Geoghegan, T. (2014). *Only One Thing Can Save Us: Why America Needs a New Kind of Labor Movement*. New York: New Press.

Gill, S. (2012). *Global Crises and the Crisis of Global Leadership*. Cambridge and New York: Cambridge University Press.

Gill, S. (2015). *Critical Perspectives on the Crisis of Global Governance: Reimagining the Future*. Basingstoke and New York: Palgrave Macmillan.

Gilpin, R. (1987). *The Political Economy of International Relations*. Princeton: Princeton University Press.

Gourevitch, P. A. (1986). *Politics in Hard Times: Comparative Responses to International Economic Crises*. Ithaca, NY: Cornell University Press.

Gourinchas, P.-O., and Rey, H. (2007). 'From World Banker to World Venture Capitalist: US External Adjustment and the Exorbitant Privilege', in Richard H. Clarida (ed.), *G7 Current Account Imbalances: Sustainability and Adjustment*. Chicago: University of Chicago Press.

Gowan, P. (1999). *The Global Gamble: Washington's Faustin Bid for World Dominance*. London: Verso.

Green, D. (1984). 'Mitterrand: From Socialism to Realism', *Economic Affairs*, 4: 23–6.

Grimes, W. W. (2001). *Unmaking the Japanese Miracle: Macroeconomic Politics, 1985–2000*. Ithaca, NY: Cornell University Press.

Grimes, W. W. (2009). *Currency and Contest in East Asia: The Great Power Politics of Financial Regionalism*. Ithaca, NY: Cornell University Press.

Grote, J. R., and Schmitter, P. C. (1999). 'The Renaissance of National Corporatism: Unintended Side-Effect of European Economic and Monetary Union or Calculated

Response to the Absence of European Social Policy?', *Transfer: European Review of Labour and Research*, 5: 34–63.

Grout, P. A., Megginson, W. L., and Zalewska, A. (2009). 'One Half-Billion Shareholders and Counting: Determinants of Individual Share Ownership around the World', 22nd Australasian Finance and Banking Conference, 18 August, available at *SSRN*, <https://ssrn.com/abstract=1457482 or http://dx.doi.org/10.2139/ssrn.1457482> (accessed April 2019).

Gustenau, G. E., Höll, O., and Nowotny, T. (2006) (eds). *Europe–USA: Diverging Partners*. Baden-Baden: Nomos.

Haas, E. B. (1968). *The Uniting of Europe: Political, Social, and Economic Forces, 1950–1957*. Stanford, CA: Stanford University Press.

Haggard, S. (2000). 'The Politics of the Asian Financial Crisis', *Journal of Democracy*, 11/2: 130–44.

Hall, P. A., and Soskice, D. W. (2001). *Varieties of Capitalism: The Institutional Foundations of Comparative Advantage*. Oxford and New York: Oxford University Press.

Hancké, B., Rhodes, M., and Thatcher, M. (2007). *Beyond Varieties of Capitalism: Conflict, Contradiction, and Complementarities in the European Economy*. Oxford and New York: Oxford University Press.

Harvey, D. (1989). *The Urban Experience*. Baltimore: Johns Hopkins University Press.

Harvey, D. (2005). *A Brief History of Neoliberalism*. Oxford: Oxford University Press.

Havrylchyk, O., and Jurzyk, E. (2006). 'Profitability of Foreign and Domestic Banks in Central and Eastern Europe: Does the Mode of Entry Matter?' LICOS Discussion Paper.

Helleiner, E. (1994). *States and the Reemergence of Global Finance: From Bretton Woods to the 1990s*. Ithaca, NY: Cornell University Press.

Helleiner, E. (2003). *The Making of National Money: Territorial Currencies in Historical Perspective*. Ithaca, NY: Cornell University Press.

Helleiner, E. (2014). *The Status Quo Crisis: Global Financial Governance after the 2008 Financial Meltdown*. Oxford and New York: Oxford University Press.

Helleiner, E., Pagliari, S., and Zimmermann, H. (2010). *Global Finance in Crisis: The Politics of International Regulatory Change*. New York: Routledge.

Hetzel, R. L. (2002). 'German Monetary History in the First Half of the Twentieth Century', *Economic Quarterly: Federal Reserve Bank of Richmond*, 88: 1: 1–35.

Hilferding, R. (1910). *Das Finanzkapital: Eine Studie uber die Juengste Entwicklung Des Kapitalismus*, Vienna: Brand.

Hilgers, M. (2012). 'The Historicity of the Neoliberal State', *Social Anthropology*, 20: 80–94.

Hirsch, J. (1995). *Der Nationale Wettbewerbsstaat: Staat, Demokratie und Politik im Globalen Kapitalismus*. Berlin and Amsterdam: Edition ID-Archiv.

Hiwatari, N. (2003). 'Embedded Policy Preferences and the Formation of International Arrangements after the Asian Financial Crisis', *Pacific Review*, 16: 331–59.

Hobsbawm, E. J. (1962). *The Age of Revolution, 1789–1848*. Cleveland: World Publishing Company.

Hobson, J. A. (1975 [1902]). *Imperialism: A Study*. New York: Gordon Press.

Holliday, I. (2000). 'Productivist Welfare Capitalism: Social Policy in East Asia', *Political Studies*, 48: 706–23.

Höpner, M. (2007). 'Coordination and Organization: The Two Dimensions of Nonliberal Capitalism.' Mpifg Discussion Paper, 07.

Höpner, M., and Schäfer, A. (2008) (eds). *Die Politische Ökonomie der Europäischen Integration*. Frankfurt am Main: Campus-Verl.

IEO/IMF (2003). *The IMF and Recent Capital Account Crises: Indonesia, Korea, Brazil*. Washington: Independent Evaluation Office, International Monetary Fund.

Ikenberry, G. J. (2008). 'The Rise of China and the Future of the West: Can the Liberal System Survive?', *Foreign Affairs*, 87: 23–37.

ILO (2014). *ILOSTAT Database*, online, <http://www.ilo.org/ilostat: (accessed April 2019).

IMF (1944). *Articles of Agreement*, online, < https://www.imf.org/external/pubs/ft/aa/index. htm> (accessed April 2019).

IMF (2009). 'The State of Public Finances: Cross-Country Fiscal Monitor: November 2009', IMF Staff Position Note, 3 November, SPN/09/25, Washington.

IMF (2010). *New Quota Tables*, online, <https://www.imf.org/external/np/sec/pr/2010/ pdfs/pr10418_table.pdf> (accessed April 2019).

IMF (2010). *New quota tables* [Online]. Available: http://www.imf.org/external/np/sec/pr/ 2010/pdfs/pr10418_table.pdf [Accessed 10 November 2010].

IMF (2011). *IMF Executive Board Discusses Criteria for Broadening the SDR Currency Basket*. Public Information Notice (PIN) 11.

IMF (2012). *Balance of Payments and International Investment Position Statistics*, online, <https://www.imf.org/external/np/sta/bop/bop.htm) (accessed April 2019).

IMF (2013). 'IMF Multi-Country Report 2013 Pilot External Sector Report—Individual Economy Assessments', IMF Staff Country Report. August.

IMF (2018). *Special Drawing Right (SDR)*, online, https://www.imf.org/en/About/ Factsheets/Sheets/2016/08/01/14/51/Special-Drawing-Right-SDR (accessed April 2019).

Ito, T. (1993). *US Political Pressure and Economic Liberalization in East Asia. Regionalism and Rivalry: Japan and the United States in Pacific Asia*. Chicago: University of Chicago Press.

Jachtenfuchs, M., and Kohler-Koch, B. (1996). *Regieren im Dynamischen Mehrebenensystem*. Luxembourg: Springer.

Jessop, B. (2013). 'Putting Neoliberalism in its Time and Place: A Response to the Debate', *Social Anthropology*, 21: 65–74.

Joerges, C., and Rödl, F. (2009). 'Informal Politics, Formalised Law and the "Social Deficit" of European Integration: Reflections after the Judgments of the ECJ in Viking and Laval', *European Law Journal*, 15: 1–19.

Johnson, C. (1982). *MITI and the Japanese Miracle: The Growth of Industrial Policy, 1925-1975*. Stanford, CA: Stanford University Press.

Johnson, C. (1999). 'The Developmental State: Odyssey of a Concept', in M. Woo-Cumings (ed.), *The Developmental State*. Ithaca, NY: Cornell University Press.

Johnson, H. G. (1971). 'The Keynesian Revolution and the Monetarist Counter-Revolution', *American Economic Review*, 61: 1–14.

Johnson, S. (2009). 'The Quiet Coup', *Atlantic Online*, <https://www.theatlantic.com/ magazine/archive/2009/05/the-quiet-coup/307364/> (April 2019).

Johnson, S., and Kwak, J. (2011). *13 Bankers: The Wall Street Takeover and the Next Financial Meltdown*. New York: Vintage Books.

Jürgens, U., and Krzywdzinski, M. (2009). 'Changing East–West Division of Labour in the European Automotive Industry', *European Urban and Regional Studies*, 16: 27.

Kahler, M., and Lake, D. A. (2013). *Politics in the New Hard Times: The Great Recession in Comparative Perspective*. Ithaca, NY: Cornell University Press.

Kalinowski, T. (2005a). Der Internationale Währungsfonds in Südkorea: Strukturanpassung und Reformen Seit der Asienkrise. Hamburg: IFA.

Kalinowski, T. (2005b). 'Erfolgreiches Scheitern: Der IWF in Südkorea', *Blätter für Deutsche und Internationale Politik*, 2: 208–16.

Kalinowski, T. (2007). 'Democracy, Economic Crisis, and Market Oriented Reforms', *Comparative Sociology*, 6: 344–73.

Kalinowski, T. (2010). 'Can Korea Be a Bridge between Developing and Developed Countries in the G20 and Beyond?', in T. Fues and P. Wolff (eds), *G20 and Global Development: How Can the New Summit Architecture Promote Pro-Poor Growth and Sustainability?* Bonn: DIE-GDI.

Kalinowski, T. (2011). 'Regulating International Finance and the Evolving Imbalance of Capitalisms since the 1970s.' Mpifg Discussion Paper, 11.

Kalinowski, T. (2013a). 'Crisis Management and the Varieties of Capitalism: Fiscal Stimulus Packages and the Transformation of East Asian State-Led Capitalism since 2008'. WZB Working Paper, 2013–501.

Kalinowski, T. (2013b). 'Regulating International Finance and the Diversity of Capitalism', *Socio-Economic Review*, 11: 471–96.

Kalinowski, T. (2015a). 'Crisis Management and the Diversity of Capitalism. Fiscal Stimulus Packages and the East Asian (Neo-)Developmental State', *Economy and Society*, 44: 244–70.

Kalinowski, T. (2015b). 'Second Image IPE: Global Economic Imbalances and the "Defects" of the East Asian Development Model', *International Politics*, 52: 760–78.

Kalinowski, T., and Cho, H. (2009). 'The Political Economy of Financial Market Liberalization in South Korea: State, Big Business, and Foreign Investors', *Asian Survey*, 49: 221–42.

Kalinowski, T., and Jang, S. (2014). 'Investigating Commonalities and Changes in Labor and Financial Relations in East Asia', *Korea Observer*, 45: 493–521.

Kanamori, T., And Zhao, Z. (2006). *The Renminbi Exchange Rate Revaluation: Theory, Practice, and Lessons from Japan.* Tokyo: ADBI.

Kasahara, S. (2004). 'The Flying Geese Paradigm: A Critical Study of its Application to East Asian Regional Development.' UNDP Discussion Paper No. 169

Katz, H. C., Macduffie, J. P., and Pil, F. K. (2014). 'Crisis and Recovery in the US Auto Industry: Tumultuous Times for a Collective Bargaining Pacesetter', in H. R. Stanger, P. F. Clark, and A. C. Frost (eds), *Collective Bargaining under Duress: Case Studies of Major North American Industries.* Ithaca, NY: Cornell University Press, 45–79.

Katzenstein, P. J. (1978) (ed.). *Between Power and Plenty: Foreign Economic Policies of Advanced Industrial States*, Madison: University of Wisconsin Press.

Katzenstein, P. J. (1996). *Cultural Norms and National Security: Police and Military in Postwar Japan.* Ithaca, NY: Cornell University Press.

Kautsky, K. (1914). 'Der Imperialismus', *Die Neue Zeit*, September.

Kawai, M., Mayes, D. G., Morgan, P. J., and Asian Development Bank Institute (2012). *Implications of the Global Financial Crisis for Financial Reform and Regulation in Asia.* Cheltenham: Edward Elgar.

Kennedy, P. M. (1987). *The Rise and Fall of the Great Powers: Economic Change and Military Conflict from 1500 to 2000.* New York: Random House.

Keohane, R. O., and Nye, J. S. (1977). *Power and Interdependence: World Politics in Transition.* Boston: Little, Brown.

Keynes, J. M. (1988 [1919]). *The Economic Consequences of the Peace.* New York: Penguin Books.

Kim, D. (2013). 'A Development Bargaining? Finance and Welfare Conflicts in South Korea', unpublished conference paper from the International Workshop on Geo-Political Economies of East Asia, 22–3 August, Seoul National University Asia Center, Seoul, South Korea.

Kim, E. M. (1998). *The Four Asian Tigers: Economic Development and the Global Political Economy.* San Diego, CA: Academic Press.

Kindleberger, C. P. (1986). *The World in Depression, 1929–1939.* Berkeley and Los Angeles: University of California Press.

Kindleberger, C. P., and Aliber, R. Z. (2005). *Manias, Panics and Crashes: A History of Financial Crises*. Hoboken, NJ: John Wiley & Sons.

Kirchgaessner, S., Politi, J., and Harding, R. (2011). 'Obama in $450bn Push for Growth', *Financial Times*, 9 November 2011.

Kittiakarasakun, J., and Tse, Y. (2011). 'Modeling the Fat Tails in Asian Stock Markets', *International Review of Economics & Finance*, 20: 430–40.

Koalitionsvertrag (2013). *Deutschlands Zukunft Gestalten. Koalitionsvertrag zwischen CDU, CSU und SPD*, online, <http://www.welt.de/politik/article122306476/das-ist-der-koalitionsvertrag-im-wortlaut.html> (accessed April 2019).

Kohli, A. (1994). 'Where do High Growth Political Economies Come from? The Japanese Lineage of Korea's Developmental State', *World Development*, 22: 1269–93.

Kohli, A. (2004). *State-Directed Development: Political Power and Industrialization in the Global Periphery*. Cambridge and New York: Cambridge University Press.

Korea Automobile Manufacturers' Association (2013). *Korean Automotive Industry Annual Report 2013*. Seoul: Korea Automobile Manufacturers Association.

Krippner, G. R. (2005). 'The Financialization of the American Economy', *Socio-Economic Review*, 3: 173–208.

Krippner, G. R. (2011). *Capitalizing on Crisis: The Political Origins of the Rise of Finance*. Cambridge, MA: Harvard University Press.

Kroszner, R. S., and Strahan, P. E. (2007). 'Regulation & Deregulation of the US Banking Industry: Causes, Consequences and Implications for the Future', in N. L. Rose (ed.), *Economic Regulation and its Reform: What Have We Learned*? Chicago: University of Chicago Press.

Krugman, P. (1994). 'The Myth of Asia's Miracle', *Foreign Affairs*, 73/6: 62–78.

Kube, A. (1984). 'Außenpolitik und "Großraumwirtschaft": Die Deutsche Politik zur Wirtschaftlichen Integration Südosteuropas 1933 bis 1939', *Geschichte und Gesellschaft. Sonderheft*, 10: 185–211.

Lahart, J. (2008). 'Has the Financial Industry's Heyday Come and Gone?', *Wall Street Journal*, 28 April 2008.

Lenin, V. I. I. (1933 [1917]). *Imperialism: The Highest Stage of Capitalism*. New York: International Publishers.

Lewis, M. (2010). *The Big Short: Inside the Doomsday Machine*. New York: W.W. Norton.

Li, M. (2012) (ed.). *China Joins Global Governance: Cooperation and Contentions*. Lanham, MD: Lexington Books.

Lütz, S. (2002). *Der Staat und die Globalisierung von Finanzmärkten Regulative Politik in Deutschland, Großbritannien und den USA*. Frankfurt am Main: Campus-Verl.

McMillan, J. (2014). *The End of Banking: Money, Credit, and the Digital Revolution*. Zurish: Zero/One Economics Gmbh.

Maes, I. (2004). 'On the Origins of the Franco-German EMU Controversies', *European Journal of Law and Economics*, 17: 21–39.

Manconi, A., Peyer, U. C., and Vermaelen, T. (2018). 'Are Buybacks Good for Long-Term Shareholder Value? Evidence from Buybacks around the World', 7 March, European Corporate Governance Institute (ECGI), Finance Working Paper, No. 436/2014; IN-SEAD Working Paper No. 2013/101/FIN, available at *SSRN*, <https://ssrn.com/abstract=2330807 or http://dx.doi.org/10.2139/ssrn.2330807> (accessed April 2019).

Manners, I. (2010). 'Global Europa: Mythology of the European Union in World Politics', *Journal of Common Market Stu*dies, 48: 67–87.

Manning, R. D. (2000). *Credit Card Nation: The Consequences of America's Addiction to Credit*. New York: Basic Books.

Marsh, D. (2009). *The Euro: The Politics of the New Global Currency*. New Haven and London: Yale University Press.

Martín, R. A., and Sevillano, J. M. M. (2011). 'Cooperative and Savings Banks In Europe: Nature, Challenges and Perspectives', *Banks and Bank Systems*, 6: 121–35.

Mearsheimer, J. J. (2001). *The Tragedy of Great Power Politics*. New York: Norton.

Menz, G. (2005). *Varieties of Capitalism and Europeanization: National Response Strategies to the Single European Market*. Oxford and New York: Oxford University Press.

Menzel, U. (1985). *In Der Nachfolge Europas: Autozentrierte Entwicklung in d. ostasiat. Schwellenlaendern Suedkorea u. Taiwan*. Munich: Simon & Magiera.

Milberg, W. (2008). 'Shifting Sources and Uses of Profits: Sustaining US Financialization with Global Value Chains', *Economy and Society*, 37: 420–51.

Milmo, D. (2011). 'G7 Rallies behind Japan in Bid to Curb Soaring Yen', *Guardian*, 18 March 2011.

Mirowski, P., and Plehwe, D. (2009). *The Road from Mont Pèlerin: The Making of the Neoliberal Thought Collective*. Cambridge, MA. Harvard University Press.

Mishkin, F. S. (2006). *The Next Great Globalization: How Disadvantaged Nations Can Harness their Financial Systems to Get Rich*. Princeton: Princeton University Press.

Morrison, W. M., and Labonte, M. (2013). 'China's Currency Policy: An Analysis of the Economic Issues', *Congressional Research Service*, 22 July 2013.

Mügge, D. (2006). 'Reordering the Marketplace: Competition Politics in European Finance', *Journal of Common Market Studies*, 44: 991–1022.

Mügge, D. (2014). 'Europe's Regulatory Role in Post-Crisis Global Finance', *Journal of European Public Policy*, 21: 316–26.

Mundell, R. A. (1963). 'Capital Mobility and Stabilization Policy under Fixed and Flexible Exchange Rates', *Canadian Journal of Economics and Political Science*, 29: 475–85.

Mussa, M. L. (2000). *Exchange Rate Regimes in an Increasingly Integrated World Economy*. Washington: International Monetary Fund.

Narr, W.-D., and Schubert, A. (1994). *Weltökonomie: Die Misere der Politik*. Frankfurt am Main: Suhrkamp.

Neal, L. (1979). 'The Economics and Finance of Bilateral Clearing Agreements: Germany, 1934–8', *Economic History Review*, 32: 391–404.

Neumann, F. L. (1981). 'Die Wirtschaftsstruktur Des Nationalsozialismus', in M. Horkheimer, H. Dubiel, and A,Söllner (eds), *Wirtschaft, Recht und Staat im Nationalsozialismus: Analysen des Instituts für Sozialforschung, 1939–1942*. Frankfurt am Main: Europäische Verl-Anst.

Nolan, P., and Yeung, G. (2001). 'Big Business with Chinese Characteristics: Two Paths to Growth of the Firm in China under Reform', *Cambridge Journal of Economics*, 25: 443–65.

Nölke, A. (2011). 'Transnational Economic Order and National Economic Institutions: Comparative Capitalism Meets International Political Economy'. Mpifg Working Paper, 11.

Nölke, A. (2015a). 'Introduction', *Second Image Revisited: The Domestic Sources of China's Foreign Economic Policies*, special issue, *International Politics*, 52: 657–65.

Nölke, A. (2015b). *Second Image Revisited: The Domestic Sources of China's Foreign Economic Policies*, special issue, *International Politics*, 52: 657–800.

Obstfeld, M., Shambaugh, J. C., and Taylor, A. M. (2005). 'The Trilemma in History: Tradeoffs among Exchange Rates, Monetary Policies, and Capital Mobility', *Review of Economics and Statistics*, 87: 423–38.

OECD (2009). *Statextracts: Central Government Debt Statistics*. Paris: OECD.

OECD (2013). *FDI Regulatory Restrictiveness Index*, online, http://www.oecd.org/investment/fdiindex.htm (accessed April 2019).

OECD (2016). *Economic Outlook for Southeast Asia, China and India 2016*. Paris: OECD Publishing.

Panitch, L., and Gindin, S. (2003). 'American Imperialism and Eurocapitalism: The Making of Neoliberal Globalization', *Studies in Political Economy*, 71: 7–38.

Park, S.-S. (2008). 'Number of Oil Cleanup Volunteers Top 1 Mil', *Korea Times*, 10 January.

Park, Y. C. (2011). 'The Global Financial Crisis: Decoupling of East Asia–Myth or Reality?' ADBI Working Paper Series, Issue 289.

Park, Y. C., and Wang, Y. (2005). 'The Chiang Mai Initiative and Beyond', *World Economy*, 28/1: 91–101.

Patomäki, H. (2009). 'Neoliberalism and the Global Financial Crisis', *New Political Science*, 31: 431–42.

Paulson, H. M. (2010). *On the Brink : Inside the Race to Stop the Collapse of the Global Financial System*. New York: Business Plus.

Peel, Q. (2011). 'Hefty Stimuli Dent Germany's "Swabian" Habit', *Financial Times*, 21 June 2010.

Peet, R. (2003). *Unholy Trinity: The IMF, World Bank, and WTO*. Malaysia; SIRD; London and New York: Zed Books; Johannesburg: Wits University Press.

Pempel, T. J. (1977). 'Japanese Foreign Economic Policy: The Domestic Bases for International Behavior', International Organization, 31: 723–74.

Pempel, T. J., and Tsunekawa, K. (1979). 'Corporatism without Labor? The Japanese Anomaly', in P. C. Schmitter and G. Lehmbruch (eds), *Trends toward Corporatist Intermediation*. London and Beverly Hills, CA: Sage Publications.

Piketty, T. (2014). *Capital in the Twenty-First Century*. Cambridge, MA: Belknap Press of Harvard University Press.

Piketty, T. (2016). *Why Save the Bankers?: And Other Essays on our Economic and Political Crisis*. Boston: Houghton Mifflin Harcourt.

Pisani-Ferry, J., and Posen, A. S. (2009). *The Euro at Ten: The Next Global Currency*. Washington: Peterson Institute.

Pistor, K. (2005). 'Legal Ground Rules in Coordinated and Liberal Market Economies'. ECGI-Law Working Paper.

Plant, R. (2010). *The Neo-Liberal State*, Oxford and New York: Oxford University Press.

Polanyi, K. (2001). *The Great Transformation: The Political and Economic Origins of our Time*. Boston: Beacon Press.

Pomeranz, K. (2000). *The Great Divergence: China, Europe, and the Making of the Modern World Economy*. Princeton: Princeton University Press.

Popper, K. R. (1992). *The Open Universe: An Argument for Indeterminism*. London: Routledge.

Putnam, R. D. (1988). 'Diplomacy and Domestic Politics: The Logic of Two-Level Games', *International Organization*, 42: 427–60.

Quaglia, L. (2007). 'The Politics of Financial Services Regulation and Supervision Reform in the European Union', *European Journal of Political Research*, 46: 269–90.

Rappaport, A., and Bogle, J. C. (2011). *Saving Capitalism from Short-Termism: How To Build Long-Term Value and Take Back our Financial Future*. New York: Mcgraw-Hill.

Reich, R. B. (2007). *Supercapitalism: The Transformation of Business, Democracy, and Everyday Life*. New York: Alfred A. Knopf.

Rhodes, M., and Apeldoorn, B. V. (1998). 'Capital Unbound? The Transformation of European Corporate Governance', *Journal of European Public Policy*, 5:, 406–27.

Rickards, J. (2011). *Currency Wars: The Making of the Next Global Crisis*. New York: Portfolio/Penguin.

Roosevelt, F. D. (1933). '*Only Thing We Have To Fear Is Fear Itself*': *FDR's First Inaugural Address*, online, http://historymatters.gmu.edu/d/5057/ (accessed April 2019).

Rosenau, J. N., and Singh, J. P. (2002) (eds). *Information Technologies and Global Politics: The Changing Scope of Power and Governance*. New York: State University of New York Press.

Rostow, W. W. (1959). 'The Stages of Economic Growth', *Economic History Review*, 12: 1–16.

Rostow, W. W. (1990). *The Stages of Economic Growth: A Non-Communist Manifesto*. Cambridge: Cambridge University Press.

Ruggie, J. G. (1982). 'International Regimes, Transactions, and Change: Embedded Liberalism in the Postwar Economic Order', *International Organization*, 36: 379–415.

Sablowski, T. (2008). 'Towards the Americanization of European Finance? The Case of Finance-Led Accumulation in Germany', in Leo Panitch and Martijn Konings (eds), *American Empire and the Political Economy of Global Finance*. Basingstoke and New York, 135–58.

Sachs, J. D., and Warner, A. M. (2001). 'The Curse of Natural Resources', *European Economic Review*, 45: 827–38.

SAPRIN (2004). *Structural Adjustment: The SAPRIN Report: The Policy Roots of Economic Crisis, Poverty, and Inequality*. London and New York: Zed Books.

Sassen, S. (2001). *The Global City*. New York, London, Tokyo, and Princeton: Princeton University Press.

Sassen, S. (2014). *Expulsions: Brutality and Complexity in the Global Economy*. Cambridge, MA: Belknap Press of Harvard University Press.

Schacht, H. (1937). 'Germany's Colonial Demands', *Foreign Affairs*, 15: 223–34.

Schäfer, A. (2005). *Die Neue Unverbindlichkei : Wirtschaftspolitische Koordinierung in Europa*. Frankfurt am Main: Campus.

Scharpf, F. W. (1999). *Regieren in Europa: Effektiv und Demokratisch?* Frankfurt am Main: Campus-Verl.

Scharpf, F. W. (2009). 'Europe's Neo-Liberal Bias', in A. Hemerijck, B. Knapen, and E. V. Doorne (eds), *Aftershocks: Economic Crisis and Institutional Choice*. Amsterdam: Amsterdam University Press.

Schmidt, V. A. (2002). *The Futures of European Capitalism*. Oxford and New York: Oxford University Press.

Schwartz, H. M. (2009). *Subprime Nation: American Power, Global Capital, and the Housing Bubble*. Ithaca, NY: Cornell University Press.

Schydlowsky, D. M. (1995). *Structural Adjustment: Retrospect and Prospect*. Westport, CT, and London: Praeger.

Seabrooke, L. (2007). 'Legitimacy Gaps in the World Economy: Explaining the Sources of the IMF's Legitimacy Crisis', *International Politics*, 44/2: 250–68.

Sekine, E. (2011). 'China's Own Version of Basel III and its Likely Impact on China's Banking Sector', *Nomura Journal of Capital Markets*, 3/2: 1–12.

Shiller, R. J. (2008). *The Subprime Solution: How Today's Global Financial Crisis Happened and what to Do about It*. Princeton: Princeton University Press.

Single European Act (1987). 'Single European Act', *Official Journal of the European Communities*, L 169, 29 June.

Sklair, L. (2001). The Transnational Capitalist Class. Oxford and Malden, MA: Blackwell.

Solis, M. (2003). 'Adjustment through Globalization', in U. Schaede and W. W. Grimes (eds), *Japan's Managed Globalization: Adapting to the Twenty-First Century*. Armonk, NY: M. E. Sharpe.

Soskice, D. (2007). 'Macroeconomics and Varieties of Capitalism', in B. Hancke, M. Rhodes, and M. Thatcher (eds), *Beyond Varieties of Capitalism: Conflict, Contradiction, and Complementarities in the European Economy*. Oxford: Oxford University Press, 89–121.

SPAHN, P. B. (2002). *On the Feasibility of a Tax on Foreign Exchange Transactions* [Online]. Bonn: Report commissioned by the Federal Ministry for Economic Cooperation and Development. Available: http://www.wiwi.uni-frankfurt.de/Professoren/spahn/tobintax/index.html [Accessed].

Spahn, P. B. (2002). *On the Feasibility of a Tax on Foreign Exchange Transactions*. Report Commissioned by the Federal Ministry for Economic Cooperation and Development, Bonn, online, <https://www.wiwi.uni-frankfurt.de/professoren/spahn/tobintax/index.html> (accessed April 2019).

Spaulding, R. M. (1991). 'German Trade Policy in Eastern Europe, 1890–1990: Preconditions for Applying International Trade Leverage', *International Organization*, 45: 343–68.

Stability and Growth Pact (1997). 'Resolution of the European Council on the Stability and Growth Pact Amsterdam', *Official Journal of the European Communities*, C 236: 1–2, 17 June.

Stallings, B. (1995). *Global Change, Regional Response: The New International Context of Development*. Cambridge and New York: Cambridge University Press.

Stiglitz, J. E. (2002). *Globalization and its Discontents*. New York: W. W. Norton.

Stiglitz, J. E. (2003). *The Roaring Nineties: A New History of the World's Most Prosperous Decade*. New York: W. W. Norton.

Stiglitz, J. E. (2013). *The Price of Inequality*. New York: W. W. Norton.

Stiglitz, J. E., and Chang, H.-J. (2001). *Joseph Stiglitz and the World Bank: The Rebel Within*. London: Anthem Press.

Stiglitz, J. E., and United Nations (2010). *The Stiglitz Report: Reforming the International Monetary and Financial Systems in the Wake of the Global Crisis*. New York: New Press.

Stockhammer, E. (2005). 'Shareholder Value Orientation and the Investment-Profit Puzzle', *Journal of Post Keynesian Economics*, 28: 193–215.

Stout, L. A. (2012). *The Shareholder Value Myth: How Putting Shareholders First Harms Investors, Corporations, and the Public*. San Francisco: Berrett-Koehler.

Strange, S. (1986). *Casino Capitalism*. Oxford and New York: Blackwell.

Strange, S. (1994). *States and Markets*. London and New York: Pinter Publishers.

Strange, S. (1998). *Mad Money: When Markets Outgrow Governments*. Ann Arbor: University of Michigan Press.

Streeck, W. (1995). 'German Capitalism: Does it Exist? Can it Survive?' MPIFG Discussion Paper, 95.

Streeck, W. (2013). *Gekaufte Zeit: Die Vertagte Krise des Demokratischen Kapitalismus*. Berlin: Suhrkamp.

Streeck, W., and Thelen, K. A. (2005). *Beyond Continuity: Institutional Change in Advanced Political Economies*. Oxford and New York: Oxford University Press.

Streeck, W., and Yamamura, K. (2001). *The Origins of Nonliberal Capitalism: Germany and Japan in Comparison*. Ithaca, NY: Cornell University Press.

Sussangkarn, C. (2010). 'The Chiang Mai Initiative Multilateralization: Origin, Development and Outlook.' Working Papers.

Tattara, G. (2006). 'Emerging Hubs in Central-Eastern Europe, Trade Blocs and Supply Chain Restructuring.' Working Papers.

Teichert, E. (1984). *Autarkie und Großraumwirtschaft in Deutschland 1930–1939*. Weisbaden: Steiner-Verl.

Tett, G. (2003). *Saving the Sun: How Wall Street Mavericks Shook up Japan's Financial World and Made Billions*. New York: HarperCollins.

Tett, G., and Hall, B. (2010). 'Sarkozy Calls for Action on Currencies', *Financial Times*, 27 January 2010.

TEU/TFEU (2012). Consolidated Versions of the Treaty on the European Union and the Treaty on the Functioning of the European Union', 6655/7/08 REV 7, online, <https://eur-lex.europa.eu/eli/treaty/tfeu_2012/oj> (accessed April 2019).

Tobin, J. (2015 [1974]). *The New Economics One Decade Older*. Princeton: Princeton University Press.

Toeller, A. E. (2012). *Claims that 80 Per Cent of Laws Adopted in the EU Member States Originate in Brussels Actually Tell us Very Little about the Impact of EU Policy-Making*, online, <https://blogs.lse.ac.uk/europpblog/2012/06/13/europeanization-of-public-policy/> (accessed April 2019).

Toyota (2013). *Vehicle Production, Sales and Exports by Region*, online, <http://www.toyota-global.com/company/profile/figures/vehicle_production_sales_and_exports_by_region.html> (accessed 17 August 2013).

Triffin, R. (1978). 'The International Role and Fate of the Dollar', *Foreign Affairs*, 57: 269–86.

United States. Financial Crisis Inquiry Commission (2011a). *The Financial Crisis Inquiry Report: Final Report of the National Commission on the Causes of the Financial and Economic Crisis in the United States*. New York: Public Affairs.

US Department of Commerce (2008). 'Corporate Profits: Fourth Quarter 2007', in Bureau of Economics (ed.), *Analysis*. Washington: Bureau of Economics.

US Department of Commerce (2014). *Leading Sectors for US Export and Investment*, online, <http://export.gov/southkorea/doingbusinessinskorea/leadingsectorsforusexportsinvestment/index.asp> (accessed 2 June 2014).

Veneroso, F., and Wade, R. (1998). 'The Asian Crisis: The High Debt Model Versus the Wall Street–Treasury–IMF Complex', *New Left Review*, /228: 3–23.

Véron, N. (2011). 'Has Global Financial Reform Run out of Steam?', Bruegel Blog, 16 March 2011.

Vestergaard, J., and Wade, R. H. (2012). 'The G20 has Served its Purpose and should Be Replaced', *Journal of Globalization and Development*, 2: 1–4.

Vogel, E. F. (1979). *Japan as Number One: Lessons for America*. Cambridge, MA: Harvard University Press.

Vogel, E. F. (1986). Japan as Number One : Revisited. Singapore: Institute of South-East Asian Studies.

Vogel, S. K. (2003). 'The Re-Organization of Organized Capitalism: How the German and Japanese Models are Shaping their own Transformations', in K. Yamamura and W. Streeck (eds), *The End of Diversity? Prospects for German and Japanese Capitalism*. Ithaca, NY: Cornell University Press.

Vogel, S. K. (2006). *Japan Remodeled: How Government and Industry Are Reforming Japanese Capitalism*. Ithaca, NY: Cornell University Press.

Wade, R. (1998). 'From "Miracle" To "Cronyism": Explaining the Great Asian Slump', *Cambridge Journal of Economics*, 22/6: 693–706.

Wade, R. H. (2002). 'US Hegemony and the World Bank: The Fight over People and Ideas', *Review of International Political Economy*, 9: 215–43.

Wade, R. H. (2004). *Governing the Market: Economic Theory and the Role of Government in East Asian Industrialization*. Princeton: Princeton University Press.

Walker, A. (2010). *Have the G20 Meetings Lost their Momentum*. BBC, 10 November 2010.

Wallerstein, I. M. (1974). *The Modern World-System*. New York: Academic Press.

Walter, A. (2008). *Governing Finance: East Asia's Adoption of International Standards.* Ithaca, NY: Cornell University Press.

Waltz, K. N. (1959). *Man, the State, and War: A Theoretical Analysis.* New York: Columbia University Press.

Walz, G., Buiskool, B. J., Collewet, M., and Koning, J. D. (2012). *Short-Time Working Arrangements during the Crisis and Lessons to Learn.* Zoetermeer: Panteia.

Weber, M. (1958). 'Science as a Vocation', *Daedalus*, 87: 111–34.

Wendt, A. (1992). 'Anarchy Is what States Make of it: The Social Construction of Power Politics', *International Organization*, 46: 391–425.

Werner Plan (1970). 'Realization by Stages of Economic and Monetary Union in the Community.' Supplement, Bulletin 11/1970. Luxembourg.

Whitley, R. (1992). *Business Systems in East Asia: Firms, Markets, and Societies.* London and Newbury Park, CA: Sage.

Whitley, R. (2007). *Business Systems and Organizational Capabilities: The Institutional Structuring of Competitive Competences.* Oxford and New York: Oxford University Press.

Wilhelm, H. (2009). 'Dummes Deutsches Geld', *Sueddeutsche Zeitung*, 8 April 2009.

Williamson, J. (1990). 'What Washington Means by Policy Reform', in J. Williamson (ed.), *Latin American Adjustment: How Much Has Happened.* Washington: Institute for International Economics.

Wilmarth, A. E. (2013). 'Turning a Blind Eye: Why Washington Keeps Giving in to Wall Street', *University of Cincinnati Law Review*, 81: 1283–1446.

Wittfogel, K. A. (1957). *Oriental Despotism; A Comparative Study of Total Power.* New Haven: Yale University Press.

Woo-Cumings, M. (1991). *Race to the Swift: State and Finance in Korean Industrialization.* New York, Columbia University Press.

Woo-Cumings, M. (1999) (ed.). *The Developmental State.* Ithaca, NY: Cornell University Press.

Woods, N. (2006). *The Globalizers: The IMF, the World Bank, and their Borrowers.* Ithaca, NY: Cornell University Press.

World Bank (1993). *The East Asian Miracle: Economic Growth and Public Policy.* New York: Oxford University Press.

World Bank (1996). *World Development Report 1996: From Plan to Market*, online, <https://openknowledge.worldbank.org/handle/10986/5979 (accessed April 2019).

World Bank (2013). *World Governance Indicator*, online, <http://info.worldbank.org/governance/wgi/index.aspx#home> (accessed April 2019).

World Bank (2019). *World Development Indicators*, online, <http://data.worldbank.org/indicator> (accessed April 2019).

WTO (2013). *Statistics Database*, online, <http://stat.wto.org/home/wsdbhome.aspx> (accessed April 2019).

Yamamura, K., and Streeck, W. (2003). *The End of Diversity? Prospects for German and Japanese Capitalism.* Ithaca, NY: Cornell University Press.

Yergin, D., and Stanislaw, J. (1998). *The Commanding Heights: The Battle between Government and the Marketplace that Is Remaking the Modern World.* New York: Simon and Schuster.

Zhang, Z., and Zhang, W. (2009). 'The Road to Recovery: Fiscal Stimulus, Financial Sector Rehabilitation, and Exit from Policy Easing'. Hong Kong Monetary Authority Working Papers 2009 (18).

Zimmermann, H. (2001). 'The Fall Of Bretton Woods and the Emergence of the Werner Plan', in L. Magnusson and B. Strath (eds), *From the Werner Plan to the EMU. In Search of a Political Economy for Europe.* Brussels: PIE–Peter Lang.

Zysman, J. (1983). *Governments, Markets, and Growth: Financial Systems and the Politics of Industrial Change*. Ithaca, NY: Cornell University Press.

Zysman, J., and Schwartz, A. (1998a) (eds). *Enlarging Europe: The Industrial Foundations of a New Political Reality*. Berkeley and Los Angeles: University of California Press.

Zysman, J., and Schwartz, A. (1998b). 'Reunifying Europe in an Emerging World Economy: Economic Heterogeneity, New Industrial Options, and Political Choices', *Journal of Common Market Studies*, 36: 405–29.

Index